'With remarkable courage, insight and access Mark Shaw takes you into the darkest corners of the ganglands, guiding you through safe houses, clandestine arms cache handovers and encounters with hitmen and informed insiders. He acts as a cicerone through the spiderweb of the gangs of the Cape Flats, the taxi violence of KwaZulu-Natal and the corridors of police power, providing context, nuance and the history of how we came to this point, with the streets ablaze with gunfire. This is a riveting story about how first as a trickle, then as a flood, police weapons flowed into the hands of gangsters and ended in bloodshed. Shaw describes how the guns gave the gangs life as hitmen were ready to pull the triggers over and over again with scant regard for the human cost. It will terrify you but it's a story you must know.'
– Mandy Wiener, author of *Killing Kebble* and *The Whistleblowers*

'Mark Shaw's finger is on the trigger. Target: the complex criminal economy. And Shaw is a deadly marksman. So enthralling you would be forgiven if you thought time had stopped'.
– Vusi Pikoli, former head of the National Prosecuting Authority

Give us more Guns

How South Africa's Gangs were Armed

Mark Shaw

Jonathan Ball Publishers
Johannesburg • Cape Town • London

Published in South Africa in 2021 by
JONATHAN BALL PUBLISHERS
A division of Media24 (Pty) Ltd
PO Box 33977 Jeppestown 2043

ISBN 978-1-86842-878-6
EBOOK ISBN 978-1-86842-879-3

www.jonathanball.co.za
www.twitter.com/JonathanBallPub
www.facebook.com/JonathanBallPublishers

Cover, design and typesetting by MR Design
Printed and bound by CTP Printers, Cape Town

To the children caught in the crossfire

In memory of Dimitri Vlassis, 1959–2019

'The trouble was that South Africa was anything but normal, it was never much of a mother, and its name on the map of Africa provoked more questions than answers. Where did it begin and where did it end? Which bits of it were "ours", and which bits of it were "theirs"? When you looked hard at the map, it seemed to be a matter not of geography but of guns.'

– Christopher Hope, *The Café de Move-on Blues: In Search of the New South Africa*. London: Atlantic Books, 2018, 120.

'The Badlands is awash with guns – 32s, 45s, Mauser Red 9s … they seep in, changing hands for just a few dollars, with ammo for cents; where they all come from is a mystery. A gun now costs the same as a catty of rice. Food inflation; firearms deflation – that's the Badlands' law of supply and demand.'

– Paul French, *City of Devils: A Shanghai Noir*. London: Riverrun, 2018, 217.

CONTENTS

PREFACE: THE ZULU

It didn't look like the kind of place where illegal weapons would be stashed – a smallish brick house with a chipped iron security gate, positioned between two windows like a rusty nose. There was a neat little garden gate, which opened with a creak. Some untidy shrubs lined the inside of the concrete wall. The security grill swung open. Expectantly, I went in.

The house was dark, with heavy velveteen curtains covering the windows. There was a white lace doily cloth covering the table, the kind that all respectable South African lower-middle-class houses had – at least in the 1970s. It was the sort of place where you would expect to find a lonely old lady sitting in the corner, watching TV maybe, waiting in vain for her grandchildren to visit.

This was a gang safe house. Our man emerged out of the shadows in the back. He had a baseball cap pulled low over his eyes. It was not his house. He didn't look like the lace doily type. The agreement we had was a simple one: he would show me something, just for the record. I would take a look, then leave. Usually I like to talk about things with people like the man in the baseball cap, but that hadn't been part of the deal. Showing and talking were clearly different transactions.

After a brief nod between us, 'baseball cap' reached behind his back and produced the gun, with a kind of sweeping motion that bank robbers in the movies use – both arms coming forward like a butterfly stroke, the weapon in his right hand, then both hands coming together, elbows slightly bent, gun pointing forward and down. He snorted under the cap. A flash of gold teeth. Then he handed me the piece. We had not said a word to each other.

The gun was a Z88 – a 9 mm pistol. It sat heavy in my hand; dull and black. I weighed it up and drew a bead on the wall of his house, squinting down the sights in the gloom at a space between a flowery poster and a painting depicting the Cape mountains. I had wanted to check how the gun had been tampered with, but the light was too dim and the owner was glaring at me. I cupped the gun in both hands, looked at it as closely as I could. Then, feeling self-conscious, and not knowing what else to do, I gave it back to him. He took it, nodded approvingly, and then padded off to a back room to pack it away.

By that point, I had spent three years talking to people about how guns that were the property of the South African state had leaked into the hands of criminals. Most had been willing to talk, but few had been eager to show me their guns. Over the years, I had glimpsed plenty of Z88s – there had been furtive gestures to a barrel poking out from a straining belt or someone pointing out a police officer's holstered gun – but until my meeting at the safe house I'd never held the gun in my hand. Several gun dealers had also shown me their Z88s. In one case, I got to see one of the earliest models, complete with its wooden box and bronze plate engraved in Afrikaans commemorating its production, like flotsam from a forgotten era. The gangster's gun, in contrast, seemed all too real-life.

Emerging from the gloom again, baseball cap said abruptly that the gun he had shown me was known as a Zulu. He had emphasised the word for my benefit. 'Here we call that gun a *Zulu.*' The Zulu was the underworld gun of choice.

I have spoken to many gangsters about the Zulu. This was a middle-level gang boss from Hanover Park, Cape Town, whom I met in 2017. Like so many others interviewed in the course of researching this book, he explained that the thing about the Zulu is its reliability. 'It is mos hard to break. We are just plain used to it.'

Just the street name, Zulu, says a lot about this weapon. It plays to a series of stereotypes in South African history, conjuring up images of rampaging impis coming in for the kill. Having possession of a Zulu is a status symbol on the gang-ridden Cape Flats, a sign of power and the ability to influence the things and people around you, if only through the deadly act of aiming it at someone and pulling the trigger. As one gang interviewee put it, while sucking air though his teeth and giving out a short chuckle, 'We sommer can kill with the best of them.' He was by no means exaggerating: by that point, the murder rate in Cape Town had reached levels seen only in parts of Central America.

What is special about the Z88 is that it is a South African gun. All of our own making. Gangsters and other criminals are oddly proud of the Z88's origins. Possessing this gun, a collective South African pride swells the chests of its rightful owners, police officers, and those they are meant to police. I can't recall how many times this came up: the Z88 was a good gun because it was a local product made for local conditions – even though the design, as I was at pains to point out, had been borrowed from other models made elsewhere. 'Yes, but it was made much better,' retorted one representative of the underworld. 'Local is lekker' applies in gangland too.

Thousands of Zulus were manufactured over the years. It was designed in the late 1980s by Lyttelton Engineering Works near Pretoria on the basis of a request from the South African Police (SAP), which had been rapidly expanding and urgently needed more guns. The '88' part indicates the year in which the first model was produced; the 'Z' reflects the surname of the chief engineer, one T.D. Zeederberg – nothing then to do with Zulus. Mr Zeederberg appears to have been something of a legend, known for his exacting standards and habit of making walking inspections of the factory to make sure that all was in order.[1]

The Zulus come in several configurations, but all have Z88 stamped on the barrel and the words 'Made in South Africa'. Earlier versions have the 'L' and 'E' of Lyttelton Engineering on the handgrip; later versions have a 'V' embossed over a target. The 'V' stands for Vektor, which would later become the Denel brand name for the handgun.

The international sanctions imposed on apartheid South Africa in the 1980s had prevented the import of guns for the police service, so Lyttelton Engineering copied the design of the Italian Beretta 92 pistol, a sleek, good-looking and durable model. Beretta would later sue for copyright infringement in a case that eventually seemed to have been quietly dropped.[2] In the violent uncertainties that characterised the last days of white rule, Zulus were bricks in the apartheid state's crumbling defensive wall. Several decades later, it is a profound irony that these guns ended up in the hands of the very people they had been designed to shoot – men like the gangster who had let me hold his gun in that dark room, vectors in a spiralling orgy of killing that was to dominate the Cape Flats from around 2011.

The guns

The Zulus were recalled from the law-enforcement front line to be replaced by more modern guns purchased from outside South Africa. Decommissioned, they were stockpiled in the police armoury from about 2000, consigned for destruction. Well and good. Another step towards achieving a safer and democratic South Africa. The government was doing its work.

But then something happened, something with far-reaching and long-term consequences for all South Africans, but particularly those in areas where gang bosses carry more weight than municipal councillors or teachers. Instead of having the guns crushed and melted down at the police storage and destruction facility in Vereeniging, a middle-aged white police officer, resentful at his lack of promotion and eager to make a quick buck, removed the guns and sold them. At first, he sold them himself, then later he forged a business deal with a former shooting buddy and police reservist who acted as his middleman and sold the guns wholesale to the gangs.

The police colonel behind the theft and sale of the weapons was one Christiaan Lodewyk Prinsloo, gun expert, sworn protector of the public and illegal flogger of state property for cash. The alleged intermediary was Irshaad 'Hunter' Laher, one-time salesman, hunting enthusiast and restaurant owner.[3] There are many others who will play a part in this story. But these two men stand at the centre.

The alleged leader of South Africa's largest criminal group, the Americans gang, Sanie American, in a remarkable recorded interview before Prinsloo's arrest in January 2015, described what was happening:

Today, people, the kids, they just wanna kill because there's too much guns on the streets. There is one source that is providing the guns for all different gangsters in the Western Cape. The same person, if he comes with 300 guns and ... you can only buy 50, then he goes to rival gangs. He sells to whatever that one can buy and whatever's left he goes to the other gangster and he sells it to the other gang. That's every second month, ... they come with three, four hundred guns ... and it's all Z88s.[4]

As it turns out, Sanie American may have been peeved that other gangs were getting their hands on the guns first, and not his gang. That was soon to change. The guns spread like a mutant cancer through the gangs. From impending destruction to distribution on the street, the Zulus and other guns began inexplicably arriving in Cape Town, reaching men like the gangster in the baseball cap. They empowered some criminal formations and weakened others, who found themselves increasingly outgunned. They were sold to numerous gangster groups until the Cape Flats was inundated with them.

And they killed. At a conservative estimate, and based on the ballistics evidence available, the guns Prinsloo failed to destroy and sold on have been linked to 1 066 murders and some 1 403 attempted murders in the period between 2010 and 2016 alone.[5] These numbers of killings mean that Prinsloo's work is, without doubt, the deadliest single crime to have been committed in post-apartheid South Africa.[6]

I began my research into the story of the Prinsloo guns, focusing on the initial cache of 2 400 that Prinsloo had admitted to police investigators he had sold to the gangs of the Cape Flats from around 2007. Over the course of the research, it became clear that this was just the tip of the iceberg of this man's crimes. From the mid-2000s until just before his arrest in early 2015, he is likely to have fenced more than 9 000 police guns to a go-between with the gangs and other criminal organisations, which have since been distributed to places far beyond the Western Cape. Guns from the police consignment have been subsequently found in Johannesburg,

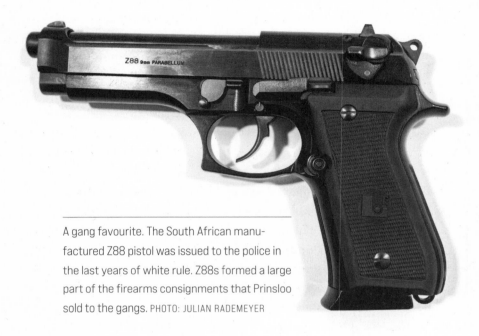

A gang favourite. The South African manufactured Z88 pistol was issued to the police in the last years of white rule. Z88s formed a large part of the firearms consignments that Prinsloo sold to the gangs. PHOTO: JULIAN RADEMEYER

Durban, Nelson Mandela Bay and elsewhere. Many of them were Z88s. Over time, this gun market moved from a supply-driven to a demand-driven one: gangsters competed with one another for access to the guns, threatening Prinsloo's intermediary with violence if he did not deliver.

Prinsloo has not been the only source. Guns have haemorrhaged from police stores at station level, from individual officers, from metropolitan and municipal police departments, and from other government departments, such as the South African National Defence Force (SANDF). Digging into the Prinsloo case reveals a litany of mismanagement and poor messaging by the police on the issue of firearms control. The critical failure of the South African Police Service's (SAPS) Central Firearms Registry contributed to the life-destroying trafficking of guns, allowing it to continue for so long. The registry's administrative systems are a shambles, while corruption has marred the issuing of firearms licences. The failures of this institution, central to the government's much-vaunted policy of gun control, have prevented any sustained attempts at equitable gun regulation, with critical implications.

The focus of this book is not just on the spread of the guns themselves, but also on a wider set of criminal market changes in South Africa that they catalysed. It is also an indictment of the police service, which has failed to implement adequate, transparent forms of gun control. This is particularly evident in sectors such as the taxi and private security industries, which blur into organised crime.

If the South African state, as the Constitution provides, is responsible for the safety of its citizens, it has failed. The guns that the state owns and controls are intended to be used to achieve the societal security promised by the Constitution. Instead, the opposite has occurred. An enormous number of state weapons, leaked to criminals because of weak internal systems, corruption and mismanagement, have been deployed in a range of violent crimes, and they are still being used.

This book is an exploration of how those guns were removed from the police stocks, the extent of the loss, how they were illegally sold, and to whom, as well as how a policy of gun control whose purpose was to reduce violence in South Africa fell apart through poor implementation, error and corruption. We will probably never know the exact number of guns that have been diverted in this way, but what we can see is their impact in the daily headlines of murders and violence in communities across the country, particularly on the streets of Cape Town. Many of these guns are still in criminal possession. Unless they are retrieved, the killing will continue.

The gangs

Besides the cost in human lives lost, the guns also triggered major changes within South Africa's criminal underworld. The guns were beginning to arrive at the same time that the illegal drug market was experiencing an upsurge in South Africa, setting off a series of gang wars, several of which continue to this day.[7]

Furthermore, it is probable that the surge of guns provided by Prinsloo specifically and the state more generally was central to transforming the illicit firearms economy. Price trends for weapons sold on the black market indicate that a cartel for illicit weapons has formed. A number of underworld dealers have colluded to raise the price of illegal guns, and they source guns from the armouries of the state and the stockpiles of firearms handed into the police. This is not of course the only source, but it has been a major one: a pile of guns waiting to be plundered. They access an almost unlimited supply of guns at a low cost, for which the underworld is prepared to pay big money. The profits to be made from gun sales rival those from drugs.

What interview after interview with gangsters has revealed is that the Prinsloo guns transformed the nature of organised crime, and ordinary people are living with the consequences. Cape Town, where most of the Prinsloo guns were circulated, is now one of the most violent places on earth.[8] The firearms were used by organised-crime groups to unleash an orgy of killing so intense that in mid-2019, the South African military were called in to patrol the city's gang-infested areas. That in itself was an important moment in the evolution of post-apartheid South Africa's security: a recognition by the government that the police could no longer manage the situation on their own because they lacked the strategic ability, were riven by internal conflicts and had themselves become complicit with the gangs.

It is something very hard to get your head around: the police and the wider state, both wittingly and unwittingly, armed criminals in South Africa, strengthening their operations and activities by giving them access to firearms, and threatening the life opportunities of many ordinary people.

Given the number of guns he was implicated in selling, the Prinsloo case is at the centre of this scandal. Hundreds of people, including women and children, died between 2007 and 2019 as a result of one man's crime: a resentful senior police officer selling millions of rands' worth of guns to fund his son's university fees. That crime should have at least sparked outrage, yet the response has been remarkably muted. The reaction of the SAPS to the case in public has been cautiously reticent – partly, I suspect, because they fear a civil case against the service for the damage done by the guns.

State-issued guns and ammunition now regularly turn up linked to crime scenes. The SAPS does not collect or publish such figures, but evidence of the link emerges from interviews. For example, a professional from a leading security company that is engaged in responding to hijackings confirmed that almost a third of the hundred guns or so that the firm has recovered on average every year in the course of its work have been Z88s.[9] Although they are often referred to in reports as unspecified '9 mm pistols', police-issue Z88s have also been used in a range of crimes and assassinations reported in the media.[10] If the police report that a 9 mm pistol has been used in a crime, it is most likely to have been a Z88, particularly if the scene is the Cape Flats.[11] State property rifles, such as R1s, R4s, and R5s, are also regularly retrieved and reported to have been used in armed robberies, cash-in-transit heists and even clashes between rival groups of illegal miners.[12] The role of the state is to control crime, but it is effectively fuelling it.

As the firearms crimes mounted and the bodies piled up in the morgues, another story emerged. The crisis caught the attention of a small group of police officers, led by two of the most unlikely cops in the country – Jeremy Vearey and Peter Jacobs, former ANC intelligence operatives, who themselves had grown up on the Cape Flats, where the guns in the hands of the gangsters were now causing untold deaths. Inside a police agency riven with ANC infighting and dysfunction, these two officers stumbled on the case of the lost police guns in 2013 and began to investigate. For all their individual heroism in taking the case forward, the resistance they faced in their investigation and their eventual removal from the case are far from comforting. In fact, the response of the police as a whole is a sobering indictment of the politicisation of law enforcement, and its eventual breakdown, under the Zuma presidency.

Much has been written about the phenomenon of state capture and how it has undermined economic growth and service delivery in South Africa. The story of the leakage of guns from the state also deserves to be seen as part of the state capture scandal. It is without doubt a reflection of the wider process of institutional breakdown that began before the Zuma administration but was accelerated by it. It is the result of corruption, poor management, incompetence and arrogance on the part of state officials, defying the imagination in the same way that the various threads of the state capture story have continued to shock South Africa. The guns-to-gangs phenomenon is a reminder, if any is needed, that for South Africa to survive, let alone grow and prosper, working institutions that operate within the frame of the rule of law are a prerequisite.

I have written this book with the purpose of highlighting these failures, not only because they are shocking, but also because we must make them right if we are to protect the lives and well-being of South Africa's citizens and the very sustainability of our democracy.

Note on the research

Articles have been written about the Prinsloo guns. But this book, which is the product of more than three years of research and over 200 interviews with gang members and bosses, gun dealers, state officials and many others, is the most comprehensive investigation into both the events around the crime and the environment that made it possible. It considers the impact that Prinsloo's guns have had on the Cape Flats, and how these deadly weapons have shaped the evolving system of criminal organisations in the country. It also examines the failed system of gun control and, as a consequence, how they fell into the hands of mafia-style groups, like the Cape gangs, and how they have fuelled violent taxi wars.

I have not referenced each interview, but make clear in the text, where appropriate and relevant for the story, the informants whom I spoke to, and when. When discussing illegal firearms and other matters of the underworld, most people want to remain anonymous, and I have honoured that. But, as I hope will become clear through the story, I have done my best to confirm the main details of the plot. During the research, I have spoken with people at all levels – very senior police officers and junior ones, street gangsters and some of the most senior gang bosses, lawyers, and the families of victims and those involved. I formally requested support and access to police officers for interviews from SAPS headquarters but never received a reply to my request. I also requested documents from government under access-to-information legislation – these were all refused or my enquiries received no response. In the end, this was immaterial, as plenty of police officers talked willingly, but they could do so only if it was agreed that they would be cited off the record.

I conducted interviews, which provided information used in the book, in South Africa in 2017, 2018 and 2019, with some follow-ups in 2020 as I finished the writing. Interviews on sensitive subjects can be quite a process, from the simple checking of a detail with a gang boss over the telephone to setting up a gun look-see, like the one described above, to a more detailed discussion with a police officer, for example. Interviews took place mainly in Cape Town, Johannesburg, Pretoria and Durban, but also in Vereeniging, Pietermaritzburg, Witbank and Nelson Mandela Bay. In several cases, people were interviewed multiple times.

Many of the incidents, events and legal cases described here are in the public domain, in affidavits, media reports and court sub-missions. Every effort has been made to ensure factual accuracy, and that interviews and correspondence with key participants are correctly reproduced and acknowledged. If there are any omissions or errors, I would welcome information that enables me to set the record straight in future editions.

CHAPTER 1

DEATH OF A GANGLAND LAWYER

Noorudien Hassan seemed to be as elusive in death as he was in life. I had tramped around the Spaanschemat River Muslim Cemetery in Constantia looking for his final resting place. The descriptions that I had received of where he lay had been relayed to me over the phone in a confusing fashion and I had sketched them out on a scrap of paper too hastily. Was the tomb by a wall or next to the path? Which one of the two adjacent cemeteries had he finally ended up in? Back and forth and back and forth I went for hours, searching among the graves in the hot sun. Until, there he was: a short granite headstone inscribed with *Noorudien Hassan (Mulla) D.O.B: 28.08.1971 D.O.D: 07.11.2016.*

D.O.D. The events of one day. Just three golden letters engraved in black granite, belying a story so complex and hard to grasp, its edges blurring into the mass of gang-related violence on the Cape Flats. One murder among thousands, each part of the massed ranks of shuffling dead, which masked the reality of every individual killing. The story of so much death meant that even the most prominent cases began to fade into obscurity, much like the toll that the blistering Cape summer had taken on the condition of this grave.

The weeds growing in the light-coloured sand over his body had wilted in the heat, splaying over the edge of the concrete boundary. An empty glass jar stood at an angle to one side, hot to the touch.

The death of Noorudien Hassan became, as I dug further and further into the story, a critical piece of history in the violent contestations that had marred life on the Cape Flats for decades. Hassan was the spider in a web, the centre of a network of communication, the holder of the critical purse strings, the indirect facilitator of the flows of drugs and guns – even if his work never seemed to touch either directly.

Assassinated lawyer Noorudien Hassan had the appearance of an affable uncle, but he was deeply enmeshed in Cape Town's underworld. PHOTO: MEGAN BAADJIES / AFRICAN NEWS AGENCY

In life, Hassan looked like a roly-poly uncle. Balding, with a thick moustache and an easy smile, he had the earnest air of someone who might be a willing member of the local school parents' committee. He was short and overweight, and wore a slightly outsized jacket, and what remained of his hair was blown out of place, a windswept character in a windswept city. If you noticed him at your local supermarket, you would not have given him a second glance.

In his professional life, Hassan was a successful local lawyer. Several people who knew him said that he was driven by money – greedy, some said. That, I suppose, is acceptable for a lawyer. But the issue in question and one that, one way or the other, had ended his life was this: the small matter of who his clients were.

Red carpet gangster funeral

In the underworld, you can tell a lot about a person by the nature of their funeral. John Landesco's seminal study of organised crime even suggests that funerals are the place where the upperworld and underworld meet, at least visibly, for the world to see. He notes that while in life the criminally connected may conceal personal ties, in death they cannot avoid disclosing them.[1] Hassan's funeral was a gathering of gangsters. Perhaps because they had read the organised-crime textbook, the police turned up too, with a camera mounted on a vehicle, snapping pictures of the attendees.

They were all there – the big-time bosses. Jerome 'Donkie' Booysen, wearing a shiny suit and tie, alleged chief of the Sexy Boys, a gang as violent and deadly as any on the Cape Flats, a stark contrast to their label, which suggests a group of teenagers outside a local disco. Donkie is an interesting character. Despite his name, the origins of which are unclear, he is reputed to be the smartest of three brothers. He matriculated with good marks and joined the City of Cape Town as a building inspector, having also developed a reputation as a good club rugby player.

But business-minded Booysen, apparently at the behest of his mother, focused on shaping the Sexy Boys into a formidable operation. Partly applying his experience at the city administration, he built a property empire, pushing down prices at property auctions and positioning himself as the sole buyer. Violence, or the threat thereof, would keep other buyers at bay and prices low. Donkie reportedly had also dabbled in the taxi industry, which required a clear head, a hard set of hands and a finger on the trigger.[2]

The Sexy Boys ventured into the turf of other gangs in a strategic way, expanding their interests in drug trafficking and dealing, and prostitution. They also provided the muscle for the inner-city extortion market, a long-standing feature of Cape Town's night-time underworld economy.

Donkie's brother Colin, a man about town in his own right, was also there, his bodyguards muscling through the crowd, openly displaying their weapons. The heavies weren't just for show. Like his brother, Colin had been targeted in a number of assassination attempts. In May 2013, he had been shot in the leg and arm outside the Sexy Boys' Belhar stronghold, his family rushing him to hospital so he could fight another day. And fight another day he did, but later, and against his own brother Donkie as the Sexy Boys split down the middle in a vicious internecine turf war over the city's lucrative extortion market that left several bodies in its wake and continues to this day.[3]

Ralph Stanfield, gangster extraordinaire, alleged leader of the notorious 28s, a black-and-white cap pulled tightly over his head, shielding his eyes, stalked around greeting mourners. Stanfield has an almost mythical reputation on the Cape Flats, helped along by clever management of the media. He and his wife, the leggy Nicole Stanfield, wear flashy clothes and like to be seen driving expensive cars, just the sort of stuff for newspaper gossip columns. Perhaps more than most gang bosses, Stanfield has an eye for politics as a protective film for illegal business.

In this sense, he learnt the tricks of the trade from an influential predecessor in gangland. Ralph had been handpicked by his uncle, Colin Stanfield. Uncle Colin, who passed away from cancer in 2004, had been integral to an attempt to bring unity among the gangs after an onslaught by a vigilante group, People Against Gangsterism and Drugs (PAGAD).[4] In the 1990s, Colin Stanfield had sat the gang bosses down together and negotiated a *Pax Mafiosa* through the formation of a new group, which was christened, appropriately and apparently without irony, The Firm.[5] With Colin in the driving seat, The Firm took the step of forming a community engagement arm, the Community Outreach Forum, or CORE, whose purported objective was to reintegrate gangsters. Their real purpose, it seems, was to improve their standing in communities and to begin to dabble in politics in the new South African democracy. CORE offered the government R50 million to pay for community outreach activities.

Ralph Stanfield quickly became a central operator in the city's gangster dealings as PAGAD began to find itself weakened following several arrests. The gang bosses kept talking among themselves, even while their foot soldiers murdered each other on the streets. Always one to keep his eye on the bottom line, Ralph was allegedly key to introducing a wave of new designer drugs into the Cape market. Having been bequeathed the family gang business empire, he showed similar traits of political savvy to his uncle's. He continued the tradition of providing cash handouts to people and paying their utility bills – Robin Hood deeds cynically designed to ensure the support of needy communities.[6]

Stanfield posed a threat to the business interests of other gangs, most notably the Sexy Boys and the Americans (the leaders of which he was rubbing shoulders with at Hassan's funeral), and a dramatic attempt was made on his life in Johannesburg in July 2017. Fourteen bullets pierced his Audi R8 sports car, severely wounding him. He survived by managing to drive himself to hospital, a fact that only enhanced his reputation as untouchable. A tracking device was later found on his car.

In the funeral congregation with Stanfield was Ernie 'Lastig' Solomon, one-time leader of the Terrible Josters gang and alleged king of the illegal abalone trade. For the occasion, Solomon had donned a bright-red shirt adorned with a real leopard skin with matching headdress, tribal leader style. Solomon had a fearsome reputation on the Flats and is reputed to have personally cut out the tongue of a man who had said that he was a coward. Among ordinary gang leaders, quite apart from the tongue-cutting legend, Solomon was seen as a gangster's gang boss (akin, I suppose, to an army officer being described as a soldier's soldier). That was because of his reputation for carrying out assassinations of rival gang members himself. It is said that he would dress as a woman so as to get close to his targets without their feeling threatened.

Solomon's funeral garb was selected to show respect to his now deceased lawyer; it was also based on his passion for Khoisan culture, an ethnic heritage to which he saw himself connected. Standing smiling in the sun at the cemetery, he projected an all-round nice guy image. 'Don't be fooled,' a gang contact of mine told me. 'He looks like a softy but I tell you he still carries a knife because there is no way that he would leave that past after killing so many people.' Solomon would later be wounded in an assassination attempt in May 2020, the result of some conflict between his family and another gang boss, possibly Stanfield.[7] He died in a hail of bullets in a second successful hit six months later.

Further down the gangster food chain was Johannes 'Bal' Abrahams (the nickname 'ball' presumably denoting his heavy-set figure). Allegedly the scourge of the gangland suburb of Valhalla Park, Abrahams was out on bail of R20 000. He had recently been arrested because of a small arsenal of 250 firearms that had been found at his home.

In addition to this small cast of VIP characters, the funeral was heaving with some of South Africa's other notorious underworld players. 'Nobody could be absent,' a police officer investigating Hassan's murder told me, 'because that would have pointed the finger at them as a possible suspect.'

The gang bosses mingled with the ordinary people of the Cape Flats, and they with the smartly suited criminal defence lawyers who had also come to pay their respects. Present among the legal fraternity was Advocate Pete Mihalik, sharply dressed as always, his chiselled features almost a stereotype of the hard man's hard defence lawyer. Mihalik had known Hassan for two decades and would himself be gunned down with a Z88 two years later while dropping off his children at posh Reddam House school in Green Point, Cape Town. He spoke warmly, several attendees said, of his friend and legal partner.

Hassan's shrouded corpse – he appeared to be draped in an embroidered gold-and-green cloth – was carried through the crowd. His sister, Haseena, told reporters that the family was still in a state of shock and disbelief. 'This is unreal and our mother is finding it difficult, as he was at her house last night.' The family were being counselled, she said, especially his two young children, 'to deal with the tragedy'.[8]

Anatomy of a killing

Hassan had been at his mother's home on the evening of 7 November for dinner. This contrast between the hard-nosed criminal lawyer and the homely son joining his mother for dinner at the family home is one that has stuck with me. I went to see Hassan's mother and brother while preparing this book. In the room where he had eaten his last meal, his mother talked about his gentleness, but she also quite unselfconsciously spoke of the respect in which he was held by his clients, the gang bosses.[9]

Just as no gang boss of reputation would dare be absent from the Hassan funeral, likewise no police officer wanted to put his name on the investigation docket of his murder. Powerful people wanted to protect Hassan's killers, or that is how it seemed to the lower-level cops tasked with solving the case. The docket went back and forth between the provincial office of the elite investigation unit, the Hawks, and the respective police stations, with little progress being made. Solving the Hassan case would not, it appeared, be a career-enhancing move.

Trying to piece together exactly what happened by speaking to several of the people most closely involved, it is as if this murder repels attention. 'It's best left alone,' a police officer told me. 'If you dig in there, who knows what you will find.'

It was a warm evening, with the long Cape summer and its holidays beginning to beckon. The first indication of trouble was an anonymous call to the police 10111 centre, which was logged at 22:20. It's unclear what exactly was said, but the caller said something like, 'The lawyer Hassan has been shot.' The call was dispatched to Lansdowne Police Station and patched through to some patrolling officers. It crackled through their radio, the two officers looking at each other, well aware of who the victim was, the bakkie careening through the turns on the way to the scene. When the officers arrived, Hassan was no longer there. It transpired that he had been taken to a nearby hospital, Kingsbury, in Claremont, but he did not make it alive.

The harassed patrol officers, according to protocol, left for the hospital to find the doctors, who were trying to resuscitate the lawyer, but to no avail.

From the beginning, the details of the incident were unclear, with some important pieces of evidence immediately going missing.

It is known that Hassan was a passenger in his new car, a silver Mercedes-Benz, which was being driven by Jaffer Dowlray. He and Dowlray, an old friend, drove away from his mother's house, weaving through a series of bends and turns that brought them into Burwood Road, Crawford. The two men drove at a leisurely speed, turning into the driveway of Hassan's house at number 147. Dowlray was a police reservist; his calmness under fire was about to be put to the test.

The house, nothing ostentatious in a predominantly Muslim middle-class suburb, stood out only because it was painted bright yellow. Hassan did not actually live there. He owned nine other houses in the vicinity but lived elsewhere with his wife. Almost nothing is known about Mehraaj. It is said, though, that she is quiet, retiring and religious. Hassan seems to have played a bit on the side too. But he liked a subservient woman at home.

The idea that Hassan lived parallel lives comes through in discussions with people around him. 'He smiles to your face but is quite prepared to stab you in the back,' someone who had worked with him said. 'He was a gentle soul,' another acquaintance mentioned. 'But was quite prepared to hire a hitman if he needed to.'

In the words of a lawyer who had known him from court, Hassan was also 'cheap'. His parsimonious nature may explain why he was visiting the yellow house, which stood empty. The only living things there were several expensive koi fish. Hassan was driving to the house to feed them. He did that most nights, even though he could have paid someone to look after the house.

What they had not noticed as they drove to Burwood Road was a white bakkie behind them. The vehicle was captured on a neighbour's CCTV camera, its tail lights glowing in the dark. As they turned into the driveway, the bakkie drew up behind them. It was 22:13. A man alighted, his movements easy and fluid as he quickly approached the passenger side of the car where Hassan was about to get out, the gun ready, pointed, held level and steady. He shot six or seven times.

Several hitmen have told me how important focus is. For the most highly practised shooters, three things are required: focus on the target and don't have any doubts once you start to move; dehumanise him or her, think of the target as an 'it', something you are just shooting at; do the job and disappear quickly, but don't run or let your adrenalin control you – move steadily while going in for the kill and getting away.

The location chosen to carry out this hit was classic. Hitman lore – and this is corroborated by academic research – suggests that the places where victims are most vulnerable are on their doorsteps and in their driveways.[10] That is where victims are less alert, close to the comfort of home. 'Your guard naturally drops as soon as you see your home or drive into the garage. That's when it's a good time,' one hitman told me.

Our hitman had only one target on that November night, and he was good enough to pull it off successfully. Dowlray, meanwhile, rolled out of the car on the driver's side, like a parachutist. He was unhurt, although severely shocked. Later, he refused to discuss the incident for fear of his own safety. There is little doubt that if he had interfered in any way, he would have been dead too.

Less than a minute later, at 22:14, the killer, a professional to his fingertips, smoothly drew in the gun and returned to the bakkie in the road, its door still open, waiting to receive him after his night's work. The vehicle then drove at a measured pace down the road – no hurry, no panic. The professional killer knows that speeding or driving erratically or not observing street signs after a kill is the route to an arrest. (In the case of Mihalik's assassination two years later, the two killers were arrested for inadvertently skipping a stop street outside, of all places, Gallows Hill, the headquarters of the Cape Town traffic police's licensing department. Had they been driving attentively, it is almost certain that they would have got away.)

Dowlray, despite his shock, appears to have had the presence of mind to drive Hassan to hospital. But too late, despite the duty doctor's attempts to revive him.

Following the call to the police, the patrol vehicle arrived promptly – a good response time of only a few minutes. Given the high profile of the dead man, the Lansdowne station commander also showed up at the scene, at around 10:40, some 25 minutes after the bakkie had pulled away from the house.

Standing around in the driveway after the killing was a group of men, some said to be linked to PAGAD. The PAGADers seemed to be in good spirits, reportedly laughing and joking at the expense of the dead lawyer and his police reservist companion.

Cleaning up

The killing bore all the signs of a professional hit. But even professional hitmen can be careless. Some important pieces of evidence provided clues. Primary among these was the fact that the whole incident had been captured by the neighbour's CCTV camera across the street, which recorded the bakkie moving slowly down the street and drawing up outside the Hassan property. What the film showed, its images flickering in grey and white, was a testimony to the professional skills of the hitman. But he had made one crucial mistake: when conducting reconnaissance of the area, he had failed to notice the camera itself.

It may have been the key piece of evidence, but the film that eventually made it into the hands of the investigating officer had been tampered with in some way to obscure important parts of the action. Most notably, the killer's face is not visible as he lowers the gun and moves back towards the car. And it's a glaring gap. Perhaps the neighbour was threatened and edited the file. Or perhaps the police officers who obtained it, or someone else involved in the case, meddled with it. It is unclear. And nobody is saying.

The shell casings at the scene had also disappeared. Removing them would have been pretty standard practice for a professional hitman. The bakkie might have made a loop back to the street to find them, or one of the first people on the scene may have removed them. Whichever, by the time the police crime specialists were milling about at the scene, they had been spirited away.

There was one piece of crucial evidence available, however, which the investigating officers thought might lead to a breakthrough: Hassan's mobile phone, which was retrieved from his car. His most recent calls and text messages could be examined to determine whether any link could be made with the killers. Had someone called, for example, to check where he was going or when he would be arriving home? The phone was booked into the police station evidence store at Lansdowne Road Police Station. It then disappeared, signed out by a detective, who, when confronted, claimed that he had in fact not done so.

The investigation then ran into a brick wall. That is, except for one other crucial piece of evidence that good police work turned up in the course of the next few days. The police managed to trace the white bakkie. If that did not resolve the killing, it did at least provide some strong circumstantial evidence as to who the perpetrators might be. As mentioned, the police had observed a gathering of individuals linked to PAGAD at the scene after the murder. The bakkie, whose registration number had been recorded on the CCTV images, seemed to be linked to people close to PAGAD.

Hassan himself was no stranger to PAGAD. The group had threatened him before. Having heavy-breathers on the phone from PAGAD was no joke. These people meant business, even if they were not quite the power in the city that they once had been.

In the past, the vigilante group had perpetrated a killing spree across Cape Town, gunning down several prominent gang bosses. The group had overstepped the mark, however, by shifting its targets in a pipe bomb campaign in the late 1990s to police, government and commercial targets. The motivation behind PAGAD turning to government and US-linked commercial interests – Kentucky Fried Chicken outlets seemed to be a favourite, and, notoriously, the Planet Hollywood nightclub, attacked in August 1998 – seemed to be an odd combination of attacking government for not responding to gangs and striking at Western-aligned corporate interests. A swift crackdown on the group followed under the government of Nelson Mandela and later Thabo Mbeki, using the remaining hard-core security instruments of the old apartheid state, now bundled under Crime Intelligence.[11]

PAGAD had split in the wake of the bombing campaigns. A more radical splinter, known as the G-Force, which had been responsible for many of the targeted killings, remained committed to violence. Meanwhile, the bulk of PAGAD continued to operate as an anti-gang, community-style vigilante group, organising patrols in mostly middle-class Muslim neighbourhoods.

There is strong evidence that the G-Force developed tendencies remarkably similar to those of the gangs against which it said it was taking action. In the first place, it appeared to develop a system of extortion of small businesses, targeting cash-generating companies, such as video shops and car dealerships, that were probably more vulnerable given that they had one foot in the grey economy themselves. The G-Force also took an interest in the drug economy, mainly by extorting payments from those involved in moving the illicit narcotics.

What emerged from speaking to gang bosses was how dismissive they had become of PAGAD. This was encapsulated in a comment made by a member of the Terrible Josters: 'PAGAD is no more and if they were …', he paused here to emphasise the point, 'that is in the past. On the Flats, nobody speaks of PAGAD … because the only thing that matters in the townships is the gangs.' His hands cutting the air, he then concluded: 'That is the long and the short of it.'[12]

In some ways, the picture was even more complex than that. Not only had the power of PAGAD weakened, but its most radical and violent parts had themselves become captured by the power of the illicit economy. There had been over time a blurring of lines between gangsters and vigilantes, and between vigilantes and adherents of radical Islam. Poor Hassan, managing his legal business, seemed to be crossing too many lines in an increasingly complex criminal economy. There is little doubt that he was on PAGAD's radar.

A premonition of death

Several people close to Hassan said that he was not himself in his final days. In fact, he was scared stiff. But it was not entirely clear why. Nobody seemed to have threatened him directly, although his family concedes that he would have been unlikely to tell them anyway, as he usually kept that sort of business to himself. He did not want to worry his mother in particular. That was why his police reservist friend was with him in the car on the night of his death. Hassan had asked him to accompany him, as he feared for his safety. Several people close to him told me that they thought that someone had got to Hassan. Someone had told him he was going to die. But I did not get the impression that his family thought PAGAD was a suspect.

Hassan had in fact escaped attempts on his life on at least two occasions. In May 2014, a bomb had been thrown at his house, all but destroying it. The perpetrators on that occasion are said to have been gangsters enraged with his 'poor service' around the delivery of people from the clutches of the criminal-justice system, although of course it is hard to discern the truth.

A couple of weeks before the murder, a man had been arrested outside Hassan's house in Burwood Road. The armed man had parked a Golf GTI near Hassan's house and appeared to be watching his movements. He had guns in his car, which an alert police patrol confirmed were state guns – a Z88, the ubiquitous Zulu, and an R5 automatic rifle.[13] Such guns could not have come from anywhere but police weapon stocks.

The police on the scene did not seem to make too much of this, not even the possession of an automatic weapon that could have been sourced only from a government armoury. An R5 rifle is a serious weapon and not one that individuals can own without a special permit. The man in the GTI had no such permit. He was arrested, yet no one seemed to put two and two together and work out that Hassan was in danger. Perhaps the police did not make the connection to Hassan because he did not live permanently at the house and they were unaware of his regular fish-feeding drive-pasts.

Stranger still was the police response. The man with the guns was arrested. But he was then released on bail and disappeared. I have not been able to get to the bottom of this. For a person arrested with an R5 state-issued automatic rifle and a Z88 to be granted bail seems strange. 'He had a clean record,' was the best a police investigating officer, whom I peppered with questions, could come up with.[14]

What also seemed strange was that the prospective hitman was spending time watching the target himself. Professional hitmen on the Cape Flats don't normally need to observe and record the movements of those they are about to kill. That can be done by others, before the hitman himself moves in. This would only be the case if a hitman is commissioned with a particular special assignment where outside knowledge has to be kept to the minimum – and the price is high.

CHAPTER 2

THE INTELLIGENCE REPORT

Hassan's family owned a shop on Lansdowne Road, a busy arterial thoroughfare, and the lawyer would meet clients there. His clientele encompassed an impressive pedigree of gang bosses, as the attendees at his funeral attested. And there were many more, including a host of gangsters for whom Hassan is said to have held money in trust. But his clients also included a number of prominent people in a variety of other criminal matters.

One was Jason Rohde, a wealthy businessman, convicted in November 2018 of murdering his wife, Susan, at the upmarket Spier wine estate near Stellenbosch (a case on which Hassan partnered with Advocate Pete Mihalik). Another was prominent Cape Town music festival producer David Forbes, accused of murdering one Toufiq Joseph, himself a murder accused, at a fuel station in 2015. And then there were three senior Western Cape police officers, including the former provincial commissioner, Arno Lamoer, who had been charged with money laundering and racketeering in a case that received national coverage. These high-profile cases are a testament to Hassan's extraordinary reputation as one of the city's go-to attorneys for people in serious trouble with the law.

Gang lawyers are an interesting crowd. Although criminological study has long suggested that a focus on primary offenders is too narrow, there is still far too little focus on lawyers who mix with the bad.[1] Some choose to go that route through family connections (Mihalik's father also did legal work for the gangs, for example[2]), but most seem to become gradually lured into representing the underworld as the money becomes easier, in the mould of Hassan.[3]

Gang lawyers mine the seams of the underworld and, as a result, often become prominent in their own right. That can be good for business: being in the news helps lure more clients. The problem is, territorial lines inevitably get crossed. Gang lawyers may take on clients who are aligned on opposite sides in vicious underworld wars and have to mediate between them. Or they might be asked to hold on to some money or weapons for a while until the heat passes. Or they may find that they know too much about a criminal business through the steady drip of information they are party to. They become like flies caught in a spider's web of potentially dangerous information and intrigue. This makes them vulnerable. Hassan is not the first – or the last – gang lawyer to die in a hail of bullets.[4] In December 2019, another Cape Town lawyer, Vernon Jantjies, who was doing 'gang work' was killed, with rumours that he died because he had failed to deliver, making him a target: 'Gang bosses are tired of paying these lawyers large amounts of money and then their guys still go to jail,' said one gang boss in the Jantjies case.[5] There have been several others too.[6]

In the months before his murder, a new client had come knocking on Hassan's door: one Irshaad 'Hunter' Laher, accused of being the crucial middleman between Colonel Prinsloo, the police officer who illegally supplied the guns from police stores, and the gangs. Hassan agreed to take on Laher's case.

Before acting as his lawyer in the guns case, the relationship between Laher and Hassan is unclear, but I was told by people close to Hassan that he already knew him and had acted as an interface between Laher and the wider gang community. Laher did not personally have good connections among the Cape gangsters, although he does have some interesting family connections, and it was Hassan who had provided him with some crucial introductions. Sitting as he did in a web of connections, it would have been easy for Hassan to have made some helpful introductions for Laher, for which, as a money-driven lawyer, he would have presumably taken a cut. There is no evidence that Hassan ever met Prinsloo, but he was likely to have been the crucial link in the Cape guns-to-gangs enterprise.

Hassan had good connections with the police. He was a fixture at police stations across the Flats. 'He would stroll in behind the counter and have a chat,' one police officer said. 'We all knew him.

He was relaxed and easy to talk to.' On the payroll of the gangs, Hassan would be dispatched to seek bail for a client or secure the release of an arrested gang member. Whether money changed hands in these exchanges is not certain, but the possibility that it did seemed to hang in the air.

Either way, Hassan's good connections with the police seem to be confirmed by the discovery of an important document. Found in his house after his death was a report that no defence attorney would or should have in his possession: an internal and highly secret police intelligence report and a police investigation diary. It could only have come from senior levels of the police.

Hassan had been rumoured to have some high-level connections in Crime Intelligence. Given how much information he had access to, it is certainly possible that Hassan may have been approached to be a police informant. Although we will probably never know, he would have been a natural choice.

The top-secret document contained details of none other than a purchase of state guns by an informant, who was named in court. (Pressure from the state has kept the name out of the public domain.) Intriguingly, the informant had been requested to obtain some of the guns under a so-called section 252A process; this is the part of the Criminal Procedure Act that outlines a process in which entrapment operations can be conducted, in cases where illegal acts, such as procuring drugs or weapons, are permitted for the purposes of an investigation.[7]

Hassan had this report in his possession but had not made use of it in his defence of his client Laher, presumably because that would have led to uncomfortable questions about how he had accessed it. After Hassan's murder, however, and on taking on the firearms case, Laher's new attorneys rifled through boxes of documents that Hassan kept on the matter. Squirrelled away among more innocuous paperwork, they found the intelligence report written by a police informant. You can almost visualise them holding it up, not sure what they had found: *What the hell is this?* As journalist Caryn Dolley has noted, the report 'contained details that would likely have sent shockwaves through gang circles and sown seeds of mistrust and suspicion among members of the Hard Livings'[8]

It was Hassan's old friend Mihalik, one of South Africa's preeminent defence advocates, a former prosecutor and an attendee at his funeral, who was instructed by Hassan, as Laher's attorney, to make the case for the defence. He demanded to know from the state whether any of the police's paid informers had played any role in the case against Laher. By using the report, Mihalik seemed eager to suggest that that the state may have entrapped his client, Laher, in the same way.

There is a lot of smoke and mirrors around this incident and it is difficult to know what to make of the intelligence report. Did it name one informant or several? What other documents were part of the collection?[9] But what we can ascertain is that the top-secret report had been an important piece in the overall investigation: an attempt had been made to purchase a set of guns to determine whether in fact guns from the police store were indeed on the streets. The guns were purchased by the unnamed informant, a gang boss or figure of repute in the criminal underworld. Such a transaction would have required knowledge and some kind of underworld trust between the buyers and sellers, something the informant could bring. On examination and testing, the guns were found to be the real thing – they were from the government Vereeniging police armoury.

What seems clear from the intelligence report, however, is only that the guns landed up in the hands of criminals. It details the purchase of guns from gangsters who had been supplied with the armoury guns. This shows how quickly the metal had moved through gang hands, although it does not implicate Laher. None of the guns specifically linked to Laher were part of the set purchased by the informant. It also raises the question: why did Hassan have the report among his files? But dead men don't speak, so in the end it is hard to know exactly how to answer this question.

Someone senior in the police must have leaked the document, and suspicion has fallen on elements in Crime Intelligence opposed to General Jeremy Vearey, the lead investigator in the Prinsloo guns case, whose informant it was who was mentioned in the intelligence report. The head of Crime Intelligence in the province, Major-General Mzwandile Tiyo, was seen as a Zuma man, or at least he has portrayed himself as one, and there had been fierce infighting in the local police.

For his part, Mihalik's strategy in his defence of Laher seems to have been to throw dirt into the circle and to demand further information from the state. The more he could acquire, the more he hoped he could trip up the police investigation into the firearms case.

If new documentation was found, a lot of other papers also seemed to disappear. This was never covered in the media, but Hassan's work diary and lists of who his clients were also vanished. Some of these documents had been taken by the police, but later vanished from Lansdowne Police Station; others disappeared from his mother's house.

There was one other tantalising detail. A reliable source passed on information that it was not only documents that had disappeared from Hassan's house: there were guns too – guns that had come from police stocks. Guns that were connected to killings on the Cape Flats. Hassan had apparently agreed to store them for one of his clients. While this could not be verified, it is, if true, a revelatory piece of information. Crime Intelligence was very sensitive on the case. Far too sensitive, it seemed. As other police officers have said, there seemed to be some powerful figures in the South African Police Service (SAPS) who had no wish to expose who was behind Hassan's death.

There was a strong interest, it seems, both in gangland and the police service, to ensure that nobody ever got to the bottom of who had murdered Noorudien Hassan, lawyer to illegal gun broker Laher. 'Scandinavian noir' crime fiction novelists could not have made the story up. In the Cape Town underworld, truth is stranger than fiction. It was all too real.

Who killed Hassan?

In trying to understand who had ordered the hit on Hassan, I set out to tap my underworld contacts. As always, however, they may well have shared only parts of the truth, or my interviewees had their own theories perhaps that they were eager to expound. And, at least in some cases, gangsters and members of the police may have been eager to promote one suspect, precisely because they did know in fact who had ordered the trigger to be pulled and wanted to obfuscate the truth. Presenting all the different theories advanced, however, at least provides as good an illustration as any of the smoke-and-mirrors world that Hassan operated in, and of the challenge of researching the workings of the Cape criminal economy.

The first theory is that the police killed Hassan. Even the fact that some entertain this theory as a possibility goes to show just how corrupt and riven by politics law enforcement in the Western Cape has become. Several people are convinced of this explanation, including some close to Hassan. Although I don't agree with their views when they are laid out in the swirling rumour mill on the Flats and the context of a general distrust of the police, they can seem remarkably convincing. If the police did have a hand, however, it is more likely that individual police officers would have acted in collusion with certain gangsters. That the police as a whole or a number of officers were responsible, acting either as an institution or some small conspiratorial group, seems highly unlikely.[10]

Fractures would appear in the police around the guns-to-gangs case, and this is also relevant here. In attempting to trace who may have killed Hassan and to galvanise the police into doing something about it, his brother made contact with anyone among the ranks of the police who would care to listen to his pleas, pressing them for a better response. In the process, he was told by senior figures in Crime Intelligence that senior police officers had killed his brother to protect police sources in light of the intelligence document that had been discovered in Hassan's house after his death. The finger of guilt, he suggested, pointed to Jeremy Vearey.[11]

Hassan's brother conceded that the police in the province were split politically along the lines of officers who supported Zuma and those who were behind Ramaphosa (who at that time had been president for three months). This in itself is a startling revelation. Could a gangland murder, and its failure to be resolved, be connected to a wider set of national political fault lines? Although he seemed to struggle to pick it all apart, Hassan's brother did promise 'big exposures' to come. For him, it was a case of a local police conspiracy submerged into a broader national one.

All of this was pure fiction and speculation, in my view. Nevertheless, it was a story that I had heard elsewhere, a different version being that the police, or at least certain police officers, had much to lose should Hassan tell all. But although there is little doubt that Hassan was instrumental in 'persuading' the police to lose a docket or not oppose a bail, there seemed little incentive for him to expose corrupt police contacts, the very sources of support upon which he relied heavily, it seemed, to get gang members out on bail.

It was reported to me that a senior police officer had said that he was glad Hassan was dead. '*Meng jou met die semels, dan vreet die varke jou*', was what he told a group of colleagues at a conference. That roughly translates as 'if you mix with pigswill, then the pigs will eat you', the implication being clear: Hassan had delved too deeply into the underworld, and had paid the ultimate price. On the face of it, the theory was plausible because of the strange triangular relationship between the police, the gangs and Hassan himself. It was hardly conclusive proof, though, that the police had done the job. But policemen whom I trust have told me that if the police genuinely wanted to solve this case, it could be done in a month. Nobody seemed too keen to do it and several detectives I spoke to expressed genuine fear of becoming involved.

The second theory, and one that is much more plausible, is that Hassan had run afoul of the gangs themselves. That would mean that one or more of the gang bosses at his funeral would have had a hand in his killing – and that's why attending the funeral was key for the killer to reinforce the impression of innocence. Who would attend their own victim's funeral? Who indeed?

A big part of Hassan's strength in the marketplace in which he operated, but also by implication his vulnerability, was that he was either a conduit for funds for gang bosses in different deals, or administered the finances of several trust accounts for competing gang bosses. 'They left money with him like a bank,' a senior-level gang member with some knowledge of gang finances said. 'And big people with big money put him in control of the rands, so I think they blamed him if money went missing or if money did not get to where it was supposed to be.' At least some of that money is alleged to have come from the purchases of guns, the very case involving Laher, for whom Hassan was acting as attorney.

On the street, the word was that the 28s gang had taken out the lawyer. Apparently, or so the story goes, Hassan had acted as the financial conduit for a big drug deal that subsequently fell apart. He seemed to have used a portion of the money already, and so found himself caught in a bind when it was demanded that he pay it back. It was circumstances like this that appeared to have led to the 2014 attempt on his life, with a senior gang figure being the main suspect in that case.

Hassan seemed to have got himself into a vulnerable position on a different issue too – the matter of organising bail. Promises were made, according to several gang-affiliated people, but the lawyer could not deliver on his promises. Money changed hands in this process, but instead of people being released on bail, they found themselves behind bars.

One of the Sexy Boys explained the process like this: 'If I pay a moerse amount of money to get four people out of prison, then I expect them to come out of prison because I know how the systems work and I know whose hands must be buttered in order for the handcuffs to come off.'

According to another gangster, this time from the 28s, 'Mense got pissed off, because some important soldiers went to prison when they were needed for important drugs deals.'

It was difficult not to feel some degree of sympathy for Hassan, imagining the endless calls and messages that he must have received as he made his way from police station to police station. The life of a gang lawyer must be tough. What Hassan was often doing was, to use gang lingo, 'springing soldiers', the people who were key to the money-making operations of the gangs. A gang may have plenty among its ranks, but only some of them could be trusted. It was therefore key to business that these guys were working, and not locked away in a cell. The astonishing thing was that Hassan was simultaneously working for competing gangs, and that in itself would be enough to breed suspicion and resentment.

An added complication in all of this was that Hassan, gang lawyer number one, was not in fact a particularly good lawyer. He never attended court, it was said, leaving things to his associate, a certain Mr Khan. Hassan was more of a negotiator, allegedly a cash bag carrier for the gangs and corrupt police officers. He sold promises of freedom, but the system could not, or did not always allow him to, deliver it. Perhaps a new cop was on duty, making things difficult, or an older one was running scared, or the price of opening the handcuffs just got a little more expensive, probably eroding his own fees. Not everything could be controlled.

The third theory is that it was PAGAD who knocked off the lawyer. This scenario is given some credence by the discovery of the link between the bakkie that carried the killer and a PAGAD gathering taking place down the coast from Cape Town in Rooi Els. As mentioned, PAGAD had threatened Hassan before, and he lived in fear of the group. Their motivation would have been to send out a grim warning to other lawyers not to get too close to the gangs, or simply to disrupt the gangs' financial liquidity by taking out the holder of so many trust accounts. But the group was not what it once had been. In its heyday, it would have claimed responsibility; in the wake of Hassan's killing, there was only an ominous silence.

A prominent gang leader in the 28s, himself a killer of some repute, told me with just a little too much certainty: 'Don't you know, Hassan was killed by PAGAD. Everyone knows that.' Given that the 28s were on the suspect list, it seemed hard to take the comment at face value. And not everyone was pointing the finger at PAGAD. I had been told with equal certainty by others that it had to be the work of the 28s. Obfuscating the truth by inserting things into the underground information flow was common practice in the underworld.

What is perhaps most interesting about Hassan and the three theories is that just about everyone seemed to want him dead, albeit for different reasons. It was even suggested that perhaps they had all acted together, each in different ways, but with overlapping and reinforcing intent.

A mysterious suspect

All this talking to gangsters and police about the case began to taint my sense of reality. It was as if the entire city was operating on conspiracy. It eroded the optimist in me, partly because the case seemed all but unsolvable, but also because people referred to it as unsolvable while pointing to possible suspects. It was a case of a riddle wrapped in a mystery inside an enigma, all shrouded by a Cape winter mist. But some of the mist blew away dramatically one morning when I was informed that a suspect had surfaced.

Well, predictably, it was more complex than that. There was a suspect, but nobody would say that on record because he was not officially a suspect. A high-level gang boss in prison had told a very reliable contact of mine who he was. Some police detectives also confirmed it was the case, although he could not be charged, at least not for the Hassan murder.

This suspect appears to be one of Cape Town's most proficient hitmen. Several police officers told me that he would work for whoever paid him, so arresting him would not necessarily expose the hand that had hired him. The suspected hitman goes by the moniker of Po. His real name is Ziyaad Haywood. He had previously been arrested and then skipped bail, in that case for the murder of a security guard, Herman Hendricks, at the China Town in Ottery in November 2016. According to witnesses, the killer had walked directly up to Hendricks and shot him in the face in cold blood, taking his gun.[12] A photograph of Hendricks in his uniform lying in a pool of blood went viral on Facebook. I visited the scene: Hendricks was shot dead in full view of several shops. CCTV cameras also captured the whole incident and police identified a suspect.

This, it turned out, was the same man who had been arrested outside Hassan's house, armed with a Z88 and an R5, a couple of weeks before his murder. If the police at the time had thought he was out for just a well-armed drive, this time it was clear that he was a murderer. There was, however, no sign of him.

Po killed poor Hendricks on Saturday 5 November 2016. Hassan was killed two days later, on Monday 7 November. It remains unclear why Hendricks had to die. By all accounts, the stolen gun has not been used in another crime. Perhaps he just angered Po, got in his way, talked to him in a manner that he did not particularly like. There is no knowing. 'He is absolutely ruthless,' an experienced detective from the Flats told me. 'A mercenary, basically. He kills for whoever pays.' There are several pictures of Haywood in the public domain, and they show a dark-eyed emotionless young man looking at the camera, in one case with extremely bloodshot eyes, in another with a large, black, bushy beard and closely cropped hair. As his reputation on the street suggests, he looks the killing type. He has committed several murders, including that of a friend who snitched on him.[13]

There is not enough evidence to prosecute Po for the Hassan murder, apparently, or the police involved feel that this would be a detrimental career – or even life-limiting – move. But I have little doubt that he is the man: at least, that is what some powerful gangsters imprisoned with him have indicated. He said so himself, and apparently didn't try to hide it. I believe them. And a police officer confirmed it, but would not go on the record, and told me it was better for my health to forget about it all.

What Po had been doing outside Hassan's house in mid-October 2016, a short time before Hassan's killing, no doubt was scoping things out. He may have been frightened off for a while, but had recovered his confidence by 7 November. (It does of course raise the question of why a hitman apparently known to the police was released on bail after having been arrested with stolen state weapons.)

Po may have been a killer, but his parents still seemed to think highly of him. His father, Moegsien, reportedly had links to PAGAD, and was a pretty cold-hearted man himself. Police suspected that his parents were sheltering him, and they returned several times to search the house, always finding nothing. On 7 July 2018, however, the police,

Ziyaad Haywood, known as 'Po', an accomplished hitman and the likely killer of Noorudien Hassan.
PHOTO: GALLO IMAGES / *DIE BURGER*

conducting a regular sweep of the house, smelled a rat. Moegsien was acting suspiciously in the bedroom as police moved near a large closet. The officers then discovered that one part of the closet could be removed, revealing a secret compartment where Po was found hiding. The media dubbed him the 'closet killer', a label that has stuck.[14] He was charged with the murder of Herman Hendricks, among others.

The closet killer was confined to Pollsmoor Prison pending trial. This hitman is an independent operator, so not gang-aligned. But, as someone who works in the prison said, he would need protection inside 'because Hassan is big. Nobody wants the truth out.' In March 2020, Po was sentenced to an effective 211 years in prison for murder, kidnapping, robbery and the illegal possession of firearms.[15]

There may not be sufficient evidence to secure a criminal conviction but there is good reason, and good authority, to believe that Po was Hassan's assassin. If Po is the killer, it does not solve the conundrum, however, of who ordered the crime. Po was just a tool – a violent, cold-hearted one, but a tool all the same. Something was rotten. And it led back to the case of Prinsloo's guns, one of which it is likely was used to kill Noorudien Hassan, a spider in his big web that linked the fancy suburbs along the southern fringes of Table Mountain where he is buried, to the exclusive apartment blocks along the Atlantic Coast, to the sprawling, gang-ridden Cape Flats.

CHAPTER 3

A PATCHWORK DEFENDED BY GUNS

There is a point where you come speeding around the contour of the mountain from the plush suburbs of Constantia and, just before you crest the hill and begin to turn to face the yet unseen city centre, the view of the Cape Flats unfolds below. At night it is a carpet of flickering lights stretching as far as the eye can see. Visitors sometimes stop their cars to take a look at this sight spread out before them. They stand on the curb, the Cape breeze on their faces, and marvel at the beauty of this city. It may not be one of the regular tourist attractions, but it is nevertheless an arresting sight to behold this man-made spread of flickering urban light.

Closer up, that glowing carpet is divided into an intricate set of spaces, a jigsaw of competing pieces of drug turf bathed in the blood of young men. Knives used to be the weapons of choice for gang violence. Guns were hard to come by and were treasured possessions, loaned out and returned to the gang boss. By about 2013, knives had been overtaken by guns. The extraordinary acceleration in murder rates that followed this shift paralleled the arrival of Prinsloo's gun consignments. One old gang member from Hanover Park said that when he went to prison in the late 1990s, the Americans in his area had only two guns between them; when he returned from prison over a decade later, 'guns were everywhere'.

After several years of accelerating murder levels, it had become a perfect storm out on the Flats, until in 2019, Latin American-style, the military were deployed to quell the gang wars and, later, the COVID lockdown pushed violence temporarily off the streets. If you take the time to drive around them, there is a sort of elusive beauty to the neighbourhoods – Vrygrond, Manenberg, Grassy Park, Heideveld, Bonteheuwel, Blue Downs, Belhar, Bishop Lavis,

GIVE US MORE GUNS

Elsies River. On a wet winter's night, the yellow streetlights illuminate ghostly shapes through the windscreen wipers. People who live there are friendly and talkative – oddly, even the gangsters. It's a hard-bitten place, but one with spirit.

That contrast is quite difficult to describe to outsiders: people will take you into their home just for a chat and a cup of tea. They needn't do it, but they do. And they will speak in hushed tones about the gangsters, or about other gangsters. And they will explain how the new democratic order has left Coloured people behind, that the jobs have dried up and the drugs and guns have arrived, big time.

The violence and criminal control that emerged on the Cape Flats during the first two decades of the new millennium are an outcome of two contradictory forces, both falling under the much-maligned label of globalisation, which has been badly managed. If Brexit and Donald Trump are two realities that globalisation can be blamed for, so is the evolution of the gangs nearer to home. On one hand was the Flats' growing marginalisation from the economy, as surrounding industries, most notably textiles, were savaged by cheaper products from Asia as the new South Africa opened up its borders to global trade and tariffs were eliminated.

At the same time, the Flats became immersed in the global drug market, driven by growing demand and record levels of global drug production. Cheap and nasty stuff to be sure, and known by colloquial names – tik/choef and straws (crystal meth); unga (heroin mix); beads/flowers/buttons (Mandrax); rocks (crack cocaine) – but still part of something bigger. In that sense, the Cape Flats is at the same time both highly marginalised and highly integrated, and its integration into the global drugs economy delinks its people from the legal possibilities that the new democratic order promised, but has not delivered to them.

Opposite | **Gang density in Cape Town, 2019** | Source: The map was produced as part of a research project by the Global Initiative Against Transnational Organized Crime that sought to count the number of gangs across greater Cape Town. The data was collected in the course of 2018 and 2019.

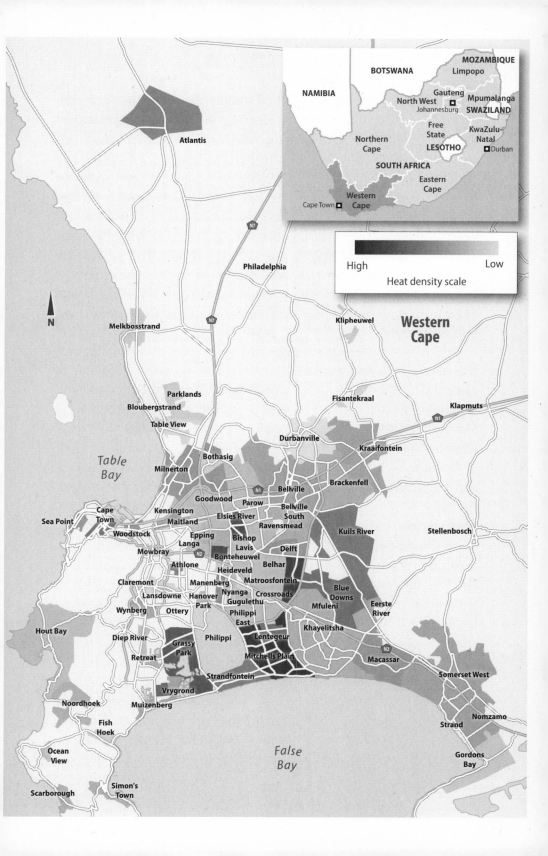

This is hard-core gangland and people die all the time. In the decade from 2010 to 2019, it was war here. The gangs control areas of land, dividing the city up into 'turf'. In some parts, a single gang is in control; in others, numerous gangs are present. The map of gang density across the city shows high concentrations of different gangs in places like Elsies River, Bonteheuwel, Grassy Park, Manenberg and Mitchells Plain. These are also areas where gang-related violence is at its most severe. In places where a single gang is in control, levels of violence are often lower. This patchwork geography of gangsterism has been shaped by two things: drugs and guns. And they are inextricably interwoven. The story of the killing can't be told without understanding the source of the firearms: the police armoury.

A gang needs turf to sell drugs and needs guns to control its turf. It is about as simple as that. Of course, you must recruit people to pack and tout the stuff, and you need hands to hold the guns and pull the trigger. And of course you need people, like the now dead lawyer Hassan, to get your worker bees out of prison. But this is the simple business model: drugs, turf and guns.

It is a model that has caused untold damage across South Africa, and the state's responses to it are largely seen as ineffective by communities. While ordinary people experience gangs in highly localised ways, the threads that tie together the supplies of drugs and violence span the country. The connections between gangsterism in Cape Town, parts of Johannesburg and Nelson Mandela Bay, as well as Durban, long a trafficking hub, are closely knit. Across the country, community frustration at the lack of state responses began to build up in early 2018. It would erupt later in the year in a series of protests, including a march to Parliament in October.

How tight a hold gangs have over their communities is evident when you speak to people. Gangsters are killers, but they are also self-styled protectors and distributors of largesse. This is what made the public outcry over gangsterism that seemed to emerge from nowhere in October and November 2018 significant. Later, when COVID struck, the gangs moved quickly in an attempt to improve their local legitimacy by distributing food parcels and cash among needy communities.

In an unprecedented move, the national government acceded to community and provincial government demands to deploy the military across the Cape Flats in 2019. This intervention does appear to have had some success in tamping down the violence, while of course it did not resolve the drivers of gangsterism, including police corruption.

In the days before the military were deployed, people had already had enough. It often seems that communities protest with depressing regularity and the state responds (particularly if elections are nearing) with the usual package of a score of fierce police officers wearing dark glasses and the promise that the gangsters will be 'klapped'; then they are withdrawn when needed elsewhere. In that community mix are courageous groups of activists, cajoling and demanding, who run the gamut of gang governance and repression. For their troubles, they sometimes get harassed by the police too.

A hard living

Manenberg is one of the beating hearts of Cape Town's gang wars. The area, less than four square kilometres in size, and some 20 kilometres from the city centre, has been torn apart by conflict between multiple gangs, led by two of the city's most violent organised-crime groups: the Americans and the Hard Livings. The conflict was at its most brutal in 2013 and 2014, when schools in the area were closed down. It flared up again in 2015 and 2016, and it still rumbles on now, the sharp crack of gunfire in the street an everyday occurrence.

Places like Manenberg may be gang-dominated but they are also where a contest is playing out for leadership between gangsters and civic leaders seeking to erode the power of the crime lords. It is often an unbalanced relationship because the bosses have more money and pose an ever-present threat of violence. That threat is not to be taken lightly: community activists are harassed in subtle and not-so-subtle ways. One prominent Manenberg activist, Roegchanda Pascoe, had her house shot up after she testified in a court case against a prominent gang boss. She was not at home at the time and her children cowered on the floor as the bullets flew. Pascoe has not been able to go home again and has relocated to protect her family.

This confrontation is a dangerous business, and activists and other civil-society members often feel unprotected by the state. At its heart it is a contest of legitimacy between those who promise the immediate benefits of money or a drug high and local leaders who promote what seems to be an unattainable vision of a community that cares for itself, that educates its children, that integrates into a city from which people feel alienated. And, apart from the threat of violence, what the gangsters offer is immediate and tangible (like the food they handed out during the COVID lockdown). What civic activists demand from the state – better policing, for example – has been promised before, but in the view of many of Manenberg's residents, has never arrived. Community leaders like Pascoe say that more guns flowing into the community have tipped the balance of power away from them even further.

The 2015/16 gang war in Manenberg is said to have originated when a member of the Clever Kids gang was killed by several members of the Hard Livings. That death seemed to be the result of the Clever Kids and their allies the Dixie Boys venturing from their usual mainstay of extortion into the more lucrative drug trade, thus sparking a spiral of violence, as the Hard Livings were having none of it.

This conflict merged with a later one when members of the Americans gang defected to the Hard Livings (who were seen to be making good money in the local drug trade), resulting in a furious and violent attack by the Americans. Those Americans who had defected later returned to their original gang (significantly, with guns they had now acquired) after a split developed in the senior ranks of the Hard Livings.

On the face of it, Manenberg is a morass of gangs. There are ten large ones and some 40 smaller ones operating in an area of less than three and half square kilometres. These complex back-and-forth conflicts with their litany of gang killings can be hard to parse, with the result that external reporting has a tendency towards the 'this is just a mess' sort, or stereotypical conclusions along the lines of 'Coloured people are naturally violent'.

Across the Western Cape, there are probably over a hundred gangs: the Laughing Boys and the Dollar Kids, the Fast Guns and the Gaza Mobsters, the Bad Boys and the Bad Rush, the Naughty Boys and the Nice Time Kids, the Mongrels and the Mal Boys. There are the Barbarian Mobsters and the Jakaranda Kids, the Okka Boys and the Pitbulls, the Yuru Cats and the Young Gifted Bastards. The list goes on.

Not all gangs, or gangsters, are equal, however. Gangs, as organised clusters of criminal activity and sources of violence, need to be understood along both horizontal lines, by their geographic spread and membership, and their vertical integration, most notably the degree to which gang bosses themselves have developed contacts within the state for protection, or externally to access drugs and sell contraband. In the latter case, for example, there is some talk that at least one gang boss has made contact with Latin American drug sources, opening up the possibility of a supply pipeline that may transform that gang's position in relation to others.

The pie chart overleaf depicts the Cape Town gangs that have the largest number of members and the greatest geographical distribution (those that are present in more than ten areas).[1] In terms of pure size and reach, the Americans remain the most dominant gang, followed by the 28s, the Terrible Josters, the Hard Livings (referred to colloquially as the HLs) and the Mongrels.

The gangland ecosystem is like a pyramid at the top of which is a handful of large and powerful gangs (the major gangs shown in the pie chart). A better description of these is criminal organisations. Below these big players are what might be called aspirant gangs. These are smaller, newer on the scene and often very violent; they operate under the radar and seek alliances with the established players. The Ghettos, Fancy Boys, Junky Funky Kids (JFKs) and Nice Time Boys fit this description.

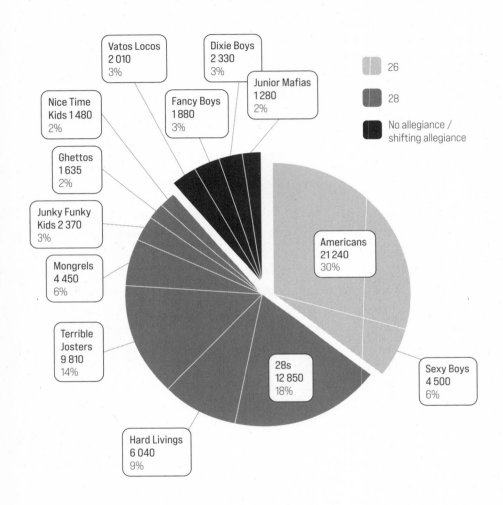

Gang membership of the most prominent gangs on the Cape Flats, 2019

SOURCE: Based on Global Initiative Against Transnational Organized Crime gang count by area conducted in 2018 and 2019.

The pie chart contains the estimated numbers of about 70 per cent of the city's gangs with a total of approximately 71 000 members. The overall estimated number of gang members for Cape Town is some 100 000, so an additional 30 000 gang members are present in smaller, less organised outfits.[2] These very small gangs are at the bottom of the gang hierarchy, often based at schools or on individual streets. They are formed and fade quickly. Their business is small scale, as they generally lack the external contacts in larger criminal networks that are essential to secure a regular supply of drugs. To survive, they inevitably align themselves with bigger, more established gangs.

The Americans, the British and the Number

As one moves from place to place in Cape Town, the multiplicity of gang names in any given territory obscures a set of bigger dynamics: the city is in fact largely divided into two competing, if internally conflictual, broad gang alliances. The brutal and often seemingly directionless killing corresponds to a series of overarching logics. This point is seldom noted in press coverage or academic studies, one reason being that gang bosses themselves prefer explanations that suggest that the gang environment is fragmented and conflictual. To describe the tight linkages between the bosses and the fact that significant criminal consolidation has occurred makes people potential targets for public outcry or law enforcement, or raises the question of why they are not apprehended. For reasons that stretch back into the founding mythology of the gangs, that division is based on the American War of Independence, which pitted the Americans against the British.

Gangs on the Flats, and in District 6, from where people were forcibly moved under apartheid in the 1960s, were formed initially as a source of community solidarity against the forces of apartheid. These were the 'corner store gangs' of the 1950s and 1960s, explains a former gangster, made up of guys who used to hang around the local shop. It is ironic to a certain extent, then, that community activists who promote a different vision of the future now mobilise against them – a new form of community organisation responding to a badly mutated older sort.

These old gangsters should not be mythologised too much, however, for which there is a tendency sometimes. They could also be ruthless. For example, they ran protection rackets (although by current standards, they were admittedly pretty tame). It was also a context where the apartheid state lacked legitimacy and there was space for alternative forms of governance. For that reason, the gangs were able to amass some power and meaning. When communities were forcibly moved and broken up by the apartheid authorities, it was the idea of gangs, and some of the old ties, that re-established themselves. As forms of social organisation, gangs were sought out as allies, both by the forces of liberation and by the apartheid state. That strengthened their prestige, upped their recognition and embedded them socially. These small gains made in a brutal and bigger war would have lasting consequences.

The origins of the opposing alliance are strongly rooted in two pieces of overlapping history and gang mythology. Gang lore on the Cape Flats can be hard to follow in its intricacies. Gang history matters to participants, although some of the edges have now blurred a bit and the mythology has been appropriated by a new and violent set of actors. Nevertheless, the symbols and labels that were adopted and internalised years ago still carry great mobilising power.

The corner-store gangs adopted a symbolic identity drawn from American mafia B-movies. The terminology they used was taken from the big screen and internalised into gang organisational principles and language. One of the earliest of these American-branded gangs had its roots in Durban. A group of hustlers, calling themselves the Young Americans, drove flashy American cars and dressed to match the look of the movie stars. Some of the Young Americans later migrated to Cape Town, which prompted the formation of an opposing gang, inevitably called the Ugly Americans. 'Ugly' was adopted, remembers one old-timer, because of the new guys' reputation for violence.

The Young and the Ugly Americans were later to join forces to provide strength in numbers in the face of several new emerging gangs who were beginning to throw their weight around. 'All Americans stick together!' became the clarion call as a period of gang mobilisation gained pace in the 1970s and 1980s. They adopted US-style symbols, such as the Statue of Liberty and the bald-headed eagle, iconography that made its way into the tattoos and graffiti that branded their identity. Given that the Americans and British had been allies in two world wars and the Cold War, it might seem strange that, as a process of gang consolidation began on the Flats, groups that opposed the Americans tagged themselves as British, adopting symbols around the Union Jack.

To make matters more complex within the gang ecosystem, a set of prison gangs had formed in South Africa under the moniker 'the Number', whose origins lie in the period of colonial control and early industrialisation around Johannesburg and Durban in the late 19th and early 20th centuries. The Number system orders gang life and hierarchies in South African prisons. Its ideology entails establishing relations with the prison authorities (known as the *lekker bandiet policy*) where treating prisoners with contempt is met with resistance from the Number gangs. The gangs have strict hierarchies and rules around the conduct of illicit activities, sexual practices and violence. The objective of the system is to create an alternative society with its own ranks, rules and regulations that are deliberately complex and inaccessible to outsiders. I have had many discussions with prisoners and ex-prisoners on the issue of the Number, and it can be very hard to follow and sometimes contradictory.

The Number gangs – the 26s, 27s and 28s – engage in a fierce process of recruitment for new arrivals in prison (as part of an overall credo of growth and prison control, partly in an attempt to structure relations with the prison authorities, including making demands for food and bedding). For ordinary prisoners, becoming part of a Number gang is often essential to survival and a route to receiving protection.

The Number system remains powerful in prison as the gangs struggle to retain solidarity and order. Outside, the symbols of the prison gangs have mutated over time, overlapping with those of the street gangs. This overlap, driven by a greater business orientation on both sides, is seen by old salts as a commercialisation of the Number, symbolised by the ability of some to purchase high rank in the Number gangs. This alignment of street gangs with the Number gangs, and the resulting clusters of gangs labelled as '26 gangs' or '28 gangs', is now central to a business model that relies on the seeking of alliances, the recruitment of new members and the holding of turf. (The position of the 27s is more complex, as they have for most part rejected the commercial orientation they see the 26s and 28s as having adopted.)

Significantly, this alignment of the gangs today – as either 26s or 28s – almost exactly mirrors the alliances between the old American- and British-aligned gangs. Thus the Americans gang is 26 aligned. The same applies to a cluster of related gangs, including the Sexy Boys, the Clever Kids and the Dixie Boys. On the other side of the divide, in the British alliance, is a cluster of gangs aligned with the 28s – the powerful Hard Livings, their allies the Junky Funky Kids, the Ghettos, the Mongrels and the 28s.

The result is that, while analysis of gang conflict in Cape Town often points to fragmentation of the gang ecosystem, whereby more and more low-level gangs are formed and older gangs splinter, there is in fact an important concurrent element of consolidation; or the grouping into bigger alliances, in the sense that few conflicts take place outside of this broad 26–28, American–British divide. Although individual gangs may have autonomy within each of the alliances, and the alliances themselves may vary by area depending on the affiliation of smaller gangs, the reality is that gang wars almost always occur between gangs in these two rival clusters. Nevertheless, there is not always a common enemy uniting gangs and directing their violence: there is also vicious internal competition for leadership within individual gangs, and, at the same time, some cooperation at a high level between bosses of different gangs. There are also several cases where aspirants within the gangs have reached across the wider divide to recruit hitmen or secure cooperation to take out the rivals above them. The killing of Rashied Staggie in December 2019 was such a case.

The big daddy

Central to Cape Town's gang history – and at the centre of one alliance – is the Americans gang. The father of the Americans is Jackie Lonte, the notorious 'Jakkals', who began to shape the gang and its role in the emerging dagga and Mandrax economy in the 1980s. He provided the foundation for what one local gang boss described as 'the city's big daddy gang'.

Based in Athlone, in the lee of Table Mountain, Jakkals recognised the need to shape his organisation according to principles of American power. The stars and stripes became the gang's motif, a shed in Jakkal's backyard known as the 'White House' was where gang meetings were held, and the gang's tattoos reflected American iconography.

The end of the 1980s saw the Americans accumulating power and, with it, Lonte grew wealthy; he drove around the Flats in a Porsche, an unheard-of display of wealth by a non-white person under apartheid. The source of that money and power was the drugs economy.

Without guns, persuasion and symbolism were the gangsters' key tools. That is one reason why gang history so closely resembles community history in parts of the Flats. The history of the gangs is one of outsize personalities who organised illegal markets and mobilised communities to support them.

Born Neville Heroldt, Lonte was a gang visionary. If you sit any older knowledgeable gang person down and have a chat, stories of Lonte will come up. Seen as the George Washington of gangland, he built the Americans' empire. Lonte positioned the gang as the source of dagga and Mandrax, which were both growing markets on the Cape Flats in the 1980s and early 1990s. (Harder drugs were few and far between at the time.) After 1994, as South Africa's barriers to world markets came down, the Americans pioneered the distribution of Ecstasy and Acid.

Lonte also built his gang empire on the symbols of American gangster movies, integrating these into the fashion, graffiti and tattoos of
everyday gangster life. The Americans soon developed a reputation
for violence as their market share expanded, and Lonte was not afraid
to use threats and force. The gangs had guns then, but not in large
numbers. Gun control was a strict affair in those days. The bosses
knew where their gangs' guns were and they were used sparingly.

In prison, the Americans had formed an alignment with the 26s.
One of Lonte's innovations was to export that prison linkage to
the streets. He is also said to have purchased his rank in the prison
Number gang instead of moving up the system, as others had done
in the past. This was an unprecedented development and the begin-
nings of the effective commercialisation of the Number system, the
exchange of money for rank, which old gang hands decry.

By 1998, the year in which Lonte died in a hail of bullets outside his Athlone home, levels of gun violence on the Flats had been
ratcheted up. Shortly before he was killed, Lonte had announced
his retirement from gang management, although, as in other cases,
there is the question whether supposed 'retirement' would have
been a cover for continued activity. Significantly for our story, it is
likely that Lonte was killed by state-issue weapons because R5 and
9 mm cartridges (presumably from a Z88) were found on the scene.

Building on the vision and commercial and political nous of their
early leaders, the Americans became Cape Town's and South Africa's
biggest organised-crime group in terms of numbers and territorial
control. Today they control turf from Ocean View in the far south
of the peninsula to Milnerton on the Atlantic seaboard, from Grassy
Park to Mitchells Plain and Strand along the False Bay coast, and
all the way to Kraaifontein in the interior. Although the main source
of their revenue today is still the drugs market, hence the need for
turf and guns to defend that ground, they have multiple lines of
business, including protection rackets and extortion (notably in the
taxi industry), the illicit abalone trade and the sale of stolen goods.

The Americans' boss is currently believed to be Igshaan 'Sanie'
Davids, often known simply as Sanie American (who is quoted

recounting the story of the Z88 sales in the preface). Sanie lives in Kensington on the Cape Flats and (predictably) claims to have retired from gang business. Sanie inherited the leadership of the Americans from his brother Kippie, who was assassinated by the 28s. He appears not to be a man to be messed with, having served a ten-year sentence for murdering a Young Americans gang member, slicing through his throat with a knife and nearly decapitating him. (In a 2014 YouTube video, Sanie speaks about how he 'used to love stabbing people'.[3]) He has seen the influence of the Americans go nationwide, and forged strong connections with criminal networks in Johannesburg, Durban and elsewhere.

Another important link in the Americans chain is Lloyd Hill, a senior gang figure based in Durban. This connection was at the initiative of Sanie American, who sought to consolidate the gang's positioning in the Indian Ocean city, given that the port is a key destination for imported drugs, which the Americans would transport for distribution in Cape Town. Hill is said to have forged partnerships with Nigerian drug dealers, initiating a system of barter in which drugs such as Mandrax are exchanged for cocaine. In Cape Town high-ranking American bosses acknowledge Hill's power; in the mother city he is sometimes known as the 'Ghost American' because his power is felt while he himself remains unseen.

The Americans have not been shy in terms of connecting themselves to political power. In 2011, a group of gang bosses met with then President Jacob Zuma in secret at his official residence in Cape Town just before local-government elections. The meeting was apparently brokered by Hill, whose Durban base had given him useful connections to the networks around Zuma.[4]

Within the broad alliance of the American gangs is one that is much in the news in contemporary Cape Town: the Sexy Boys. Now allegedly led by Donkie Booysen, this gang is a busy, savvy and violent outfit. Donkie's mother, a hospital cleaner who moonlighted, selling dagga on the side, was convinced that the way to riches and success was to subvert a system that had been stacked against her. She was a tiger mother with an alternative definition of what success stood for.[5] Despite conflict between the Booysen siblings, the Sexy Boys rose to prominence in the 1980s and have carved out a substantial network across the Cape Peninsula and the Flats. The gang has been connected to targeted violence and extortion of nightclubs and restaurants.

Over time, all superpowers decline, and by the late 1990s a new set of challengers were emerging in gangland to disrupt the prevailing order dominated by the Americans and their allies.

CHAPTER 4

BATTLE LINES DRAWN

The Americans had been the dominant Cape gang since the 1970s, but they would find themselves confronted by a new and powerful foe, led by the notorious twin brothers Rashied and Rashaad Staggie. The evocatively named Hard Livings emerged in 1983 and 1984 in Manenberg.

The HLs, as they are known, and the gang's business-minded sibling leaders, are said to have splintered from the Americans. Tired of paying the role of middlemen in Manenberg, the brothers seized control and formed their own gang. For the Americans, that painted a large target on the back of the gang and the Staggie brothers. In contradistinction to the symbols of American power, the Hard Livings branded themselves with imagery redolent of the British empire – the MG sports car and the pound sign – as well as the symbol B13 (a reference to Bungalow 13, where a prominent gang leader known as Bobby Mongrel, the founder of the Mongrels gang, which is aligned to the Hard Livings, lived in District 6).[1]

The Hard Livings, as the name suggests, were not afraid of using violence; indeed they needed it to win and retain turf. As a result, Manenberg has been a war zone ever since their formation, a close-quarters and extraordinarily vicious battle between the old-order Americans and the newbie Hard Livings. The battle lines between the two were drawn, and each of their respective allied gangs joined in the fray. The guns that began to flow in would fuel that conflict.

The brothers' strategy, given the tightly controlled territory that they set themselves up to challenge, was to flood their areas in Manenberg with drugs. The ensuing profits would then allow them to expand. At the same time, the Staggies needed to elicit community support, mafia-style, so they distributed largesse to residents in the form of food hampers and cash, a tactic that the Americans would emulate. Building on their Manenberg base, the Hard Livings expanded across the peninsula. Today, although they have a smaller geographic base than the Americans, they have a presence in Mitchells Plain, Grassy Park, Bonteheuwel, Belhar, Maitland, Woodstock and the city bowl.

The Staggies' dramatic rise, and the way they co-opted the community, made them the prime target of PAGAD, which was just beginning to flex its muscles in the new democratic order. In August 1996, just over two years into the term of President Nelson Mandela, the vigilante group arranged a large gathering and sought to deliver an ultimatum to the brothers at a house in Salt River known for being a hub for drug sales. At first, neither brother was there, but Rashaad Staggie later arrived on the scene. In a dramatic lynching, which was widely publicised, PAGAD members shot Rashaad and then burnt him to death. Photos taken during the incident show him dressed in a green-and-white jacket, slumped over the wheel of his car, blood running from his ear. He was later dragged from the vehicle and a petrol bomb was thrown at him, setting him on fire. Now badly wounded, in one final effort, Rashaad ran down the road like a human torch, before finally collapsing in a gutter, where he died. The burning gang boss became a potent symbol of the power of PAGAD at the time.

One of the reasons that the Hard Livings were targeted by PAGAD was that they were an enormously disruptive presence on the Cape Flats. What was less visible, though, was that the newcomers' disruption of the gang ecosystem was enabled by their access to guns, which they also sold to their affiliate gangs, the Laughing Boys, the Ghettos, the Terrible Josters and the Junky Funky Kids. The Mongrels would also join the alliance, although they had initially been fierce rivals to the Hard Livings. All of these allied gangs were able to acquire guns from the Hard Livings, enabling the alliance to expand its territory, threatening the city-wide power of the Americans. The Mongrels were to play a critical role as the first conduits through which the Prinsloo guns would be distributed to the Cape Flats.

Plundering state guns was not new business for the Hard Livings and they were innovators in this respect. In 2004, Rashied Staggie was arrested and convicted for a burglary at the Police Public Order Unit's armoury at Faure near Cape Town. According to insiders, the gang had long identified the state as the easiest way of sourcing weapons in bulk rather than one by one in suburban burglaries; obtaining the guns was a means to greater power and also profit.

Taking his place in the family gangster dynasty, Rashied's son, Abdullah Boonzaaier, has risen in prominence in the gang leadership, although was said to be aggrieved that he did not get the top position when Rashied Staggie went to prison. (Boonzaaier is in fact Rashaad's biological son, whom Rashied adopted after his brother's murder.)

In prison, Rashied Staggie claimed he had found religion. Word on the street, however, suggests that he remained closely involved in gang activities and that his religious proclivities were just a cover. In research on gang violence in Westbury, Johannesburg, Staggie's name came up repeatedly as the major supplier of drugs and guns to the area.[2] One gang member who knew his movements said, 'That's just bullshit' – in reference to his proclaimed conversion to the faith, 'because he is still selling drugs.'

In December 2019, Rashied Staggie was assassinated in the same street where his brother was killed in 1996. His death and the rumours that continue to circulate as to who was responsible provide an insight into the complicated rivalries of gangland. Several well-connected sources suggest that it was Boonzaaier who organised his uncle and adoptive father's assassination. The son allegedly felt that he had been passed over for the lucrative leadership of the Hard Livings and partnered with rivals in the Terrible Josters to clear away the competition. The Terrible Josters and the Hard Livings are aligned against the broader American alliance, so this could well be a case of an aggrieved prince removing the king.[3]

But the complex rivalries between the two main alliances are never far away, and Staggie's killing is an illustration of how senior gang leaders negotiate with one another while at the same time competing in a deadly game. Before Staggie's murder, he and Donkie Booysen operated in rival alliances, but they were related by marriage and are said to have discussed how to deal with Nafiz Modack, an underworld upstart who will pop up at various points in the guns story. Modack was apparently muscling in on an area of business, the crime-ridden tow truck industry, where Staggie and Booysen had a joint interest.

Mongrels in the ghetto

An important member of the Hard Livings and broader British alliance of gangs, the Mongrels are one of the oldest gangs in Cape Town, originating in District 6 in the 1960s and 1970s, making them a member of the 'gang aristocracy,' as one police officer put it. The Mongrels were among the first to have access to the Prinsloo guns. In the unstable world of gangland, having guns would lead to a war over control of the gang – and then over greater reaches of the local drug economy.

In the period of forced removals, members of the Mongrels were dispersed across the Flats. The boss, Bobby Mongrel (real name Ismail April), seems to have built the organisation's operations through the crucial transition period of the 1990s. Mongrel was killed in 1998, probably by PAGAD, although a rumour has persisted that his death was the work of the Americans, who were trying to muscle in on the Mongrels' turf. Bobby died also at the hands of guns stolen from the state.

Over time, in a series of internal coups and assassinations of middle-level leaders beginning in the late 1990s, a certain mysterious Du Plooy is said to have risen through the ranks and now leads the Mongrels. 'The gang basically went to war with itself,' commented one insider. A spasm of violence followed as different factions inside the Mongrels sided with other gangs. That culminated in the assassination of Frederick 'Hansie' Heynes, one-time top dog of the Mongrels. Du Plooy emerged triumphant.

Du Plooy appears to be something of a criminal innovator in his own right. The Mongrels are flush with guns. One of the reasons for its internal battles is that opposing factions have been armed, rather than guns being held centrally. Having guns has also made the gang increasingly a force to be reckoned with in the battle for drug turf. In the interwoven set of alliances and behind-the-scenes agreements, gang hitmen are subcontracted to do the killings for gangs that they are not aligned to. The politics is byzantine, the violence brutal.

The nature of deals between bosses, and how these are read on the ground in relation to what are understood to be 'established' alliances, is a reminder of the inherently unstable nature of the gangs and their alliances. It is not unknown for cooperating gangs to steal guns or drugs from one another, or for rival gang bosses to sell guns to one another. As a member of the Americans described it, 'this now puts the Mongrels in Ottery with their own Mongrels in Hanover Park because it's mos what you call in English a conflict of interest … because you have the main gang boss, Du Plooy, making millions from drugs, so he wants to keep this moving, but maybe Ses and Kop want to side with the Laughing Boys over some stupid kak. So you now have a massive gang war between opposite gangs and even in the same gang.'

Also closely aligned to the Hard Livings are the Ghettos, whom one might describe as a transition gang, in the sense that they arose out of the immediate opportunities that the shift to democracy in South Africa provided. Like the Mongrels, the Ghettos were key in the sale of police guns to gangs by Prinsloo. Street wisdom says that the Ghettos rose to prominence under a gang boss called Seg, who seems to have two things going for him: his access to weapons, and connections to Chinese Triads and Nigerian networks, smoothing the supply of drugs into the areas that the gang controls.

Although the Ghettos are a comparatively new gang, they have shown impressive growth since 2015, particularly in the context of a tightly controlled drug market in Cape Town. One reason for this is that Seg has posted lieutenants to several neighbourhoods around the city to try to carve out a greater share of the drug market. These apparently include such characters as 'Miley' in Factreton, and 'Gryssie' and 'Duncan' in Hanover Park. Seg has also sought to invest in legitimate businesses, primarily the taxi industry, as well as property, although rival gang members say these are in fact just merchant houses from which to expand his drug business.

Seg appears to have an established reputation for violence. One member of the Ghettos told me that Seg apparently attacked one of his own 'soldiers' because he had heard that an American gang member had slapped the soldier and insulted Seg in his presence. As a punishment for failing to defend the name of the gang, Seg reportedly stabbed him eight times.

Gang wars: The Americans against everyone else

Among these broad and fragile gang alliances, conflict has sparked a series of wars that have over the years pockmarked several parts of the city – particularly Manenberg, Mitchells Plain, Hanover Park and Elsies River. There are multiple smaller conflicts, often connected, but it would be probably fair to say that these have been the arenas of the four major gang wars since around 2015. It's quite difficult to pin down the exact causes of the conflict in each case. What often occurs is that a single incident, such as a fight over a girl or between individuals from opposing gangs, triggers a set of pitched battles between opposing gangs.

Gangs, in my experience, are acutely aware of the body counts. A killing often precipitates revenge killings as opposing gangs mobilise. It is a vicious circle. It has been confirmed that the availability of guns has transformed these conflicts and their ferocity. Media reporting on gang wars on the Flats is sporadic, so piecing together how the conflicts have unfolded is difficult. But one of the common features of almost all of the major gang wars on the Cape Flats is that the Americans gang is involved. That is a feature of its size and geographic spread, and the fact that the 'British' gangs aligned with the 28s have sought to expand into the drug sales market, which the Americans regard as their monopoly.

Since 2016, for example, this has played out in Mitchells Plain in a vicious conflict between the Americans and their affiliate gangs, and the Mongrels and Ghettos, who are aligned to the Hard Livings and the 28s. Gang conflicts in Mitchells Plain are often hard to interpret at first flush; this is because of the size of the area and the fact 'the Plein' has many active gangs.

It takes a while to understand what first sets things off. In the Mitchells Plain case, a young girl was 'touched' by the brother of someone with influence in the Ghettos. The result was a conflict ostensibly to revenge this slight, but with the strategic objective of widening the turf on which the Ghettos could sell drugs. How this functions is not always clear: do gang bosses see a conflict and then use it for their own purposes, or does that initial spark get channelled almost automatically along the fault lines of drug selling, given how central this is to gang funding? All these factors probably apply to some degree.

In Mitchells Plain, things got rapidly out of hand. When a Ghetto member was killed by the Americans, tensions increased further. The Mongrels, still smarting from losing drug turf in a skirmish with the Americans in 2015, joined with the Ghettos, as did at least one other smaller gang. The Spoilt Brats, who had been contesting drug turf with the Ghettos for some time, took up arms for the Americans, with whom they were allied. So did the Sexy Boys, although this was not public, and was justified on the grounds of their joint allegiance to the 26 prison gang, and because the Americans had been supplying the Mitchells Plain chapter of the Sexy Boys with firearms at the time.

This conflict has now developed into an ongoing war, even if incidents appear to be only sporadic. Attempts at achieving a lasting truce between the gangs have failed, partly because it is unlikely any gang will obtain clear control. 'The gang bosses,' a local observer of the conflict with strong gang connections explained, 'feel that if they let down their guard, their opponent gang will dominate them and they therefore stand to lose millions in the process.'

In such a tight contest for control, access to guns has become key over time. One of the main reasons the Ghettos and their affiliates have managed to take on the Americans in Mitchells Plain is that they have been well armed. 'They have grown into a substantial gang with credible networks and access to heavy firepower,' said a leading Americans boss.

The war between the Americans and the Mongrels in Hanover Park, where the murder rate has increased substantially since 2011, reads like a copy of the gang conflict in Mitchells Plain. Hanover Park, long notorious for its violence, poverty and drug use, has been marked by a conflict over the last three years between the Americans and the Ghettos, and a parallel two-year war between the Laughing Boys and the Americans. The first war is said to have started over a spilt bottle of beer which led to an altercation, which led to revenge, which led to the wider conflict, now defined as one that hinges on drug turf. Gangs like the Laughing Boys and the Mongrels, because they see the Americans as the main threat to their drug sales, all sided with the Ghettos, following the established system of alliances. Approximately 40 people are said to have been killed in the course of the Hanover Park wars, although several say that the number is likely to be far higher.

In Elsies River, a small community that is inundated with gang activities, conflict rumbled on from 2014 to 2017, dying down in the last few years. This war is between the 28s and the Americans. Again, the immediate cause and the fault lines of the wider conflict in Elsies River are eerily similar to the above two cases. A 28s gang member is said to have stabbed a member of the Americans in a fight over drug turf in Mitchells Plain and then fled to Elsies River, where this entrepreneurial individual began building his own drug business, breaking an agreement that the 28s would not intrude on the Americans' turf there. The Americans killed him.

In retaliation, the 28s targeted the Americans and the gang war in Elsies River escalated into a series of attacks and counter-attacks. This conflict, again a broader reflection of how seemingly isolated gang wars in different places are seldom separated from the bigger picture, was in fact part of the wider tension between Sanie American and Ralph Stanfield of the 28s. The roots of the conflict between these two business-minded gang bosses allegedly lay in the contested drug markets of Mitchells Plain. In Elsies River, the conflict mutated into one between the 28s, with the support of the Terrible Josters, and the (American-aligned) Sexy Boys, who maintained an extensive infrastructure of drug trafficking and sales in the area.

This was followed by another conflict in Elsies River in 2016, this time between the Americans and the Cisko Yakkies. This is said to have been related to a failed deal following the theft of several outboard motors. The Cisko Yakkies had participated in the robbery and demanded a share of the profits. The businesswise Americans had paid a Yakkie with fake R100 bills. He went ballistic, stabbing an American gang member several times. Very soon, the war had developed into one around drug turf, drawing in the 28s. About 17 people were killed.

The need for guns

I have long tried to understand why gang bosses would deliberately foster or sustain violence, given that it disrupts their business operations (drug sales, mainly). What is the advantage for gang bosses to engage in protracted warfare? A community leader in Elsies River tried to explain: 'They make so much money, these gang bosses, that there is no way they are going to stand down. You must have a street reputation to survive in this business and if you stand down it means anyone can mess with you and take food out of your mouth.' Violence, in other words, is part of the business model, and thus conflict – and by implication the need for guns in what effectively escalated into an arms race – became characteristic of how gangsterism operated in the Western Cape from around 2013. Attempts have been made to negotiate a *Pax Mafiosa* to reduce the violence but these efforts have seldom gained traction. In the ordinary course of business, where looking strong is critical, gang bosses have no interest in peace.

The logic of illicit markets is that, generally, a single powerful actor emerges over time. In the case of the Cape Town underworld, there is good reason to assume that the Americans have been the largest and most sophisticated criminal operation, and the one with the broadest territorial reach. They have also received surprisingly little attention from the state's law-enforcement apparatus. Insiders claim this is because the Americans have developed strategic links with state actors and while its mid-level men may go down, senior ones are protected.

As I have argued, almost all conflicts take place across the fault line that constantly destabilises peace between the two gang alliances. As is evidenced in the case of Manenberg, where the Hard Livings first took on the Americans, much of the conflicts across the Cape Flats have consisted of a series of emerging groups challenging a prevailing criminal order. The outline of the gang wars in the four areas mentioned above suggests this is a recurring pattern.

The ability of other gangs who join forces with the 28s and the overlapping British alliance to arm themselves and undercut the market share of the Americans and their 26 alliance is a key reason for the ongoing violent instability in the city. To achieve that, the up-and-coming groups needed to get their hands on guns, and more guns.

Links to the centre

Predictably, violence that occurs on the margins of the city receives far less attention then killing that occurs in the central business district. From late 2016 onwards, while the killing on the Cape Flats in the gang wars continued apace, media coverage began to focus on a series of violent incidents in the city centre. Here, groups were mounting a challenge to the established players in the protection economy, effectively extortion, which focused mainly on clubs and pubs.

This established criminal economy deploys private security companies to extort businesses in the city's night-time leisure economy. Those that do not comply with the payments have their businesses trashed or staff threatened by gangsters roped in from the Flats. It is also tied to the drugs trade: providing 'protection' is effectively also a front for selling drugs. The link between a protection racket providing club security and drug sales is long established elsewhere. But there was an added twist in South Africa.

A private company involved in this business, which had been linked to Cape Town businessman Mark Lifman, with strong underworld links, used the Sexy Boys of Donkie Booysen fame (or proxies for the gang) as its enforcement arm. It was an ingenious system – registered security companies were the front for gang-style threats of violence. Booysen and Lifman were closely integrated as business partners.

It's worth recalling here that the Sexy Boys are aligned with the prevailing organised-crime power in the city, the Americans, and that the Americans have considerable investments in the drug retail markets in the city centre and Sea Point, where the extortion economy is in full swing. The system is lucrative, and there is some evidence that those behind it were eager to roll it out beyond the clubs and pubs scene, to businesses more broadly.

The extortion market has long been a source of conflict, as numerous criminal factions challenge each other for its control. This economy has been the prime driver behind a series of high-profile assassinations in the city since 1994, including that of Cyril Beeka, murdered in 2011, and the notorious underworld figure Yuri the Russian (ironically, a Ukrainian), who was murdered in 2007. (His young daughter was also killed in the shooting.) In two recent incidents, bouncers at prominent venues were stabbed to death, and although arrests were made they could not be linked to the main masterminds of the extortion scheme.

Since 2017, however, it has become clear that the prevailing order in the extortion economy is under threat. The split that has generated the challenge seems to be within none other than the Sexy Boys themselves, as brothers Donkie and Colin fell out. However, as with so much underworld business, there is a lot of smoke and mirrors.

A new figure aligned to Colin Booysen is allegedly behind the disruption: Modack, who appeared to have come from nowhere. Modack's roots seem not to be in the gang world. (In this respect, he resembles Cyril Beeka, also an outsider who later broke into the underworld establishment.) Modack and Beeka were reputed to be close, and the former has drawn on a network of people around Beeka as a platform. There is some evidence that he is or has been a paid informer for the state – at least his cellphone records show contact with high-ranking police officers, and allegations have long been made that he is acting for interests within the intelligence community. Modack has denied this.[4]

The Crime Intelligence and other police bosses arrayed against Vearey, the original chief investigator in the guns case, have documented links with Modack. They also appear to be the source of the stories that Vearey was behind a police plot to kill Hassan. Modack is also linked by marriage to the main suspect in the guns-to-gangs case, Laher.

Mihalik, the murdered lawyer, was also linked to the extortion economy, with allegations that he acted as a mediator between the extortion groups and, more ominously, that he had been a key figure in the racket itself by acting as an intermediary, negotiating payment with prominent Jewish businesses on the Atlantic seaboard.[5]

People on both sides of the two overarching gang alliances had links to the networks around Zuma. Sanie American and his cohorts had met with the president, and the Americans have long been seen to have state connections, hence the sense that senior bosses are untouchable. Lifman has been photographed attending an ANC event with Zuma and was a VIP guest at his birthday party in 2014.[6] On the other side of the gang tracks is Modack, who has been reported by the media to have met with Zuma's son Duduzane, and is linked to senior police officers who are regarded as having been connected to Zuma.[7] There is a history in South Africa of political elites playing both sides of the underworld for their professional and, where necessary, personal gain.

However, the vicious extortion turf war in central Cape Town should be put into perspective. It should be interpreted in much the same light as all of the other gang conflicts, whereby a group of challengers attempt, with figures in the state administration providing support, to upend the prevailing order dominated by the Americans, who, in turn, have their own grouping of backers in the police. These arrangements are based on money changing hands. The chances of success look slim. State action against Colin Booysen and Modack may neutralise the challenge. And, in any event, the authorities are bound to crack down on violent activities in a city-centre economy that is heavily reliant on tourism and entertainment. Lifman has been targeted by the tax authorities[8] and is reportedly now seeking business opportunities outside of South Africa.

The last few years have seen a number of challenges to the dominant criminal order, with a pattern of conflicts drawn across the battle lines between two broad alliances that characterise the city's underworld: the 26-aligned American-linked gangs and the 28-aligned Britishers. It is all part of a wider cycle of violence that began to escalate from 2010/11. The guns were already flowing to the gangsters by then.

CHAPTER 5

THE FLOOD OF GUNS

When discussing how the Cape Flats eventually became inundated with police guns, gangsters are eager to make an important point, and in this they are unanimous: a surge of weapons may have come from around 2007, linked to the gun armoury stocks infiltrated by Prinsloo and sold on to the Cape Flats gangs. But these were by no means the first nor the last police guns that the gangs would lay their hands on.

Prinsloo was not setting a precedent. A fairly steady flow of police-issue, state-owned guns had begun to seep into the gangland environment in the late 1990s in small volumes. Later, a steady flow of more professionally tampered-with guns seems to have started around 2004, according to one prominent gang boss. After that, the really large consignments began circulating by 2007. The later bulk supplies were stolen and marketed by Prinsloo.

The guns Prinsloo accessed from the Vereeniging armoury came from three sources. Firstly, older-issue police guns were withdrawn from service and consigned to the armoury store to await destruction. These were mainly the ubiquitous Z88s so beloved of the gangs. Secondly, guns handed in by the public during firearm amnesties were transferred to the armoury. Finally, there were guns that had accumulated in police stations, in so-called SAP 13 stores (the unlucky 13 coming from the designated form that needed to be filled out when a gun found a home there). Guns in the SAP 13 system included those confiscated during ordinary policing as well as guns that had been used in crimes and were being kept for purposes of evidence in upcoming court cases. Over time, the contents of the SAP 13 stores were transported to the central armoury. But these police gun stores have always been notorious for poor record keeping and the leakage of guns, many of which made their way back onto the street without being transferred to the central armoury.

Accessible data, however, strongly suggests that, for some time before Prinsloo flooded the market, accelerating the guns-to-gangs trade, the police service had been slowly leaking weapons to the gangs. What could have been happening? The best way to begin is to draw some conclusions from the police's own statistics.

Data on lost and stolen police guns is divided into two categories: the first is reports of individual officers who have lost their guns or had them stolen; the second is the disappearance of guns from SAP 13 station stores. There is no data on guns lost from the SAP 13 stocks. Significantly, the Prinsloo guns fall into neither of these two categories, as these were guns taken from the stores waiting to be destroyed.

According to police data for guns lost by or stolen from individual officers, the numbers since 2001 have been volatile. Between 2001 and 2004, the average number was just below 1 000 a month. There was a sudden and significant increase from 2005/6, and the numbers peaked at just over 3 850 weapons for the 2006/7 financial year.[1] This was followed by a sharp decline and then another sudden increase in the 2009/10 financial year, when the figure was just over 3 220 lost or stolen firearms.[2] The numbers then quickly revert to their pre-2004 level, and indeed show a further decline, with 505 guns being reported as lost or stolen by the police for 2018/19. These surges and declines can be seen in the graph.

The reasons for the huge increases in firearms registered as lost or stolen between 2004/05 and 2009/10 are not clear at first. (To reiterate, these are not the Prinsloo guns, as he was removing them from the police armoury under the pretext that they were to be destroyed, so these would not have made it into the SAPS figures for missing or stolen police firearms. These are the weapons of serving police officers.)

Making an accurate interpretation of the figures is clouded by the fact that SAPS firearms data contains notorious discrepancies.[3] However, a number of former and serving senior police officers who were involved with firearm data were clear that large numbers of police guns were going missing in this period.[4] One of the reasons was a growing market among the criminal fraternity for police guns. Without effective controls, there was the opportunity to sell guns to criminal networks, who had in many cases established links with the police for that very purpose. Meanwhile, a process under way across the country for older or damaged police guns to be handed in so that they could be reconditioned or destroyed probably contributed to the illegal sale of these weapons. Given that corrupt police members knew there was a market for the guns, a few sought to sell them, subsequently reporting them as lost or stolen.[5] They would then be replaced with new firearms.

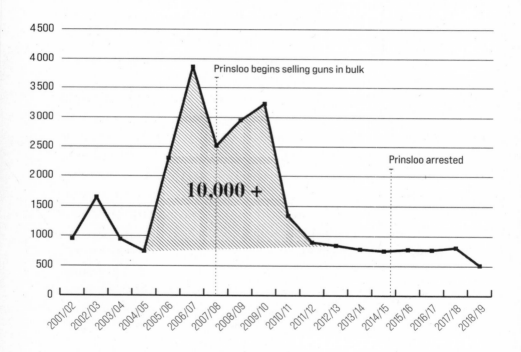

SAPS firearms reported as missing or unaccounted for, 2001–2019

Source: SAPS annual reports, SAPS management presentations to the Portfolio Committee on Police and parliamentary answers by SAPS through the Minister of Police.

Police firearms seem almost never to disappear while their owners are on duty. When firearms are reported as stolen, said the station commissioner of a large station, 'the circumstances will sometimes be questionable. You feel that they are lying.'[6] Said another: 'A lot of members allege that they are robbed on their way to work or home'.[7] Police officers working with two firearms, say a Z88 and an R5, are particularly vulnerable to losing one.

What seems significant is that firearm losses have been reported in particular stations. At the time of the increased losses, some stations had no cases, while others had a lot. That suggests not just poor station management, but that a local criminal market in firearms is likely to have sprung up around certain stations. Once one or two police guns had been sold, word would get out, and it seems probable that approaches to customers were made on a wider scale. It is simply not conceivable that firearm losses would be clustered in the same police boundaries for any other reason.

Another piece of evidence suggesting that police guns are sold rather than lost is that they are almost never recovered. Intriguingly, the recovery rate for lost or stolen civilian guns is considerably higher than for police guns. In 2009/10, for example, the police reported that 66 per cent of civilian guns were recovered, while the recovery rate for police-issued firearms was astonishingly low, at 7 per cent.[8] The most obvious explanation for this huge discrepancy is that a number of police guns recorded officially as lost or stolen have in reality been sold illegally to a criminal buyer.

In all, the data suggests that some 10 per cent of SAPS guns – again this excludes the Prinsloo guns that he removed from the armoury as well as those that disappeared from SAP 13 stores – may have been lost or stolen over the last two decades.[9]

Aside from what we can assume from police gun data, gang members have themselves long reported that they bought guns from members of the police service, and that this exchange was happening before the flood of arms that were sold by Prinsloo. One senior gang boss told me: 'You make a big thing of Prinsloo, but before that, you would find lots of cop guns on the street for sale. The only difference with what was to come later was that these guns were not so professional filed [their serial numbers removed]. When the Prinsloo guns hit the street, they were all filed in exactly the same way. I am talking a clean filing that was neat and precise.'

As opportunistic police officers sold their weapons to criminals, it is quite possible that the practice started to become gradually more widespread, and that criminals became aware of a market for police guns and approached officers to negotiate a price – a case of a shift from push to pull marketing. It is also not unlikely that Prinsloo knew about the gathering pace of this burgeoning market, and that may have sown the seeds of the idea of selling guns to gangs in greater bulk. There is also some suggestion that he tested the market with small quantities of Z88s.[10]

If there have been cases of police weapons and ammunition being sold because of inadequate controls to prevent it, the likelihood of weapons seeping out of the SAPS 13 evidence stores is even greater. Data here is sketchy and the police claim it cannot be pulled together into a national figure, but it is likely that the SAP 13 stores are places from where guns can be spirited away.[11]

What is clear is that there was already a considerable market for police guns before Prinsloo came on the scene. In that sense, he was less a market innovator than a bulk supplier in a pre-existing market. One reason why he thought he might get away with it was that there were already police guns in circulation. The small flood was about to become an inundation.

First a trickle then a flood

Tracing the flow of the Prinsloo guns and linking this gun market to changes in organised crime and increasing levels of violence is a tough task. There are still many questions, their answers buried alongside people like the unfortunate Hassan, and concealed by the country's most powerful criminal bosses, who have little incentive to talk. Nevertheless, understanding the phenomenon and impact of the guns is still possible: it can be gleaned from information elicited in snippets of discussions with gangsters who are willing to engage and others who know about the movement of the guns, from the families of victims, and by closely analysing and re-analysing data of death and injury on the Cape Flats.

It is difficult to gauge precisely when the Prinsloo guns began to reach their end market, partly because, as explained, these were not the first police guns to make their way into the hands of gangsters. Prinsloo has never had the opportunity to explain his actions in public and is likely to have sold many more guns than he has admitted to the police. Gang members' memories are sometimes vague, often deliberately so. I pressed different people on different dates and times to try to ensure as accurate a picture of the guns as possible. What follows is a solid assessment of what actually happened, as far as I can ascertain, based on many accounts.

Police guns, with their serial numbers professionally removed to conceal their provenance, began to appear in circulation on the Cape Flats from around 2007, and certainly by 2009 their presence had become noticeable. By 2010, the trickle of guns had turned into a flood. The two major rival gang alliances, outlined earlier, would shape the flow of the guns, as it escalated into an arms race between the gangs (and the same happened in gang areas in Johannesburg and in Nelson Mandela Bay). By 2010 and 2011, the Flats were ablaze with gunfire, which would leave a pile of bodies in its wake. The number of police guns that made their way to the gangs is much higher than is public knowledge. So too the number of deaths that they caused.

The Prinsloo guns were procured by gangs on the Cape Flats in two waves. In the first, Laher, Prinsloo's alleged intermediary, seemed eager to get rid of large consignments and approached the gangs after obtaining their contacts, most likely from Hassan. Later, the model changed and the gang bosses allegedly reached out directly to Laher, who contacted Prinsloo, and the gangsters would send couriers to Johannesburg to fetch their merchandise.[12] The first phase, several senior gang members said, was akin to 'a total service package'.[13]

I wanted to find someone who could tell me how it actually

worked in practice. I met Timothy, a member of one of the big gangs, at the Rhodes Memorial Restaurant. It may seem like an unlikely place to talk about guns, but, aptly enough, the restaurant does have a partial view over the Cape Flats, which stretched into the distance, masked that day by a haze of January heat. We picked over our food while Timothy recounted his experience of a gun transaction.

Interviewing gang members is always an interesting experience. Timothy was withdrawn and careful with his wording, reserved even. A gold tooth flashed in his mouth as he spoke. He wore the latest US-style leisurewear and an expensive pair of ankle-height basketball shoes. He evidently had access to money, but likely nothing invested for the long term. With considerable self-awareness, he told me that he came from a long line of local fruit sellers ('we have made good money'), and that he had had career choices other than crime.

Sometime in 2010, Timothy said he heard his gang boss speaking on the phone to arrange a gun transaction. It seemed important and there was some tension in the air. The Flats were smouldering as the gang wars raged; more guns could give any gang a leading edge. 'I am trusted by the boss,' Timothy said, without any sense of irony as he told the tale to an outsider, something unlikely to be met with approval by the gang's top dog. 'He said to me that we have a good consignment of guns and that I must come with him and others to help.' The deal was to take place a few nights later.

That evening, the boss produced a 'big block of money', which seemed to be the fruits mainly of local drug payments, and the gun retrieval team got into a bakkie. Not being too high up in the ranks, Timothy was told to lie flat in the back of the bakkie. Another car followed at a distance.

The guns were to be exchanged for the cash in an area of open ground near Mfuleni, a settlement some 30 kilometres from Cape Town. Mfuleni borders Khayelitsha, with the white surf line of the False Bay coast a little further to the south over the sand dunes. Mfuleni also lies close to an intersection where the N2 meets the R310 to Stellenbosch. It is also close to the R300, which crosses the rump of the peninsula to reach the N1 to Johannesburg.

Mfuleni is a good place for a secret transaction. There is rough ground to provide concealment from prying eyes and it is within reach of two major highways. It is also away from the immediate hustle and bustle and attention of the city, and several escape routes beckon, not only the highways, but also into the surrounding township and along the secondary roads towards Stellenbosch and the N1.

With Timothy lying on the bakkie's floor, the gang delegation drew up in a field. It was dim. Timothy was told to wait in a shallow ditch, which he remembers was lined by trees that swayed as he squatted there. Tired of waiting, he lay on his back. Eventually, a pair of headlights pierced the dark and another bakkie pulled up. Timothy was not present to unload it, but once it had driven off, he was summoned to load the merchandise into the boss's vehicle. He remembered the containers in which the guns were packed very well: they were military-style ammunition boxes that had official government seals on them. There was no doubt these were state-issue guns.

The story gets a bit hazy here. But safe to say that the boss needed to be protected, so he seems to have been picked up in another car and followed at a distance behind the bakkie with the guns. If caught, Timothy would have to take the fall. He accepted that as part of the job; he had done lots of courier work before.

Back at a safe house, the boxes were cranked open. This was on the outskirts of the Cape Flats in one of South Africa's ubiquitous security villages. The contents of the boxes were all Z88s. The serial numbers had been filed off so thoroughly that Timothy remembers that in some cases the internal springs of the guns' magazines could be seen. The irony of housing a cache of criminally acquired guns in a housing complex specifically designed to protect its inhabitants from crime was lost on Timothy. A safe house with access control is, well, a safer house.

Timothy's gang sold the Z88s for R4 000 each, he said. There was keen demand for the guns at that stage. Later, the price would fall and then rise again dramatically.

Gang pollination

If you want to talk guns, the Cape Flats are full of willing characters. Take Petros, whom I met in the back of my rental car in a side street in Hanover Park. While not strictly a gang member, Petros has good gang connections in several of their strongholds. He seems to have especially close ties to the Americans. Petros is a big, friendly, smiling man with the gift of the gab and the habit of talking expressively with his hands. We met him by chance, as he was walking down the street. My guide told me to pull over, telling me that this was someone I should meet. After a short introduction, Petros clambered into the back of the car as if assisting researchers was his civic duty.

Petros was familiar with the police guns. Sometime in early 2012, he had been summoned to the Ottery Spur, a place of some significance in the gun story. There he had met with a man whose identity he did not disclose to discuss buying some guns he could sell on to the gangs. While much is unclear – and he was not saying more – Petros was in fact working under commission for the Americans, although, as it turned out, he interpreted that brief fairly loosely. Whether his contact with the mysterious man in the Ottery Spur was passed on from his American contacts, or he had obtained the opening himself, was not explained.

After his meeting over a Spur burger, Petros headed for Johannesburg. The aim of his trip was to collect 'the pieces' that had already been paid for and head back with them to the Cape. Given airport security, taking the guns back by plane was not an option. Petros explained that the trick was to look inconspicuous. So he took a duffel bag and after meeting the contact in Johannesburg, he packed 50 guns into it ('mainly Z88s but also some .357 Magnums'). He then calmly boarded the City to City bus for Cape Town. Hiding his guns in plain sight, explained Petros, was the best plan. He put the heavy duffel bag in the overhead compartment, just far enough away from his seat to be able to deny owning it in the unlikely event that the police boarded the bus. He chuckled at the thought, hands moving up and down: 'All those guns on a passenger bus. Nobody knew a thing.'

When the bus pulled into the station in Cape Town, Petros scouted around for signs of police, then heaved the bag off the overhead shelf and disembarked, lugging his load. He phoned his contact in the Americans, who came to fetch him. The guns were taken to Hanover Park and sold on.

Petros had a good deal going: he had bought the guns for R1 500 each and sold them for between R3 000 and R3 500 – '100% profit, so not too bad,' he told me proudly, grinning from the back seat, his hand coming to rest on my shoulder as he said 'profit'.

In all, Petros made four trips to Johannesburg. If he returned each time with 50 guns in his bag, and each gun was sold at an average price of around R3 200, the stash was worth something like R640 000 in gangland. Taking into account his costs, he must have made about R300 000 for his efforts – a respectable take for a good middleman with the right sort of connections and nerves of steel. In my conversation with him, Petros did not seem to have given much thought to the ultimate costs. The price in blood and trauma would be much higher on the street.

There are probably a few reasons why Petros got a lower price for his guns than Timothy's boss. Gang leaders with real muscle, like Timothy's, were in a position to set the price – a form of inter-gang extortion really ('you buy these guns at our price'). More 'junior' gangs were therefore eager to find cheaper guns, and Petros, with his network, would have had inside knowledge of this. In any event, by the time Petros began selling, the Flats had become so swamped with guns that the price had fallen. Later, prices would rise again as the bosses formed a price-setting cartel.

As mentioned, Petros's main client was the 26-aligned Americans gang, who were desperate for more weaponry as gang war escalated in the Cape in 2012. But Petros is not the sort of man to look opportunity in the eye and refuse. He also said that he sought out the leadership of the 28-aligned Hard Livings to see if they would also have an interest – and, more importantly, cash on hand. They had both. With little compunction, Petros closed some more sales, but this time to the enemies of the Americans and some of their allies.

It's not something that he would tell them, although he implied that they probably suspected what he was up to.

Petros's account of the gun trade was particularly interesting because of this ability he had to cross the gang divide with neutral colours. Gun runners like Petros were described by a member of the Hard Livings as bees pollinating different flowers: '*Hy kan mos van een blom na 'n ander vlieg en daar sit.* [He can fly from one flower to another and sit there comfortably].' The pollination image meant selling guns, an interesting metaphor under the circumstances: guns gave gangs life.

Petros may have run out of luck in late 2018. I was told that his house had been raided by the police. Guns and hand grenades were found on the property, and he was arrested. He is adamant, my connection to him told me, that the guns had been planted at his house. A doubtful story surely. Someone must have snitched.

Speaking to people like Timothy and Petros, experts in the merchandise that they were buying and selling, I realised how widely known it was that the guns came from government stores. For the gang members who dealt with these guns, the telltale sign was how professionally the serial numbers had been obliterated from the guns. It is an important detail, and one that was reiterated during a discussion with a gangster of violent repute in Manenberg, let's call him Duiwel. Presentable and neatly dressed, and in his 30s, Duiwel carried a revolver on him and described himself as knowledgeable when it came to firearms. He told me that the guns had been put through 'an industrial MacGyver', a reference to an American TV character who devises all sorts of makeshift solutions to problems he encounters while hunting down or escaping from the bad guys. But these MacGyver solutions had been applied to the police guns on a factory-scale production line, the serial numbers having been removed by someone professionally and with good equipment. The implications were clear for Duiwel, largely because he had also spent time removing serial numbers from stolen firearms. That is what made the new consignments turning up on the streets of the Flats so unusual.

As the guns began to circulate more widely across the Flats, Duiwel said, ordinary gangsters and even some in the wider community got wise ('raak wys') to the fact that these were not the usual run-of-the-mill stolen guns. They had all had their serial numbers removed in the same professional way. It was therefore clear that they were from the same government sources, and in the case of the Z88s most likely from the police armoury itself.

It's hard not to be startled by the reaction of some in gangland when it became known that these were police guns. It seemed to present an opportunity for blackmail. Duiwel described it like this: 'So I think that's when some people realise that these guns that came from Joburg and the police ... and that naai became a problem ... so when it comes to the wrong person and with too many people knowing ... he is gonna cause kak for you. He maybe wants a piece of the money.'

In retrospect, it seems almost amazing. As the gang wars scaled up from 2011 onwards, it became widely known among ordinary gangsters that there was a growing number of firearms circulating that were property of the state. The supply of state-owned guns to the gangs had been going on for some time. But what was at first a comparatively small stream seemed to have assumed much larger proportions by 2011.

It really began 'pumping' from 2008 to 2011, said one Cape gang boss, while a gang member from the Hard Livings said, 'These guns come to us maybe in 2008 ... [I remember] because I got a gun in 2008, it was a 16 shooter, a Zulu ... a police gun – because you know how they file those guns.'

A community leader, who wanted to remain anonymous, pointed to 2009 as the key year: 'So you can say that guns were circulated to gangs before 2009, but at a lower level. You see a spike in 2009 in gang violence, with gangs more confident to use their new guns.'

This is confirmed by gangsters and several community leaders on the Flats. 'It picked up momentum here in 2008/9, when you see a definite wave of guns coming for the gang bosses to buy,' said a gang hitman, now in prison. A Petros-like delivery man would fetch them direct from source.

The police guns kept coming for several years, until at least 2014, most sources suggest. For example, a member of the Clever Kids from Manenberg told me that his gang had acquired guns from the Americans from 2008, but that by 2014 they had managed to secure a Petros-style direct channel for themselves.

The violent and gang-afflicted Johannesburg neighbourhood of Westbury, which had been marked by violent community protests in 2018 against the gangs, seems to have played a key role in the gun trade to the Cape. Some guns appear to have been sold to gangsters in Westbury who have Cape connections, while there is also evidence that police guns delivered in the Cape made their way back to Westbury. But from 2009, and until as late as 2012, most of the guns were delivered directly to Cape Town, arranged by an intermediary with direct links to Prinsloo.

CHAPTER 6

ARMS RACE

The guns from Gauteng that Prinsloo was selling began to arrive in Cape Town in several large consignments. Who the first recipients were provides an interesting story of the power dynamics in gangland. Most significantly, Laher, the alleged marketing middleman, apparently quickly came under pressure from the gangs themselves, eager to get their hands on the new source of weapons.

How exactly it worked remains unclear. It is possible that the first trickle of guns made it obvious to those who were observing – which would have included all gang bosses worth their salt – that a supply was available, and then, as it became clearer that police guns that Prinsloo sourced were 'for sale', larger consignments were ordered. But everyone is in agreement: the person who was supplying the guns was an outsider, and he needed an in. In my view, an outsider looking to make such broad introductions for the sale of guns would need an insider with many connections. Someone with a Rolodex of potential points of sale, someone at the centre of a web. Perhaps someone like Noorudien Hassan. From numerous interviews, there is consensus on one thing: the trafficker who was flogging the guns approached multiple gangs. The message went out – 'we have guns for sale'.

The first major consignment, sometime in 2011 or 2012, was delivered to the 28s alliance through a smaller 28-aligned gang, the Ghettos. The Ghettos had been Hassan's long-standing clients. The connection seemed to be through a contact that had been made with a senior figure in the 28s. The 28s gang itself were to buy large numbers of weapons to build up their arsenal. It was not only that the 28s had the right contact with the supplier – they were also able to produce the money quickly. Liquidity was important in securing the guns. As a senior gang boss told me while sipping a cooldrink at Canal Walk, a huge shopping and entertainment complex near Cape Town. 'It was advertised around, at least to some gangs. Guns went to who was most ready and who paid. Laher did not have specific gang links but he made contact through someone in Cape Town: It was not about relationships, it was about [the gang bosses] who had the most money.' Someone had spotted the gap.

The connection between the small leadership group of the 28s gang and the person supplying the guns from Gauteng soon solidified. It helped of course that they had cold hard cash. The Ghettos, a 28-aligned gang, were both central to channelling the deal and the main recipients of the first consignment. It was a batch of 200 guns and the 28s alliance absorbed them all. It included Z88s, but there were also .353s and .303s, and R1 and R5 automatic rifles.

As in the Mfuleni gun deal recounted by Timothy, the merchandise was delivered directly to the gangs in Cape Town. It was, as one leading gangster described it, 'all arranged as a package'. News spread quickly.

Several people emphasised that the Americans were for some reason slower off the mark than the Stanfields, one explanation being that the Americans did not have cash on hand. That is surprising, given that the Americans are the biggest organised criminal group in South Africa, bar none. That they should not have cash is odd. Perhaps even big criminal groups have cashflow problems. One possible reason for their illiquidity could be that the Americans have several devolved satellites of power, perhaps making it harder to bring the cash to the centre. The 28s are smaller, more cohesive and focused. They had spotted an opportunity and were able to seal it with money.

There is another intriguing aspect to the first batches of gun sales: why did none of the gangsters suspect it might have been a set-up, an entrapment operation, particularly since the individual who seemed to be acting as the interface did not have a gang affiliation? I posed that question to one prominent gang boss. He just laughed. 'We know the cops are corrupt. We would have heard if it was some sort of operation against us.' It was said lightheartedly, but it is a chilling condemnation of the integrity of some elements within the police service.

Another senior gangster had told a slightly different story: the introduction had come from someone whom the gangs knew, but who was too compromised by his association with them to be part of any police operation. That person, a community activist with close ties to the gangs said, was Hassan.[1]

What is fascinating is what happened next. As the 28s armed themselves and offered to sell guns to others, including gangs outside of their alliance, the Americans began to get nervous. Gang intelligence systems are remarkably well developed. 'We knew someone was bringing guns in because we could see more guns on the streets,' a senior American gang boss explained. Inquiries were made: 'We asked around on the ground who had guns and where they came from.' The Americans then apparently paid a visit to the Ottery Spur – the source, it seemed, of all guns. This must have been a fascinating meeting. The gangsters, who are an intimidating crowd, spoke with the person whom they had identified as the gun supplier. 'We confronted him,' one of them told me, 'and told him that the next consignment must come to us.' The supplier was a businessman, the same gangster said: 'He did not seem surprised when we appeared in his door.' That businessman was Laher.[2]

The American gang boss may have been softening some of the details in his story somewhat. An impeccable source said that although there was no violence or threats of violence, the gangsters who visited the Spur 'showed pictures' to the businessman of his wife and family – photos that had been taken at home and at school. The implied threat was clear: the next consignment must go to the Americans, and no one gets hurt.

And so it did: R300 000 was allegedly paid directly into the account of the businessman who they claim had access to the guns. The consignment that followed was said to have included Tokarevs, which have a magazine capacity of 16 bullets. The Tokarev is a hardy weapon formerly manufactured in the Eastern bloc for the Soviet military. The gangsters were pleased: this gun rivalled the more easily available Z88 and was highly prized. The street price for a Tokarev at the time was in the order of R16 000. The consignment also contained Z88s and .38 specials. The latter, a careworn Cape hitman explained, is a gun favoured for hits in closed spaces, 'like in a nightclub' he suggested with a shrug of the shoulders. The gun is relatively small and does not eject the shell, thus leaving less evidence.

The Americans' consignment (the third one overall) was delivered directly to a house in Mitchells Plain – a door-to-door service. A fourth consignment was to follow, this one also delivered directly to the Americans.

A fifth consignment reportedly made its way to the Fancy Boys, a gang initially aligned to the 26s. By that time, they had split into two factions, one aligned to the 26s and the other to the 28s. Factionalism led many to be recruited into Ralph Stanfield's 28s, explained someone who was in close contact with the gang's leaders. The Fancy Boys had become what is referred to as a cross-number gang, a bridge between the two gang alliances, a bridge over which guns moved in both directions. The guns that were sold to the Fancy Boys were most likely sold on to other gangs in both alliances.

It seems that the distribution of the guns followed a particular pattern: they were delivered to the two main cores around which the two alliances revolved – Ralph Stanfield's 28s on the one side and the Americans on the other. Both then redistributed the weapons to their allies. The guns crossed the divide to opposing gangs through groups like the Fancy Boys, who swung both ways.

It would appear that a kind of self-regulation was at play. The 28s had positioned themselves to receive the first supplies, as we have seen. The Americans then moved quickly to take advantage of the gun-supply channel. An arms race ensued, but one that then bought a degree of balance to the system. If only one alliance had been supplied with guns, the picture for the other might have been bleak.

The agreements worked out in gangland can seem strange. I suspect that the 28s knew the Americans were moving in to get weapons of their own. No gang member whom I spoke to seemed to be perturbed that other gangs were securing their own firearms. I can't quite put my finger on it: gangs are extremely competitive around drug turf, which is why so many soldiers die, but at the same time there is a live-and-let-live attitude. Part of this can be explained by the fact that there is a very different arrangement between gang members fighting out gang wars with their rivals, and the bosses, who know each other and meet to divide up the market.

The guns the cops klap with

Curiously, it seems the 28 gang members wanted the Z88 not because of its reliability, but because of its brand name. As a senior member of the 28s in Mitchells Plain said: 'I think the 28s like the Z88 because it has an 8 in it ... so the 28s klap with Z88s'. That does not mean that the other gangs did not want Z88s too. A member of the Sexy Boys said they saw it as a 'number one gun'. 'Some people', he said, 'say maybe this gun shoot nice because it don't jam. ... It depends on how you like your ice cream, strawberry or chocolate? Which gun is better? But I know the Z88 was a favourite.'

But there is another more compelling – and in my view much more disturbing – reason why gangsters preferred the Z88. There are the technical reasons of course: it is a reliable pistol, and a 16-shooter, reducing the number of times the magazine needs to be replaced in a gang fight. It is also easy to fit a home-made silencer to it. But there is a psychological reason too: the gangs wanted the Z88 because the police used them. 'The police klap with those guns,' said one gang boss's lieutenant, 'so we want to too.' A member of the Clever Kids from Manenberg articulated it like this: 'Here, in Manenberg, the Zulus are the favorites. I can say it's that gun because that is what the ouens want to shoot, it's a 16-shooter and it's mos what the boere [the police] shoot with ...'

Using the Z88, a government-issued gun used by the SAPS, seemed to imply a parity in the mind of the gangs with the police, the very instruments of state security. This was not lost on gang members, who are likely to suggest that one of the 'services' they bring is a degree of security in the communities where they are dominant.

A more sinister reason is that the gangsters also style themselves as being in partnership with the police. And, after all, was it not the police who had been supplying the gangsters with weapons? The language that gangsters use to describe the supply of guns is highly revealing. They don't talk of rogue or criminal elements in the police, they talk of 'the police'. 'It's a cool thing for the police to sell their guns back to us,' a member of the Sexy Boys said. A gang member from the Terrible Josters put it this way: 'Hey [this gun] is from the police ... we are working in partnership with the police because they are scared of us and they know they must give our guns back.'

What is equally astonishing is how widely known it was among the community that the police were supplying gangsters with guns. 'At first it was a hush thing,' said a prominent member of the 28s, 'but after a while, you see, everyone knew because when the gattas [the police] raid for guns, we must hide these guns with the people here in Mitchells Plain. The people are nogal not stupid here in Mitchells Plain ... they are all wys [canny and knowledgeable], so they knew that the guns came from the police.'

There was another reason why the community knew that there were new police guns in circulation: they were told by the gangs to hide the weapons. Another 28s gang member made the cynically logical analysis that because drugs are so deeply embedded in the community, and because guns are linked to drugs, ordinary people in gang-afflicted areas had little choice but to be involved in concealing weapons for gangsters.

'I knew,' another gang member said, 'because we had cops on the take ... so we knew it was police guns, and stupid gangsters also spread that message into the community.'

That the police were supplying guns to gangsters on the Flats seemed well known by at least 2012 or 2013. How could it be that the police, who were seizing guns during that time, were unable to determine that something was horribly wrong? Data from the police on illegal possession of firearms and ammunition shows consistent increases in the amounts of guns and ammunition found nationally and in the Western Cape.[3] Surely it would have been clear from an inspection of the guns seized that many were originally police weapons?

Police weapons or otherwise, that there was a mounting security crisis on the Cape Flats must have become even more starkly self-evident as the murder rates began to escalate dramatically from 2012 onwards.

This is war

Possession of guns has always been central to the power that gangs can project. They guard their gun stores with great care. Before the gun supply escalated, a gang boss would ensure that his guns were stored and loaned out to the foot soldiers only when needed, in the event of gang conflict or turf wars. When the fighting was over, the guns would be retrieved and stored safely again. Displaying a gun was a special status symbol. Few rank-and-file gang members possessed guns or had the wherewithal to own their own. Although there were some guns among the gangs back in the mid to late 1990s, they were not common, and smaller gangs possessed only a limited number and, in some cases, none at all. Their scarcity (and the fact that only the bosses were likely to carry them) endowed guns with potent symbolism.

Gun control within the gangs was ruthless. Gang members who did not return a gun could expect a beating or much worse. To abscond with a gun would have made you an instant target for an angry gang boss – not a good position to be in on the Flats. Guns were just too valuable to be floating around, and stocks were carefully monitored.

Before the mass arrival of state guns, the weapon of choice in gangland was the knife. 'You see,' said an Americans gang member who has served prison time for murder, 'maybe only one or two [gang members] had guns and the others in the gang had knives or pangas … but now as they push more guns onto the streets, things become woelig [restless and busy].'

By 2012, the guns flooding the streets of the Flats had indeed transformed the gangs.

A member of the 28s gang expressed it like this: 'Ja, obviously here we run because we got the guns and [you] mustn't fuck with us because we sommer kill you because we all have guns. It's not like back in the day when maybe two people had guns. Here now we all *trap* [operate] with a gun each so everyone is dangerous, so they call me Mister Moenie Mors Nie because they know that I don't fuck around ... me and my crew shoot you full of holes.'

Having guns also gave gangs an advantage in the recruitment market. Said a man from the Ghettos: '[T]he membership of the gangs it swell because the youngsters all want guns, so they join the gangs that got the guns or they join the gangs that was getting the guns, like the 28s or the HLs. And if we were supplying the guns we could see how it affect the gang because that gang got bigger and more violent.'

The experience of wider gun possession on the Cape Flats correlates with a series of studies carried out elsewhere. These show that when young men possess weapons, often in a gang context, it increases their bravado and the likelihood that they will engage in violence. In the neutral language of academia: 'Participation in [all types of] violent delinquency increases during periods when adolescents carry weapons, and decreases to pre-carrying levels once adolescents abandon their weapons.' In short, gangsters with guns means much more violence.[4]

'Do you think people gonna *slap* when they got big guns to make them stronger,' a young gangster said. 'In the end, this gun means a lot of power but also, my broer, it means a lot of death here for my people ...' Gang sociology, as accurate as the academic kind.

Enough ammunition to fight a war

Gang members and bosses have confirmed repeatedly that whereas getting guns in the underworld is not such a significant challenge, obtaining large stocks of ammunition is sometimes tricky. Tricky, perhaps. But not impossible. The first source of ammunition is of course the local gun shop or firearms dealer. Buying large quantities of ammunition by going from dealer to dealer is, however, a

'Prinsloo guns'
Former police Z88s
displayed on a car seat
on the Cape Flats by
a gang member. Their
serial numbers have been
professionally removed.

time-consuming task, particularly for the enterprising criminal looking for larger volumes, or the armour-piercing variety, not available
from gun shops. There can be only one source for such requirements:
the state itself. There is extensive evidence that state ammunition is
deployed by criminals. Controls around ammunition are even less
rigorous than those that apply to firearms. Investigating officers and
private-security personnel who respond to cash-in-transit cases and
hijackings suggest that state ammunition is now widely used. Some
state ammunition carries identifiable markings, and these shells are

often found at crime scenes.[5] At the risk of sounding cynical, the first stop for ammunition is your friendly local police station. The available evidence suggests that significant amounts of ammunition have gone missing from police stations and SAPS 13 stores. In answering a parliamentary question in August 2019, Police Minister Bheki Cele told MPs that the SAPS had lost 9.5 million rounds of ammunition over six years. That is enough to fight a small war. Which is precisely what it is being used for in the underworld.[6]

The arrival of the guns coincided with changes in Cape Town's and South Africa's drug economy. There had been clearly confirmed increases in the volumes of drugs entering South Africa since the early 2000s. On the Flats, methamphetamine use – in the form of the ubiquitous 'tik' – soared from 2005 onwards. Systems monitoring drug users seeking treatment noted 'rapid increases' in the middle of that decade.[7] Huge profits were being made and as the market began to solidify, holding gang turf became central to money making. A police station commissioner on the Flats said that 'the biggest motivator for getting hold of guns was that [the drug market] was no longer simply about Mandrax and dagga', and that tik had transformed the local drug economy and dramatically increased profits. Because of tik's highly addictive nature and the constant, growing demand for it, the need to dominate turf where buyers lived was key to money making.

After tik came cheap heroin as a new wave of Tanzanian dealers entered the Cape economy, selling to the gangs who had already carved out their turf by selling tik.[8] There was money to be made with the influx of new drugs. But without weapons, there was no way for new entrants to break into the market. By 2012, a triangle of drugs, gangs and guns had made the Cape Flats a killing field.

Police statistics show that the murder rate in Cape Town increased from 2010 onwards. In that year, Cape Town metro's murder rate coincided exactly with the average rate in all of South Africa's main cities, at just over 40 cases per 100 000. (The national rate was in the mid-30s.) While the average numbers of the other metropolitan areas began to decline and then stabilise in the five years that followed, dropping below the 40 deaths per 100 000 mark, the figure for Cape Town skyrocketed. At first, the change was slow and steady, but by 2012 and 2013 the numbers began to spiral upwards, stabilising at a high level in 2014/15. (See the graph, which compares Cape Town homicides with the national rate.) By 2017/18, the homicide rate for the Cape Town metropolitan area had peaked at over 70 murders per 100 000 people.[9] Those numbers are astonishing, placing Cape Town among the most violent places on earth, including war zones.

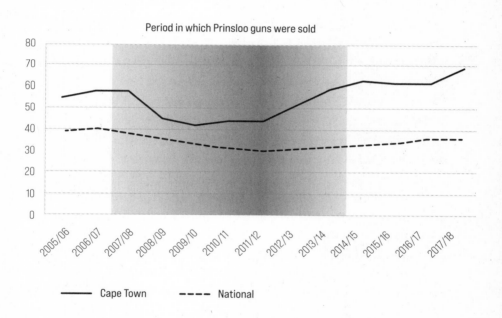

Cape Town's murder rate, showing upswing since 2011

Sources: Data used by the South African Cities Network for its 2018/19 State of Urban Safety in South Africa Report, thanks to Anine Kriegler.

Note: The data is a recalculation of police data to match metropolitan boundaries and the number of residents. See Anine Kriegler and Mark Shaw, *A Citizen's Guide to Crime Trends in South Africa*, Jonathan Ball, 2016.

What is even more stark is the concentration of the violence in specific pockets of Cape Town. Manenberg's murder rate peaked above 70 murders per 100 000 from 2014 to 2016. Delft passed the 100 mark in 2014 and continues to experience high rates (reaching approximately 150 murders per 100 000 inhabitants in 2018). Elsies River shows phenomenal levels of violence, with an estimated murder rate of over 102 deaths per 100 000 from 2014, peaking at over 133 in 2018.[10] With one exception, Syria, where the death rate peaks above the 200 per 100 000 mark, in the majority of contemporary war zones (Somalia, Afghanistan, Yemen and Iraq), the conflict death rate is well below 100 per 100 000.[11]

In terms of raw numbers of murders, the sharpest increase in killing occurred in Delft, Mfuleni and Mitchells Plain. The reported number of murders in Mitchells Plain tripled from 2009/10 (at 54 cases) to 2013/14, when it reached 156. In the case of both Delft and Mfuleni, the numbers doubled: from 72 in 2009/10 to 163 in 2014/15 in the case of the former, and from 72 to 154 in the case of the latter.[12] Across the Cape Flats, most neighbourhoods had a 100 per cent increase from 2011 to 2012.[13]

The highest proportion of those killed have been young men and children. The subtext of much media coverage is that innocent children have been caught inadvertently in the gunfire. This is greeted with almost universal scepticism by the hardened gangster community. Children may be innocent, gang members told me, but it is not by accident they are killed: children are an essential part of the local drug economy, acting as transporters and lookouts.[14] A community leader agreed: 'It is easy to say that the children were innocent in the big picture, but when you zoom in, you will see that they are connected to the gangs and targeted by rival gangs.' Gun fodder. The police investigation into the stolen Prinsloo guns would later connect hundreds of deaths of children ballistically to the police guns. Whatever the gangsters say, many innocent children have been caught in the crossfire.

Data from mortuaries and various studies from the dedicated group of academics and health professionals who focus on this issue in Cape Town suggest how important the flow of guns has been in transforming the nature of violence. The overall impact of the flood of Z88s and other guns has had a considerable impact. Larger-calibre guns, such as the medium-sized Z88 (a 9 mm gun) and the larger .375 Magnum, both contained in the illegal consignments of guns delivered to the gangs, are likely to have ratcheted up the death rate. Comparative studies show how weapons such as these significantly increase death rates in contrast to other smaller-calibre weapons, such as .22, .25 or .32 firearms.[15]

One of the first indications of the extent to which the growing number of guns transformed the Flats is evidence from mortuary studies, which indicate the decline in deaths from knife wounds and the increase in gun-related homicides. This directly correlates with what gang members have said in interviews. Statistics from the Salt River mortuary, which serves only a part of the Cape Flats, show a dramatic upswing in firearm-related deaths between 2012 and 2014 among victims between the ages of 10 and 24, rising from 93 to 198 cases. Most significantly, the number of gunshot cases at the mortuary overtook deaths caused by sharp-force instruments (knives) from 2013 to 2014, with a steady growth in gunshot cases from 2012.[16]

This is confirmed by the experience of community and civil-society activists on the Flats, who have battled the impact of violence for years. One hard-pressed community activist who has always spoken openly to me said that the presence of guns had increased the violence 'dramatically' since 2009. It also greatly increased the costs, not only in deaths, but in the medical care required for badly injured young men in particular.

What is perhaps most depressing about all of this is that this sudden upswing in violence occurred in a context in which violence on the Cape Flats had been declining for several years. Academic study after academic study had noted the decline, musing on the causes, observing in particular that a reduction in guns in circulation – a result of the implementation of the Firearms Control Act in 2004 – appeared to have had a notable impact on reducing incidents of gun-related homicide.[17] 'Where have all the gun deaths gone?' asked one study by a prominent group of researchers writing in the prestigious *South African Medical Journal*.[18]

That was, as the community activist pointed out, the calm before the storm – it was all to change from 2009 on the Cape Flats. It was like the Flats had been starved of guns for a number of years, and, like a drug addict, had slowly began to recover, and then there was a rush of the stuff – and then an overdose. Later, in 2018, some of the same authors who had asked where all the gun deaths had gone looked back over homicide trends to 2013 in Cape Town and concluded gloomily that their findings demonstrated 'the dramatic effect of increasing firearm availability to criminals directly' and that the 'evidence of guns being placed with gangs suggests that the gang conflicts arose from the increased supply'. They attributed excess mortality in this population to 'increased exposure to illegally obtained firearms'.[19]

What seems to have remained consistent, however, both before and after 2009 is that few cases of gun-related homicide are solved. Determining case resolution figures is always a complex business given the difficulties of tracking individual cases over several years through both the investigative and court phase. But when it has been done consistently over several years, in the case of gun-related homicide the results are shocking: a study of firearm homicide cases at the Salt River mortuary in 1999 showed a conviction rate of 7.21 per cent; that had dropped to 5.69 per cent ten years later.[20] Up to 2009, gun violence had been declining in Cape Town for several years, so, in theory at least, fewer cases offered the prospect of a greater and quicker conviction rate. By 2015, the case load would be significantly higher, measured in hundreds more bullet-ridden bodies now being brought into the mortuary.

CHAPTER 7

COPS ON THE SPOT

I t was early 2013, the Cape Town summer heat warping the roads and pavements of the Flats. Things had also been getting hot in gangland. At this point guns were being made readily available to violent gangsters in large consignments from the armoury stocks. The increasing availability of firearms meant the number of fatalities was beginning to rise alarmingly on the Cape Flats. Prinsloo's arms-to-gangs business was at its height and the guns in the hands of the gangs were starting to exact a deadly toll. Prinsloo himself, whose objective was simply to shift the guns, was unaffected by the extent of the death and destruction now under way and delivered by his hand.

But, as is so often the case in South Africa, just when you are nearing despair, an unsung hero appears. Although, as with many South African heroes, the story is always a bit more complicated, the hero also flawed, the truth not as clear as when it first appears, greying on the edges, blurring the lines between good and less so.

The flawed hero in this case is a police officer working at Manenberg Police Station: Constable Lutfie Eksteen. Eksteen is a small cog in a massive organisation of over 120 000 people, in the lowest of the lowly ranks. In my experience, most constables get on with their job with the aim of paying the rent and staying alive. Many of them, as researcher Andrew Faull explains in a fascinating study, would rather be doing another job, and, for them, the police service is something of an accidental occupation. What's more, a good proportion of new constables, Faull explains, were themselves in conflict with the law before they decided to play for the other side. That probably gives them a unique perspective on police work – a classic case of how it takes one to know one. Over time, they develop a grudging acceptance of their policing role, while the ties that bind them to their communities, and South African society more generally, shape their actions.[1]

For officers working in the Cape Flats communities, police work pressures are magnified exponentially. Eksteen comes from the same community that he polices. One of the challenges in such conflictual situations is that, because gangsterism is embedded in the officer's environment and circumstances, he or she can't ever quite escape its compromising influence. Indeed, the police use their connections to do their job, or what they see as their job, whether that is serving the community and the police or helping the gangs, depending on the circumstances. 'I know several young police officers who face that challenge,' a police captain from the Flats told me. 'It's very hard, and one compromise is enough to ensure you get trapped over time.'

Eksteen, while maintaining local connections in Manenberg, his home town, worked in Operation Combat, a major police intervention in the Western Cape, but with a focus on the Cape Flats, that had been initiated in 2012 as gang violence began to escalate. Combat was designed to take down the gangs by targeting the leaders and by cutting off the gangs' supplies of arms and drugs. The operation was led by a gregarious police general called Jeremy Vearey.

One of Vearey's biggest successes would be the May 2015 conviction of one George 'Geweld' Thomas, a hard-core gangster boss of the 28s, known, as his nickname suggests, for almost unspeakable acts of violence. Thomas received seven life sentences after being convicted of over 50 charges, including murder, attempted murder and extortion. In 2013, as the guns flowed, Thomas was still facing trial.

Eksteen is in his mid-40s, tall and well built. In an online photo, he can be seen posing with a police-issue sub-machine gun. In another, looking every bit the proud cop, smartly dressed, he is standing next to a new Anti-Gang Unit police car. He wears a pair of glasses, dark in the sunlight, masking his eyes. Some of that is for show, though, because when you meet Eksteen he is friendly and forthcoming. It was Eksteen who detected the first police guns on the streets: these were the breadcrumbs that would put Operation Combat investigators onto Prinsloo's tail.

Eksteen maintained a number of contacts in gangland. One of the reasons that this was possible was that his brother was a member of the Americans, and Lutfie is said to maintain links to other gangs too, most notably the Clever Kids. 'He knows a lot about gang dealings,' a community leader in Manenberg said. You can sense the grey blurring around the edges here. Rumours of gang association, and the ever-febrile politics of the Western Cape police, must have prevented his promotion from constable.

He has been known, according to one person close to the gangs, to pick up members of the Hard Livings for petty crimes while he is on duty and then drop them off in the heart of another opposing gang's territory. The Hard Livings are in the rival gang alliance to that of his brother's gang, the Americans. The veracity of such stories is difficult to judge, but the general impression is that Eksteen is a good, reliable cop with the right intentions, tainted perhaps by connections that weigh heavily on his actions. In that respect, he resembles police officers all over the Cape Flats.

A community worker in the area who has always proved to be a trusted informant has said, however, that if there is trouble between gangs, she summons Eksteen, constable or not, and he sorts things out. Although she concedes that it is probably wise to remain wary of him.

Eksteen had also suffered because of his work, a reminder of the consequences of policing the Cape Flats. It is an enormously dangerous job. In October 2014, as the guns-to-gangs investigation was moving forward, Eksteen's 71-year-old mother, Shamiela Eksteen, was gunned down and killed in the family home in a hit that appeared to be targeted at Lutfie himself. His brother, Mansoor, was wounded in the attack.

Constable Eksteen's network of informers seemed to reach like tentacles into key parts of the gang ecosystem. During his interactions with them, at some point, sometime early in 2013, information about volumes of police guns that had been flooding the

Flats must have come up. Of course, Eksteen would have been well aware that police guns were not a new thing in gangland. But what seemed different in this case was the sheer number of guns. When Constable Eksteen got wind of the fact that there were significant numbers of what appeared to be stolen police guns on the streets, he did not report it to his immediate superior, as might have been expected, suspicious that the police line of command was tainted and that the information might leak to the wrong people in the SAPS. These were police guns, after all, and there seemed to be large numbers of them on the street. Eksteen instead phoned a trusted police general directly. (He was not known for respecting the reporting lines – he had contacts higher up the food chain.) That police general was Jeremy Vearey, leader of Operation Combat, and widely known in Cape Town as a highly vocal member of the service. Vearey would become the central SAPS player in the guns story. Project Impi, the guns investigation itself, would initially fall under the auspices of Combat.

Eksteen was close to Vearey. When his mother had been killed, it was Vearey whom the family had appointed as their spokesman. Vearey had vowed to hunt down the killers and bring them to justice. Given that Eksteen is somewhat of an unconventional cop, having a powerful protector was necessary to 'save his butt when he crosses the line', in the words of another policeman who has worked in Manenberg. Eksteen's link to Vearey was to prove critical in the guns investigation.

The story of the people behind the guns investigation says a lot about the way in which policing in South Africa now works – or perhaps has always worked. Information generated by the bureaucratic apparatus of the police service, official documents and parliamentary briefings may be important, but even more telling are the networks that police officers are meshed into. By the time the guns investigation got under way after Eksteen's report in early 2013, the police in South Africa had become increasingly divided into opposing factions, neither trusting the other. This was largely a function of the Zuma years, and given the linkages to corruption and mismanagement within the SAPS, internal police politics would become a crucial feature of the guns-to-gangs case as it moved tentatively forward in 2013, and then more rapidly in 2014.

Information about the police guns had starting dripping through from the Manenberg gang community to Eksteen; Vearey had been alerted, and an attempt was made to determine just how widespread the problem was. It's important to recognise that at this point the scale of what they were dealing with was not immediately clear to the small group of cops in the know.

But it still does not explain why it took so long for the police intelligence system to ascertain that hundreds of stolen police guns were on the streets. Court documents suggest that it was in 2010, three years after Prinsloo began selling guns, that police ballistics in the Western Cape discovered that tampered police firearms had fallen into the wrong hands.[2] The most likely explanation for the time lag is that crime intelligence information gathering and analytical capacities had declined to such an extent that either the system had failed to collect crucial information or the pieces were simply not put together higher up in the command chain.

Vearey, by all accounts, kept his newfound knowledge close to his chest. He had long learnt not to trust too many people in the police. One person whom he did share it with, though, was an old colleague in arms, Peter Jacobs. Like Vearey, Jacobs was a former ANC intelligence operative. Both spies turned policemen. Jacobs was at the time the deputy provincial police commissioner for the Western Cape. Vearey and Jacobs make an interesting pair: Vearey expressive and talkative, Jacobs quiet and reserved.

Vearey is a former schoolteacher and, if it weren't for the police uniform, you could still visualise him explaining some concept to a class of young learners. He retains something of the teacher in him: didactic, but also open, willing to explain. He is also blue-blood ANC. Arrested during apartheid while a teacher and operating undercover as a member of uMkhonto we Sizwe (MK), he was convicted of terrorism in 1988 and spent a year and a half on Robben Island. He was released as South Africa's negotiated settlement got under way

Jeremy Vearey, a teacher turned activist. Sharp-elbowed, ambitious and relentless, he was the SAPS general at the centre of investigating the 'guns to gangs' case. GALLO IMAGES / *DIE BURGER*

and took up a post in the ANC's Department of Intelligence and Security in the Western Cape. He was responsible for VIP protection, and in photographs of the period when Mandela visited the Cape, you can see him talking to a pressing crowd, with Table Mountain looming grey in the background, or moving ahead opening the way for Mandela, walkie-talkie in hand. A man in motion.

Recruited into the reforming security establishment after democracy, Vearey's rise was rapid. Based on his past experience, and presumably to ensure the ANC had eyes and ears in the right places, he managed a covert crime intelligence unit in the Western Cape from 1995, moving up the ranks to coordinate intelligence at the provincial level from 1997. By early 2000, he was in charge of a SAPS gang investigation unit, rather bluntly called 'Slasher'. Rising through a series of other commands, he was appointed as police station commissioner in his own neighbourhood, Elsies River, and then cluster commander for Mitchells Plain, one of the busiest stations in the country.[3] Members of the community police forum there told me that Vearey had been an exceptional station commissioner, transforming the place.

Like all police officers from the Flats, however, there were rumours about Vearey's possible links to the gangs, and his actions have been dissected by the Cape Flats rumour mill for signs of allegiance. There is conspiracy talk that he favours some gangs with the refrain that he 'grew up in a gang area' used to imply that. It's this blurring around the edges that always seems to accompany whispered discussion about happenings on the Cape Flats, which leaves you nervous and jumpy, like you are being watched. While I understand how the network of acquaintances and contacts can lock you into a local way of thinking, I doubt Jeremy Vearey is a corrupt cop. But time will be the judge.

The shadowy world of Western Cape police politics was fully on display in the run-up to the appointment of a new provincial police commissioner during 2019. Vearey was in the running, but patently didn't have the backing of the DA provincial government. A story in the *Sunday Times* that detailed a recording of Vearey engaging in corruption turned out to be fake, presumably placed by his opponents within police Crime Intelligence.[4] In the end, he was sidelined for the job. That did not reduce his public profile, however. Media savvy and independently minded, Vearey is the only general whose postings on Facebook seem to run independently of SAPS official communications. 'He seems to operate under different rules,' said a close observer, with whom he has a vexed relationship. 'It would simply not be tolerated with any other police general.'

Jacobs is much harder to pin down than Vearey. His more reserved character befits a man in his position: he is now head of Crime Intelligence under Cyril Ramaphosa, appointed to clean up the house. Jacobs, in a crumpled suit, a cloth cap on his head, has a George Smiley sense of watchfulness about him. He is not one to talk much and he gives very little away. 'You can get close,' an acquaintance of his said, 'but never too close'. Reserved, publicity-shy, observant, almost grandfatherly, he is a foil to the exuberance and energy of Vearey.

Jacobs left South Africa as a young man in the mid-1980s as political conflict ratcheted up, and as a member of MK he was involved in several operations in the country.[5] His steely silence in real life is reflected in the scant information that can be found on his background. But what is clear is that Jacobs is no pushover and is certain in his beliefs. He believes in the power of the state, a person who is close to Jacobs said: that the state needs to enforce the law, otherwise we can't operate as a country. On the public record, however, is the fact that after his arrest, he was tortured by the notorious apartheid police officer Jeffrey Benzien. After his arrest, Jacobs was deemed by the apartheid security police to be evasive in his answers and was subsequently brutally tortured into giving up information. This included the repeated use of the notorious 'wet bag', where the oxygen-starved victim is often left unconscious or dead. Benzien's chilly words still echo down the years: 'Peter, I will take you to the verge of death as many times as I want to, but here you are going to talk, and if it means that you will die, that is okay.' Jacobs was also subjected to electric-shock treatment.[6]

After the transition to democracy, Jacobs joined the SAPS and rose up the ranks, beginning as the head of airports and seaports, then did a stint as commissioner at Khayelitsha's huge, busy and troubled police station. He occupied posts in the police intelligence environment and in a unit responsible for tackling organised crime. He was eventually promoted to the position of deputy provincial commissioner for operational services in the Western Cape. In that capacity, he gave evidence to the commission of inquiry into inefficiencies at the Khayelitsha station, discreet as ever on the stand, politely demurring when asked to provide information on his new role as provincial head of Crime Intelligence.[7]

Good cops, bad cops

Operation Combat, the Vearey-led anti-gang task force of which Eksteen was part, 'pissed off' the various cluster commanders in the Western Cape, according to several senior police officers. In the SAPS system, a cluster commander is a big cheese, overseeing the policing services for a particular area. Operation Combat went over the heads of these senior officials, interfering in their area of operations. Vearey bypassed them, establishing relationships with local police officers whom he pulled into the operation, which was working at a provincial level.

Under the provincial police commissioner at the time, Arno Lamoer, the way in which the operation was run had been protected. Lamoer is something of a tragic figure in all of this. A career cop, he was central to protecting the initial stages of the investigation before being suspended, tried and convicted on charges of corruption. Lamoer's removal from office would open up opportunities for a new provincial commissioner who was much less sympathetic to the investigating duo. But under Lamoer, and with his support, Jacobs had been appointed as deputy provincial commissioner to run interference for Vearey, smoothing egos and talking down the cluster commanders. What seemed to have evolved was a highly networked, if occasionally disorganised, operation, which worked much more effectively than the stodgy clusters at bringing together information and acting on it. While it was left unstated in SAPS official explanations of Combat, the idea was that Combat would be as dynamic as the gangs themselves, pulling together intelligence and following it up with good detective work, to try to close cases that would damage the gangs. But it was essentially an information and activity network that operated parallel to ordinary policing structures. It worked but it also put a target on Vearey's back in the police bureaucracy.

Both Vearey and Jacobs have been accused of acting politically in their policing careers. Their struggle background raised questions as to whether they had acted in the interests of the ANC or as impartial enforcers of the law. When the ANC was in power in the Western

Cape, the then Democratic Alliance (DA) mayor of Cape Town, Helen Zille, made accusations that both Vearey and Jacobs had either given instructions for, or been involved in, her arrest. Zille was paid out for wrongful arrest after being taken into custody in 2007 after an anti-gang march that she had been leading in Mitchells Plain veered off course. Vearey denied that he was involved, accusing Zille of 'Stratcom' tactics, a term deliberately meant to imply that Zille reflected the old order.[8] Either way, arresting the mayor in a protest whose objective most citizens had sympathy for would prove to be a career-limiting move for Vearey.

The relationship between Zille, who was later to assume the premiership of the Western Cape, and Vearey has remained frosty, inflamed by several incidents over the years. The tension between the two, and between Vearey and the DA, has festered on. Vearey, never one for reticence, has engaged in open disagreements with the premier of the province, the member of the province's executive council (MEC) for community safety, Dan Plato, now Cape Town's mayor, and the city's current head of safety and policing, J.P. Smith. Vearey's public persona is in many ways unprecedented in South African policing, either before or after apartheid. It is likely that this cost him the plum job of provincial police commissioner, as well as more senior jobs at national police headquarters, including that of national commissioner, because he is regarded as too outspoken and not easily controlled.

The open rancour between the SAPS, in the shape of Vearey, as well as some other officers, and the DA provincial and city governments is itself a product of declining levels of safety and the alarming homicide rate in Cape Town. Given that policing is a national responsibility, provincial politicians have been eager to point out that the SAPS has been failing the Cape's citizenry. The more conspiratorial (Zille included) have also made the argument that an ANC government itself has been deliberately causing insecurity in the Cape, including by protecting prominent gangsters. The police ministry's own clumsy handling of the Khayelitsha Commission into poor policing only fed that impression.

Vearey writes a widely read blog and has written a book in Afrikaans about his life. The book starts with a fascinating line: '*Dis die ding met groot lesse in die lewensloop, jy leer dit altyd op ongeleë tye, onverwags, met 'n ontnugtering wat jou kinderlike onskuld verpletter.*'[9] (That is the thing about big lessons in life: you learn them always at inconvenient times, unexpectedly, with a disillusionment that crushes your childlike innocence.) Could that line apply to Vearey's relationship with the ANC, as the movement began to creak and splinter 20 years into democracy? Were the weakening of the police and the spilling of guns onto the streets of Vearey's home town acts of state carelessness of such extremity that they rivalled the excesses of the apartheid state itself? Having found the source of the guns, he was blocked at almost every step by other former ANC members as he tried to bring the case together.

The factional politics within the ANC, which has been the stuff of daily news for many years, began in the Thabo Mbeki era, worsening under the destructive leadership of Jacob Zuma. It had huge consequences for the police. Zuma, in order to protect himself from prosecution, sought to appoint a series of allies in key positions within the SAPS. He was aided in that by chronic leadership instability at the top of the police, brought on by his desire for it (a destabilised police being unlikely to mount an effective investigation into his activities), as well as the corruption that now dominated the service.

Zuma appointed two former SAPS and homeland police officers to senior positions. Richard Mdluli, a one-time Security Branch cop on Johannesburg's East Rand, was elevated to the critical post of head of Crime Intelligence. There Mdluli, apart from ensuring that he could siphon off enough money for his own needs (maintaining, for example, a girlfriend in a police safe house), ran interference for Zuma, becoming one the most feared men in the police and the country. Crime Intelligence resources, it has now been shown, were used by Zuma to neutralise his enemies. Crime Intelligence would become one of the centres of what is now known as 'state capture'.

Secondly, at the specialised investigative unit, the Hawks, Zuma appointed the grossly incompetent Berning Ntlemeza, with the sole purpose of blocking any investigation against him and anyone from whom he was receiving favours. The Hawks became derisible, ignoring serious organised crime and instead pursuing politically inspired 'investigations' into Zuma's enemies. It was a case of policing as politics.

At around the time that the Project Impi team were investigating the sources of the stolen firearms, public perceptions of the then police commissioner, Riah Phiyega, were at an all-time low. Criticised for lacking police experience and being a poor manager, Phiyega would be suspended in October 2015 following the inquiry into the deaths of protesting miners at Marikana three years earlier. She had been a political choice, seen as more likely to be influenced by gaining political advantage (or avoiding damage) in the Zuma regime than by policing professionalism.

Vearey and Jacobs went to see Phiyega in mid-2014 to brief her on their operation and ensure that she knew what might be coming down the line. The Project Impi investigators were now paranoid about whom they could trust. If firearms were leaking out of the police system in large numbers, it was possible that senior police could be involved. For reasons of security, they met Phiyega at a hotel away from the prying eyes in the SAPS headquarters in Pretoria. They explained to her the possibility that the gun-trafficking case might well implicate senior police officers. Phiyega listened to them in silence and then asked questions. Her instruction to Vearey and Jacobs was that the investigation should continue no matter who would be swept up by it. This is to Phiyega's credit, whatever other criticism has been levelled at her.

During the Zuma years, tensions in the service increased dramatically. Good cops were pushed aside or quietly retired. The likes of Vearey and Jacobs navigated the space cautiously, conscious of who held and did not hold power. Officers like them were increasingly isolated, as the president, always alert to people's vulnerabilities, drew on those with a tainted past. Vearey was clearly aligned to the non-Zuma camp of the ANC, a perception reinforced by the fact that he had been responsible for recording a damning statement made by former MP Vytjie Mentor in which she said that the Guptas had offered her the job of Minister of Public Enterprises. When the statement was leaked to the press after it had been sent to the office of the by then notorious Ntlemeza, fingers were pointed at Vearey. He has argued in a sworn affidavit that the statement was 'recorded routinely by members under [his] command'. This, he concedes, fuelled a narrative that he was involved himself in factional politics.[10]

In the destabilised environment of the Western Cape police, battle lines were drawn as the crisis during the Zuma presidency intensified. It was hard to follow the byzantine politics within the SAPS as each grouping sought to out-position the other. On one hand were the likes of Vearey and Jacobs (as well as several other officers, such as the Western Cape's highest-ranked female officer, Brigadier Sonja Harri); on the other was the province's head of Crime Intelligence, another former ANC operative, and seen as Zuma-aligned, Mzwandile Tiyo, who had been involved in tapping the phone of the then provincial commissioner, Lamoer.

Tiyo, who has links with Modack,[11] came under suspicion later for being appointed, after pressure from the pro-Zuma camp, without the correct educational qualifications (he did not have a matric) and lacking a security clearance.[12] He brought poison into the provincial police, according to an officer I regard as neutral in the dispute, developing a set of dubious relations in the Cape underworld. Tiyo, no doubt identifying Hassan as a key node for information exchange, seemed to have developed a link with the lawyer before his death and maintained contact with dead man's family afterwards. As mentioned, he told them that Vearey had been involved in the lawyer's murder.[13]

This political and professional tension puts into perspective the nature of any police response to reports that potentially huge quantities of state guns were now on the street in Cape Town. Distributing guns to promote violence was something of a hallmark of apartheid 'policing'. Vearey and Jacobs must have been acutely conscious of the enormous consequences of what they thought they were seeing, both in the cost for ordinary people on the Cape Flats, and politically too. But shaking the police bureaucratic tree was likely to have an impact both on individual careers and on the case itself.

Walking on eggshells – the guns investigation

At the time of writing, Constable Eksteen is still out there on the streets. You can question Eksteen's background and his alleged gang connections, which explain, reportedly, his lack of promotion, but there is little doubt that his phone call up the chain to Vearey was the first step in opening up the case. Perhaps it would have been broken open in other ways, but perhaps not. Whatever his flaws, Lutfie Eksteen played a crucial role.

And, as he recognised, looking for the source of large quantities of police guns in the hands of gangsters requires some careful steps. Who would be in the know? Would the very senior police who might have power to oversee the investigation be in a position to stop it? The question was even more important in the fraught political environment of the SAPS. A wrong move or the wrong person hearing about the investigation could be damaging. Vearey and Jacobs had to proceed carefully and quietly with their investigations.

The police intelligence net was cast wider, sources were squeezed for information and reports emerged about a mass of Z88s circulating in Hanover Park. The story was still pretty hazy: informants suggested that the guns had come from dirty cops in KwaZulu-Natal. Given where the story would go later, this was an interesting piece of information to put out there, but it was not, as it happens, the truth. It was probably a deliberate falsehood that had been fed into the rumour mill.

Vearey and Jacobs devised a plan. They would, in the context of an intelligence operation, try to buy some guns from gangsters in Hanover Park who seemed to be letting on that they had new firearms. The guns were acquired in a judicially sanctioned operation, a judge of the High Court having given permission for it to go ahead. The newly acquired Z88s were sent for testing.

Meanwhile, as mentioned earlier in the book, a critical intelligence report had been found in the home of murdered gang lawyer Noorudien Hassan. Although nobody will say for sure, it is almost certain that the secret document that mysteriously found its way into Hassan's possession was an internal police report detailing this Hanover Park entrapment operation. Someone within Crime Intelligence must have leaked it to the criminals. If there is anything that shows just how sordid the environment within the police service had become, it has to be the leaking of a top-secret police report on the case to a lawyer who was defending the main suspect in the illegal gun sales. The secret report did not implicate Prinsloo, and detailed only local gun sales, so whoever leaked the report could not disrupt the investigation further up the chain, even if he had wanted to. But leaking the report was probably a more localised strategy to undermine Vearey by disrupting the investigation.

If fellow officers within Crime Intelligence could not be trusted, events on the street in 2013 and 2014 started to yield some important pieces of evidence as gang shoot-outs proliferated: the guns themselves. One development in the gang war was to be of immediate benefit to the police. Gangsters started throwing their guns away. Gang members told me that given that there was now a growing reservoir of guns, many gangsters had got casual with them. In the past, gangs had protected their arsenals with their lives. Now, with guns everywhere, nervous shooters would let off a few rounds, then drop their weapon and run. Gun discipline had all but been thrown to the wind because there were so many to go around.

A concerted effort was made to collect these weapons. Vearey reportedly visited various stations, telling local officers to be alert to such guns. Piece by piece, seized guns began making their way to the provincial ballistics labs as officers on the street found them or confiscated them from gangsters. It was all done below the radar at first, an intelligence operation driven by personal contacts in Vearey's networks.

Ballistics tests indicated that all the firearms had been tampered with in the same manner. In the course of late 2013, Vearey and Jacobs brought into their team a detective known for his professionalism and reliability, Lieutenant Colonel Clive Ontong. The whole operation to trace the guns remained secret: Ontong, in a sworn statement, later recounted that the operation had been enacted 'in a covert manner because of the sensitivity of the case being investigated'.[14]

Ontong was a policeman with a long background in gang investigations. He had most recently been tracing a gang of hired killers called, appropriately enough, the Mobsters. This group rented themselves out across the Flats to any gang or individual who could pay. The Mobsters also seemed to have purchased police guns for themselves, and some of these had been acquired by the police. Ontong was told to report to Vearey and Jacobs, and keep everybody else out of the loop. Another trusted policeman close to Vearey, Sergeant Jeffrey Witbooi from Manenberg, was also brought on board. More trusted Crime Intelligence operatives were added, blending detectives and undercover operatives. From the provincial Directorate of Public Prosecutions, two advocates were added to the task force.

The group, as mentioned, was named Project Impi, perhaps a hint of a hoped-for connection to KwaZulu-Natal.

CHAPTER 8

THE MAN AT THE CENTRE

P roject Impi battled forward. Progress was frustratingly slow. By 2014, however, it had at least become clear to Vearey and Jacobs, from ballistics tests performed on weapons they had seized, that many of them had been expertly tampered with to remove the serial numbers, so that they could not be linked back to the SAPS firearms database. A large portion were Z88s, meaning they could have come from only one source: the police. There were by this point dozens of cases of guns that Vearey's investigative team had seized and were now in police custody – a virtual arsenal.

Like a crime scene investigation movie, examining the seized firearms provided a repository of key evidence. The ballistics experts in the laboratory who were working with Project Impi investigators made a crucial discovery: based on tests and discreet inquiries made back to the firearms database, 22 of the weapons were linked to a batch that had been marked for destruction. Of these, 19 guns had previously been in service with the SAPS; the remaining three had been in private hands and then voluntarily handed over during a gun amnesty. Determining the guns' source therefore proved to be a simple process of elimination. Police-issued guns, primarily Z88s, had to be disposed of in the main SAPS armoury in Vereeniging, by law. The 19 police guns could only have come from one place: that armoury. Checks were made that eliminated the possibility that they had leaked from Western Cape police stores.

There were also important clues to be had from the three non-police guns that had been seized. From tests, it was determined that these guns, rifles in this case, had been listed on the system as having been destroyed. They had clearly survived. Alterations had been made to these weapons to mask their ballistic fingerprint and create a new paper trail.

It is easy to get cynical in this story about the police and to assume that everyone in the service is corrupt. After all, on the face of it, police guns were being sold to criminals for personal profit and the effect was death on a frightening scale – which it is precisely the police service's strategic mission to prevent.[1] But working away in the system, in the ballistics laboratory, was one police gun nerd who was fulfilling his duties properly and with due rigour. Lieutenant Colonel Lukas Visser is a pedant, according to several police officers who have worked with him. And he was furious that guns that were appearing in the Cape Flats could have come from only one place.

'The firearms environment attracts detail-orientated guys. Visser is one of them,' a colleague of his observed. 'The penny dropped,' said one of the investigators in the Prinsloo case. Visser, by all accounts, was the key to the door.

The net closes in

The police ballistics environment is small; everybody knows every-body else and what they do – or should do. It must have been a painful realisation to Lieutenant Colonel Visser, who had examined the way in which the firearms had been altered, each with their iden-tity markings professionally removed, that these guns were coming from the centre of the SAPS's own gun-control system. Visser con-cluded that the guns were being altered by a professional gunsmith within the police. The source could have been one of only a tiny handful of people: only two or three gunsmiths employed by the SAPS would have had the expertise to obliterate the ballistic serial numbers. That revelation must have been shocking in the extreme.

The police armoury in Vereeniging was placed under surveil-lance. The team watched and waited. The first round of the battle of expertise may have been won, and the Project Impi team's file of information was growing by the day. By this point, they appear to have developed a source who provided crucial information, but there was still no direct evidence to tie anyone to the case. Then, in January 2015, some five years after the flag had been raised about the presence of police guns on the Cape Flats, Project Impi had a breakthrough. The SAPS's main weapons expert, Colonel Christiaan Lodewyk Prinsloo, who was also responsible for the armoury, was spotted by surveillance teams removing boxes from the firearms stores and taking them home. Visser had been right on the money.

As Project Impi operatives watched, Prinsloo was seen visiting a shooting range close to his home in Vereeniging. From this suspicious behaviour, they inferred that the guns might have been tampered with at the range. The trap was closing.

But he wasn't the only one in Impi's sights. Prinsloo had worked at the armoury with a colleague, David Naidoo, also a full colonel at the time. Naidoo is an intriguing, if distasteful, figure in all of this. It was Naidoo who had first spotted the gap and began selling firearms to criminals, and not Prinsloo, who had followed Naidoo's lead. He had seen Naidoo leave the facility with a pair of pistols in a rosewood box one day, probably in 2005 or 2006. The pistols were heritage items of some value for the active firearm collectors' market. Prinsloo approached Naidoo to ask what the hell was going on. But instead of reporting Naidoo, Prinsloo joined him in his game.

Naidoo 'is an alcoholic with family problems who needed the money', a police investigator said. It turns out he also had a serious gambling problem and kept a mistress in secret, so he had two households to maintain, someone who was close to Naidoo added. In contrast to Prinsloo, however, Naidoo seems to have escaped sanction altogether, quietly disappearing from the unfolding story. Seemingly, how he managed to do this is by talking to police investigators, effectively selling Prinsloo out. 'Naidoo is basically a coward,' said one of the investigators who spoke to him. 'He realised quickly which way the wind was blowing and signed a 204 and told us everything.' 'Section 204', refers to the part of the Criminal Procedure Act that makes provision for a witness to be granted full indemnity on a charge should they testify for the state, and the court judges this to be frank and honest.

Apparently, the threat of losing his pension convinced Naidoo, a weak and vulnerable man, to collaborate with investigators. In my opinion, Naidoo had been in contact with investigators well before the arrest of Prinsloo, being encouraged to take the 204 option in exchange for immunity.[2] He told all he knew and walked away, pension intact.

This process, a form of plea bargaining, can sometimes mean that those whom the police close in on first, and who agree to speak, are likely to receive less punishment than those whom such testimony exposes. It has been criticised for providing incentives for the police to go this route rather than investigate a case to its full extent and prosecute all those involved. Indemnity in exchange for information is a necessary tool in the arsenal of the criminal-justice system, by providing opportunities for people to come forward and declare what they have done or what they know. But it also means that the punishment does not fit the crime. Naidoo, who had been involved in the weapon sales himself, got away scot-free without the prison sentence and opprobrium that would later rain down on Prinsloo's head.

Once investigators had begun to snoop around the armoury and ask questions elsewhere in the SAPS, Prinsloo began to get very nervous. He was asked to hand over his SAPS firearms store keys, as an investigation was under way. Tension developed between Naidoo and Prinsloo, as it became clear that Prinsloo might be exposed. Nevertheless, and despite the fact he suspected that he was being watched, Prinsloo continued peddling the guns and arranging their transport.

Now armed with enough evidence to nail Prinsloo, the Project Impi team obtained a warrant to enter and search his home. On 16 January, the search team found what they had been looking for: they discovered 750 rounds of ammunition at Prinsloo's home that had been removed from the police stores. He was arrested later that day.

A broken man

Prinsloo wasn't just any policeman. When it comes to guns, he was the SAPS's top expert, widely consulted and eager to give advice. Ten years earlier, for example, when anti-gun lobbying group Gun Free South Africa had reviewed the 2005 firearms amnesty, one of the experts they consulted was Prinsloo.[3] That Prinsloo would later sell some of the very guns that had been handed in during that amnesty would have struck most people engaged in the debate as unthinkable. When the Hawks launched their investigation into Dave Sheer Gunsmithing and Firearms, a gun dealer who had allegedly dealt in stolen ammunition, Prinsloo was consulted.

Prinsloo had three decades' experience in dealing with gun-related matters, going back to the old apartheid era of the South African Police. He was an expert at interpreting the new firearms legislation introduced in the late 1990s, and an all-round go-to guy on gun matters within the SAPS. A senior police officer who worked with him over the years said that Prinsloo could tell by looking at the markings and serial number where a gun had been and even its history.

There are telling fragments of this expert side of Prinsloo in media reports. In 2005, he is quoted citing the numbers of guns handed in during the firearm amnesty of that year. 'We confiscated 256 unlawful firearms in this period,' he said. He continued, 'We think there are about 400 000 of these inherited firearms in the country.' Then a final flourish: 'Prinsloo said the amnesty was an ideal opportunity for people to surrender inherited firearms whose licenses had not been renewed.'[4] Prinsloo himself owned 12 firearms.

Prinsloo had the demeanour of a teacher at your average South African high school – tall, balding and, at the time of his arrest, sporting a neatly trimmed moustache and large gold-rimmed glasses. His clothes were unostentatious. He did not have an extravagant lifestyle – no fast cars or over-designed houses. History could be his subject, or science perhaps, and some rugby coaching in the afternoon. Someone who had knowledge and opinions, and was ready to share them. The banality of evil may be an overworked phrase, but it applies here. He was 54 at the time of his arrest.

I spoke to numerous people who had been acquainted with Prinsloo, and the same picture emerges each time: Prinsloo was considered 'an expert', a word that is used again and again. He also seemingly regarded himself as one; he had a high opinion of himself. That, in itself, may not be an unusual attribute, but in the changing context of policing in South Africa it was to make Prinsloo vulnerable. The SAP had been a key instrument of state control and Prinsloo was an up-and-coming officer in the 1980s when the country was virtually in a state of civil war, just before the violent convulsions that marked South Africa in the final days of white rule, with the police on the front lines.

Prinsloo began work in the Vaal Triangle (an industrial hub some 70 km from Johannesburg), which was badly affected by the township revolts of the 1980s and had a long history of conflict. Sharpeville, scene of the notorious March 1960 massacre by police, is nearby, as is Boipatong, a township in which a 1992 attack by Zulu hostel dwellers, supported by police, led to a major crisis in negotiations between the ANC and the National Party government.

Prinsloo was later appointed station commander at De Deur, a town just north of Vereeniging. Apart from a conviction for a driving offence in 1981 when he was 20, Prinsloo's record was spotless.

Prinsloo once told a close acquaintance that he had served time in the notorious apartheid police Security Branch. I have not been able to confirm this but my own hunch is that it is probably bravado. But he did stay on in the police service after the transition, bargaining that his particular expertise would be something that would set him moving up the promotions ladder – whoever held political power. In any event, it was clear to him that there were few peers in the police who had his level of expertise in firearms. The state clearly needed those skills as an ambitious programme of firearm amnesties and crime prevention got under way.

Prinsloo became a resource in the service for any firearm-related inquiries, for those tasked with investigations into police officers, gun dealers and others suspected of violating the Firearms Control

Act. He had a close relationship with the Central Firearms Registry (CFR) and frequently spoke at public forums convened by the CFR. The so-called Designated Firearms Officers for the province, who processed licence requests at station level, reported to Prinsloo. He was also responsible for the police armoury. 'He was always the cleverest person in the room,' an official who worked with him said. 'Other police officers would defer to him.'[5]

Prinsloo may have stayed on with the police in the democratic era after 1994, but he wasn't rapidly promoted. In 2005, he was a superintendent under the civilian ranking structure that was then in place, equivalent to a lieutenant colonel. He was later promoted to a full colonel. Ten years later, in 2015, the year he was arrested, he held more or less the same position. For an ambitious man with a high opinion of himself, this sluggish career trajectory must have rankled. Could the system not see his expertise? Would he make brigadier or even general before he was forced to retire? Did he not deserve that?

For most of this period, Prinsloo seems to have lived in Arcon Park, a lower-middle-class suburb in Vereeniging. His house, which he bought sometime in the mid-1990s, was a neat and tidy 1970s bungalow. A single tree at the end of the driveway and an expansive, well-tended lawn at the front. A line of flowers was planted along the fence in summer.

It is not an unpleasant place to live, away from the immediate hustle and bustle of Johannesburg, and with the farmlands of the Free State stretching beyond the river to the south. The local primary school is around the corner and there are well-stocked shopping centres nearby. Having resided there for a long time, Prinsloo and his wife, Helena, a few years his junior, maintained a network of friends in the area.

Despite the seemingly normal suburban life, there were some worries at home though. If Prinsloo was ambitious for himself, he also had ambitions for his two children. By 2015, they were in their mid and late 20s. The youngest was at university, an achievement of which the family seemed particularly proud. Placing value in education is not at all unusual for police officers. Many don't want their own children to join the police, and aspire to a better life for them. Since police recruits in South Africa are seldom university graduates, many want their children to go to university to study to get ahead.[6] For Prinsloo, there were university fees to pay, a strain for a man on a colonel's salary.[7] Prinsloo's eldest child also had special needs, which added to the mounting family expenses.

Friends reported, though, that the Prinsloo family seemed to be doing okay, even thriving. Although there was some belt-tightening in the era after the financial crisis of 2008, for the Prinsloos there were new cars, overseas holidays and some upgrades to the house. Prinsloo paid for his son to attend a R50 000 professional hunting course – all signs that the good colonel was looking after his brood. Some who knew him now express their suspicions, but that is easy after the fact. To all intents and purposes, Prinsloo was a model police officer and an expert in his field, not a killer with blood on his hands.

Prinsloo was warned about his arrest and knew it was coming, explained a lawyer close to the process. He broke quickly under questioning. In any event, he was in a fix: stolen ammunition had been found at his house and Naidoo's snitching had implicated him. Oddly, he did not seem bitter about his arrest. 'He was ready to face the consequences from the beginning,' someone very close to him at the time said.

While he was still in the police cell, and before he had access to a lawyer, he gave the police a statement and agreed to assist them in future sting operations. He had been caught red-handed, as well as grassed on by Naidoo. There were not many legal routes for escape.

In his conflicted way of thinking – which went something like this: I committed a crime that was clever in its execution, but I am also a policeman – Prinsloo was almost waiting to be caught. He knew that investigators were snooping around. Perhaps he even expected it. He offered no resistance and began singing. The policemen who did the interviewing also noted that he was remorseful. He did not attempt to deny what he had done and told his former colleagues the whole story.

When his arrest became public, the outside world seemed scarcely able to believe it. Although she had already been briefed on the investigation by the lead officers, Phiyega seemed stunned by the news. It was a feeling that was generally shared: 'Most people in firearms circles were shocked when he was arrested,' said Martin Hood, the go-to lawyer and guru when it comes to cases involving guns. 'A lot of people in the firearms community would approach Prinsloo when they had a problem and he was known as a guy who would not only listen to complaints but also get involved in solving problems. He was not known to be corrupt.'[8]

At this point, the best option by far for Prinsloo was to turn state witness. In fact, there was little choice, as he was already cooperating with the police before he received legal advice. In July 2015, he was rearrested on a set of new charges. (The January charges had related only to the ammunition found at his house and he had been released on bail.[9]) Between his second arrest and application for bail, which was granted for R20 000, and his brief trial, Prinsloo spent over a year talking with the investigators. From policeman to prisoner, the slope was a rapid one, reflected in Prinsloo's appearance on arrival for his first hearing in July 2015 and his later appearances in April and June 2016. He had visibly aged in one year, the neatly trimmed beard of 2015 now a long, grey, scruffy mass.

The large consignments of guns that Prinsloo had supplied to the gangs were not in fact the first firearms that he had sold. Police officers involved in his interviewing said that he admitted having sold smaller quantities of guns from the armoury for several years before finding a willing buyer who would be the intermediary to the gangsters of the Western Cape.

Prinsloo also showed himself as nothing if not entrepreneurial, quite apart from selling firearms. A good example is the case of the Dave Sheer Gunsmithing and Firearms Exchange mentioned earlier. The Hawks had consulted Prinsloo on this case a few months before his arrest. What the investigators did not know then, however, is that after suspects in the case had been arrested, Prinsloo had helped

Former police colonel Christiaan Prinsloo in court, grey-bearded and exhausted. Previously the SAPS's all-knowing gun expert, now a broken man whose life is threatened. MEGAN BAADJIES / AFRICAN NEWS AGENCY

them behind the scenes to prepare their case, highlighting problems with the prosecution approach and pointing to loopholes. After several delays, that case was still due to go for trial at the time of writing in the Kagiso Regional Court.

This entrepreneurial streak was apparently not new. I have been told that Prinsloo once took payment to make dockets disappear when he was station commissioner at De Deur. There are other alleged small incidents: agreeing to take guns for the armoury 'off the record' from people, and a predisposition to do a favour or two, like telling collectors which firearms from deceased estates were becoming available. (Collectors would then approach the families directly.) Although Prinsloo did not ask for any payment for this information, 'the lines became a bit blurred', according to a leading light in the hunting fraternity, who said that Prinsloo would accept invitations to go on hunts without having to pay.

At some point, Prinsloo seems to have lost all his scruples, a fact several imply was linked to his being passed over for promotion in the SAPS. Prinsloo told the investigators that from 2007 he had begun to sell weapons to intermediaries in large quantities. By that time, his methodology was well established. He was exceedingly careful. He did not want to deal with lots of criminals looking for guns and haggling over the prices. 'Prinsloo did not want an audience,' a police investigator said. 'He goes to the right guy. He goes to a single line.' That all made sense. Prinsloo would sell the guns in bulk to a single person, who would then worry about the distribution. That would keep him one step away from the unpredictable and volatile gangsters. No gangster I spoke to had ever been in direct contact with Prinsloo. His connections to Durban are less clear. Guns from the armoury were delivered there, but that intermediary has so far remained shrouded in mystery.

Prinsloo would deliver the guns to his connection in Cape Town, allegedly Laher, offloading them from his bakkie into a waiting vehicle. He liked to do the deliveries himself to keep the circle of those in the know to the barest minimum. It seems hard to imagine: Prinsloo, in an official police bakkie, driving down to Cape Town, alone with his thoughts, the back of the vehicle packed with guns that would then be delivered to some of the most murderous gangs on earth.

In June 2016, a year and a half after his first arrest, Prinsloo entered into a section 105A plea and sentence agreement in the Belville Magistrate's Court. Having done so, he was sentenced to imprisonment for 18 years, a shorter term than he would have otherwise received had he not agreed to work with the state. In Belville that day, it was clear that the case had taken its toll. There is a photo of him in court sitting on a bench, his head lowered, hands clasped together, alone.

A small but angry protest gathered outside the court during his appearances, mainly women, their anger palpable: 'Prinsloo has our people's blood on his hands.' The courtroom was packed as his sentence was handed down. One community leader, Saldeelah Petersen, in an emotional statement, said that the guns that Prinsloo had sold 'to our communities' had led to 'over 170 000 killings ... and counting. We have decided to take a stand, this will not disappear.'[10] A church minister, Reverend Major, added, 'I ministered on the Cape Flats for 12 years and I buried too many children who were shot. Enough is enough. The fact that Prinsloo got 18 years is not enough ... I want [him] to be charged with mass murder.'[11]

During the short trial, Prinsloo was surrounded by armed police. There was good reason, too: his evidence was likely to incriminate not only the intermediaries to whom he sold the guns, but also potentially some powerful bosses in gangland. 'He is a marked man from every angle,' Vearey said. 'He can never live in public again.'

He was right. With the sentence handed down, Prinsloo effectively vanished from view. He served the first part of his sentence at Obiqua Prison near Tulbagh in the Western Cape. In the course of researching the book, I heard several rumours as to his whereabouts. Some said he was in prison, others that he was in a witness-protection safe house. At the time of writing, he had not appeared in court again to give evidence for the state against Laher. For his part, Naidoo was quietly suspended from the police on full pension and then slipped from view.

Shortly after Prinsloo was charged under the Prevention of Organised Crime Act, the Asset Forfeiture Unit went to the High Court to
seize his assets. These would then be held by a court appointee until
the case was finalised. The seized assets included his house, pension,
cars and firearms. Travel and university fees seemed to have eaten
up most of the money, and Prinsloo did not have an extravagant
array of properties or other possessions that could be taken. A deal
was ultimately struck between Prinsloo's legal team and the state,
under which Prinsloo retained ownership of most of his possessions, including the house and cars, which had been paid off, but
forfeited just over R1 million of his pension. He was particularly set
on ensuring that he still had his police pension in order to be able
to provide for his family while he was in prison. Symbolically, his
firearms were forfeited to the state, although his son was allowed to
purchase one of these back, a hunting rifle. Given the extent of his
crimes, it was a good deal.

It is reasonable to ask why Prinsloo was treated with such leni-
ency. The answer is that the investigators were eager to arrest and
prosecute his intermediary to the gangs, for which they needed
his cooperation. In return, Prinsloo negotiated a favourable deal,
so that his wife and sons would be financially secure. It was also
agreed that he would not serve his sentence with other prisoners – it
would be too dangerous. That was the bargain.

In October 2020 Prinsloo was reported to have been released
on parole, having served only three years and ten months of his
eighteen-year sentence. It is a shockingly short time in jail given
the scale of his crimes. I had myself been told of threats to his life
and a Correctional Services spokesperson made the same point to
the media. News24 subsequently published two photographs of
a man who looked like Prinsloo shopping in Vereeniging.[12] If it
was Prinsloo, he seemed to have little fear for his life. It was later
revealed in response to a parliamentary question that Prinsloo had
been placed under witness protection.

What is astonishing is that Prinsloo did not at the time seem to
acknowledge the consequences of his actions. He even admitted that

he would have continued selling the guns if he had not been caught.[13] Prinsloo showed remorse, but only for breaking the law, not for the deaths that the guns had caused. Perhaps that was too hard for him to face. One story that he did spin to try to justify the gun sales was that he had not known that they were going to the gangs. In at least one account that I have on good authority from someone who had dealings with him, Prinsloo said he thought the firearms were going to private security companies that were guarding ships off the coast of Somalia. These companies were not in a position to get licences for the volumes of guns they needed. Their modus operandi was therefore to acquire guns illegally and then to pitch them overboard once the ships had successfully passed through the danger zone. That sounds like a cover story, a justification that must have quickly crumbled. I don't believe it has any truth.

The psychology of a criminal

He may have seemed calm when the handcuffs were slipped on his wrists, but in the years before his arrest Christiaan Prinsloo was an angry man. It's hard now to see him as an upright cop in uniform: all the pictures in the public domain show an almost Robinson Crusoe-like figure, frail and sloping forward as he walks. But that was after his fall. Before it, he saw himself as undervalued: an acknowledged expert but with seemingly no hope of promotion in a police organisation where non-white officers were on the up and up.

Other white policemen have told me how they became reconciled to the reality of post-apartheid policing. Those close to retirement saw it as a question of serving their time and moving on, and there were rare cases of white officers who still saw their job as a calling, promotion or not.

Prinsloo fitted neither of these categories. Instead, he resented a system that he saw as aligned against him. If he was not likely to be promoted, then he would quite literally make the system pay. A former intelligence officer close to the investigation provided an interesting insight. For him, Prinsloo had the classic set of vulnerabilities of someone who defects to an enemy intelligence agency, or perhaps turns to crime. One of my police contacts compared Prinsloo to Dieter Gerhardt, the South African naval officer who volunteered his services to the Soviet Union and was arrested in the early 1980s by the FBI after selling apartheid South African and Western military secrets. 'They had a remarkably similar profile,' he said.

What makes people susceptible to an approach from an intelligence service is sometimes summed up by the acronym MICE: money, ideology, coercion and ego. There is still some debate as to the motives behind Gerhardt's espionage: was it an ideological act of someone who opposed apartheid, the action of an outsider who harboured a grudge, or money? In Prinsloo's case, his betrayal by the system certainly seemed to weigh heavily on his ego, but he was also drawn to cold hard cash. He believed he warranted greater recognition and he needed the money.

Whether Gerhardt and Prinsloo are comparable is questionable: one was a paid spy, the other a corrupt policeman. Nothing I have heard from many discussions around the case, including with those who knew Prinsloo well or interviewed him, suggests that he acted ideologically, in that he may have wanted to distribute guns so that black people could kill each other, or to make the government look incompetent and unable to control gang violence. This was, however, one interpretation, that had often been debated on the Cape Flats itself.

'Prinsloo was not racist. He just thought he could beat the system because he was cleverer than it,' Vearey told others involved in the gun debate at the time of his arrest.[14] Given Vearey's background and acute sensitivity to issues of race, that seems a reliable interpretation. Prinsloo was most likely to have been motivated by ego and money, ticking two of the MICE boxes.

The Gerhardt–Prinsloo analogy has some merit, in that it is easy to see how Prinsloo could have been driven by a sense that he was an outsider in a system that had chosen to ignore his talents. That made it an easy step to persuade himself to commit crimes that would benefit him personally. Such internal reasoning is impossible to prove, of course, but presumably Prinsloo felt justified in screwing a system that he felt was stacked against him. It was perhaps less a form of revenge than it was of taking something that he felt was rightfully his.

And there is an interesting piece of evidence that seems to reinforce this. We know that Prinsloo was extremely angry that he had been promised the rank of brigadier but had lost out to a black officer. At least in Prinsloo's telling, he had to clean up the work that his newly promoted colleague had failed to do properly. He had been promised a promotion, indeed he felt he was owed it. The system had failed him, so he had little compunction in undermining it.

Prinsloo had one other vulnerability that we also know about: he was short of cash. You could see the self-justification: the crime was really just about getting back what was due to him. He would not be the first or the last to justify corruption in this way. Greed justifies things in criminal minds. The earlier signs of an entrepreneurial Prinsloo, offering up information in exchange for a free hunt invite or allegedly losing a docket for cash, were indications that he may have been motivated by money long before his ego frustrations with his lack of recognition by the system. In the end, it was a combination of vulnerabilities: greed, expenses to meet, a lack of recognition for his brilliance, a way to screw the system that was screwing him – all rolled into one.

CHAPTER 9

THE HUNTER AND THE COLLECTOR

The primary objective of the police in persuading Prinsloo to talk was for the investigation to home in on any intermediaries he may have used to sell guns to the gangs and other criminals. Perhaps Naidoo had connections that opened the way to sales in KwaZulu-Natal, but it seemed to be Prinsloo's own efforts that established the link he needed to sell guns to the Cape Town gangs. The Project Impi officers were hoping for a direct connection to the gangs; perhaps a prominent gang boss had been the intermediary, they hypothesised. But Prinsloo, who had never worked in the Cape and had never had any direct contacts with gangsters, would not have had such connections.

How exactly the idea to sell guns to the gangs originated is unclear. What seems to be the case is that Prinsloo began discussing the issue of the guns in the police stock with an acquaintance of his. This was Irshaad 'Hunter' Laher, a local Gauteng businessman who subsequently moved to Cape Town and was in contact with Hassan. Laher had been a police reservist when Prinsloo was the station commander at De Deur. The two knew each other well from those days, although relations have now soured – unsurprisingly, given what ensued.

But that was all in the future. Laher, who had originally lived in Vereeniging, moved to Cape Town in 2005. I don't believe he moved south for the express purpose of selling guns, although his introduction to the Cape Town milieu may well have got him thinking about market opportunities. Perhaps Prinsloo raised the idea while Laher was in Johannesburg. Or they had a phone call. Either way, the fact that there was a considerable surplus of guns in police stores bound for destruction was an attractive business proposition – money for jam. Both would have been aware that there were many police guns in illegal circulation. It might be easy to remove the guns in bulk, but who would they then sell them to? Who would value large consignments of guns and have the money to pay for them? Somebody must have hit on the idea of the Cape Town gangs as the ideal market. Laher did not have direct connections to the gangs either, although he did, as noted earlier, have an interesting family link to the underworld. And, like Prinsloo, he seemed to be a man of enterprising outlook. He was not called Hunter for nothing.

The hunter

Prinsloo and Laher seem to have been acquainted for some time before the gun trafficking began, not only through their policing connections, but also apparently in the game-hunting fraternity (the source of Laher's nickname). Although by no means a firearms expert of the calibre of Prinsloo, Laher also has a good knowledge of weaponry. The two shared a taste for guns; their time at De Deur Police Station and, later, their meetings at the shooting range enabled them to bond over a mutual interest. Laher belonged to the South African Hunters and Game Conservation Association, and has been an active member of a local shooting club in Kenwyn, Cape Town.

Laher has an intimidating presence; he is a tall man, his hair closely cropped, and he wears a beard. He was born in 1975, so at the time he allegedly went into the guns-to-gangs business with Prinsloo in 2007, he was 32. When first appearing in the dock he was in his mid-40s, older and perhaps wiser. In court, Laher now cuts a forlorn figure. He has often appeared hunched and scruffy-looking in a blue windbreaker, the hood pulled well forward to mask his face.

He appears to have been looking to negotiate a venture. Laher's business interests over a number of years span seven companies of which he has been registered as a director. Four of the companies were registered in a two-year period, 2004 and 2005, while the remaining three were registered in 2010 and 2011, in the time just before the gun transfers began. One of the companies, Aspar Properties, owns six pieces of real estate.

After he had moved to Cape Town, Laher purchased three restaurant franchises, all popular South African brand names: two Spurs – the Twin Peak Spur in Ottery (the venue used for a number of meetings where gun deals were discussed) and the Eagle Eye Spur in Observatory – and a Nando's in Athlone. In the first exchanges of weapons, Prinsloo drove to Cape Town in his bakkie, stacked with guns. His destination was the hamburger joint in the Ottery mall.[1] Later, when the story broke, and given the public outcry and threats of a boycott, Laher sold his shares in the restaurants.

The Laher family residence is in the suburb of Rondebosch East (across the busy M5 highway from the plusher area of old 'white' Rondebosch), which borders on Athlone and Lansdowne, where Hassan was murdered. Like Prinsloo's, it is nothing special – a pleasant suburban home, marked out by two large palm trees in the garden. Over the years, the house has been renovated and additional features added, including security features. A paved driveway runs down to the street. It hardly fits the Hollywood stereotype of the home of someone who is accused of being a major gun dealer.

In 2010, Laher was shot at his home during an armed robbery, which forced him to spend eight months in a wheelchair.[2] It is hard to know whether this is connected to the guns case. Laher had been threatened by gangs looking for more guns, so it is possible that there is a link. Laher, a practising Muslim, registered for Hajj, the pilgrimage to Mecca, in 2014.[3] At the time, he was allegedly involved in moving multiple consignments of guns into the Cape Flats.

Before Hunter became the hunted, however, and after Laher and Prinsloo had apparently hatched their plan, Laher must have needed a route into gangster territory. He had no connections, except for one person: Nafiz Modack, who is his brother-in-law. Tahiera Modack, Laher's wife, is Nafiz's sister. However, there is no evidence to suggest that Laher drew on his brother-in-law to find an entry point into the gangland market. When Prinsloo begun moving the guns, Modack was not yet on the scene.[4] What Laher probably needed was someone with a contact list of the key people in gangland – in much the same way that he would need a database if he were selling plumbing parts to local businesses. Laher navigated himself to a person with known links to numerous gangsters, but not a gang member himself. As a businessman, Laher, I suspect, would have had a sense that he needed someone who could make several introductions, acting as a reliable intermediary. Who better to approach than a lawyer who represented the gangs?

Laher must have met Hassan when he first arrived in the Cape. Within the close-knit Muslim business community, he would most probably have been directed to the lawyer's door after a few enquiries as to who knew some gang people in town. Laher and Hassan became very close, several people who knew them emphasised. Laher was often at Hassan's house. There is a photo of them together: Laher, head bent forward in the windbreaker, Hassan with his back to the camera in a grey patterned pullover, his bald pate prominent. 'I thought he was just a businessman,' someone close to Hassan said. When things got really tight and the police began to close in on Laher, Hassan moved to being Laher's defence lawyer.

First name out of Hassan's Rolodex was probably a gang with whom he had long-established links. Hassan had begun his career representing the Ghettos. They were a small outfit, but ambitious and eager to establish a place for themselves. To do that, they needed guns.

It is likely that one of the first contacts whom Laher approached was an interesting character called Shafiek Raban, who was linked to a gang that called itself the Junior Mafias.[5] It cannot be said for sure that Hassan hooked up Laher and Raban, but I consider it highly likely, given that the Junior Mafias were the route to the Ghettos.

The Junior Mafias were not your average street gang. For a start, they were based in Woodstock, outside of the usual gang territories of the Cape Flats. They were also, unusually, not affiliated to any of the Number alliances. Initially aligned loosely to the 26s, those ties faded fast as they sought out new allies in an attempt to position themselves better in the Cape illicit economy. In the end, 'money was their alignment', someone with a contact in the gang told me, 'and the

Former Spur owner Irshaad Laher, the alleged 'guns-to-gangs' middleman. He almost always appeared in court with a blue windbreaker, the hood shielding his face. GALLO IMAGES / *DIE BURGER*

Number became secondary'. 'They were with us once,' an American gang boss said to a contact of mine, 'but they struck out on their own.'

A 2007 study suggested that 'membership of the Junior Mafias was increasingly regarded as something like doing an M.B.A. in Criminal Business Management'. It was a group that 'ditched gang-ster dress and tattoos for designer outfits, gelled hair and the latest model BMWs'.[6] An upwardly mobile gang, they sent their children to smart southern suburbs schools rather than the gang-infested institutions on the Cape Flats. Their criminal focus was the property development industry, impregnated with a healthy dose of fraud and extortion. In October 2017, Raban was to die as a result of an underworld disagreement around a property transaction. He was shot, execution-style, while sitting in his new BMW behind the Fat Cactus restaurant in Mowbray.[7]

Raban was the sort of guy whom Hassan would have known, and he would have been a good conduit for Laher. Shady businessman combined with gangster – as his own death attests, violence was still liberally applied in the sector where he made his money. Raban was the sort with whom you could sit down and come to an understanding, do a deal. He had another important advantage too: the Junior Mafias were close to the Ghettos, who did their dirty enforcement work for them. Raban, the deal maker and front man, probably went to the Spur to pick up the guns and duly handed them on. The Junior Mafias received some of the guns themselves as a 'management fee' for acting as the intermediary.

The Junior Mafias' connections to the Ghettos would prove crucial. In Hanover Park, the Ghettos had a small presence and without access to new weaponry they would have been crushed by the dominant gang in the area, the Americans. Raban provided the link that made acquiring those guns possible. Under pressure, as reported earlier, the Americans then later came looking for the source of the new guns and allegedly sat down with Laher in the Spur, sharing some pictures of his family with him.

There is a final irony to the story of Raban. After he was assassinated, Raban's family could not retrieve his body from the oversubscribed Salt River morgue, which was by then clogged with the bodies of young men killed in the ongoing gang wars, many of them with wounds inflicted by the stolen guns themselves. His anguished wife was traumatised by the wait. Did it dawn on her that her husband may have contributed to the violence that caused the delay at the mortuary? Raban's mother-in-law captured what many Muslim families must have felt: 'At the end, we had to accept because there is nothing we could do about it.'[8]

Bosses as gun dealers

Laher, I am told, was not doing business with just any gang *laaities*: he was talking to the bosses. 'The gun buying was for the top people. If anyone else got involved, they would end up dead,' a middle-level gangster told me. And, as we saw earlier, when gang bosses found out that Laher was the middleman for the guns, they allegedly approached him directly, issuing some not-so-subtle threats if he didn't procure for them some of the sought-after stash. The bosses needed guns to strengthen their own gangs, but, importantly too, guns were an item that could be traded profitably, particularly if you could buy cheap and sell dear.

I have spent some time trying to understand the pricing system for illegal guns on the Cape Flats. (A more detailed overview can be found in the annex.) There was one price for when they were bought, often in bulk, and another price for when they were sold on. From gang boss to customer the mark-up was significant. On their arrival, at first the price of guns dropped briefly, because of the sudden injection of surplus supply, but then it rapidly began to rise again as the bosses sought to up the price and then fix it at highly profitable levels.

Gang bosses knew they were buying guns cheap. Why did Prins-loo and his accomplice not just up the price? After all, they were in the business of making money too. I suspect the answer is that they were not aware of the street price and that the gang bosses drove a hard bargain (without much subtlety, on occasion, as seen). Although the prices varied according to the type of weapon, it was often the case that the price for bulk purchase was set above the legal amount for guns (so, essentially a premium was charged for their being illegal) but below the price they could be bought for second-hand. This was the case for the Z88. Going on 2019 data, the gun could be purchased for around R5 000 in the underworld. (This is several years after the Prinsloo/Laher consignments, when Z88s may have been even cheaper.) Meanwhile, the legal price for the same firearm in 2019 would be R6 750 new and about R3 850 used. A gang boss could sell an illegal Z88 for around R15 000, a robust mark-up.

Gang bosses couldn't believe their luck with Laher. Buying guns others had stolen in bulk and were willing to sell cheaply drastically reduced front-end costs while allowing the bosses to profit by reselling the weapons at a premium. For some time, the profits from selling guns came close to those to be made from drugs. 'It was also easier,' one gang member who was involved observed. 'One of the best reasons being that when you sell a gun, you sell it to another gang member, not like drugs where you need an outsider [a member of the public].' The incentives to sell guns are also reportedly higher than offered by the drugs market on a transaction-by-transaction basis, and far less messy. 'You don't have to have all these tik lollies and deal with crazy addicts and turf wars, you just shop the pieces out to as many people who will buy at that price,' someone close to the process said.

One result of all of this is that gang bosses sought to stockpile guns for slow release onto the market – 'containers full' is how one person close to several bosses described the volumes.[9] It makes economic sense, in that the underworld firearms market is now flooded with guns. By controlling supply and agreeing on prices among major sellers, it is possible to make more money in the long run.

Gang bosses' aim is maximum profit, and it is possible that in a hidden market there is more latitude for upping prices, given that there is not full transparency in pricing at all times. Interviews suggest that there has in fact been a degree of price fixing and collusion between key bosses. Several key bosses have purchased large quantities of guns, knowing that if they flood the streets, prices will drop. The bosses, it seems, agreed between them to keep the prices high and to put some guns into storage as the volumes entering the market increased.[10]

Project Impi strikes again

Laher was arrested in June 2016 and released on bail of R100 000, considerably higher than the R5 000 that had been set for Prinsloo. Testifying at the hearing, Clive Ontong, one of Project Impi's senior investigators, said that police had confirmed that Laher had paid Prinsloo R120 000 in December 2014 for another consignment of weapons. Laher was said to be particularly interested in obtaining handguns, notably Berettas, and police-issue Z88s. At a later stage, Ontong said, Laher had also asked Prinsloo to deliver R5 automatic military-grade rifles.[11] That delivery had never occurred, as Prinsloo was arrested shortly afterwards in January 2015 and had already begun to provide information to the police.

Laher responded to the charges in an affidavit. He claimed to have known that police were watching him. He said that he kept weapons for safety and for recreational activities. Laher also emphasised that he had cooperated with the police since Prinloo's arrest in January 2015.[12]

Unlike Naidoo and Prinsloo, Laher had no chance of copping a plea. The state seemed determined to press its case, even though it moved forward at a snail's pace. In appearance after appearance, Laher appeared in his hoodie jacket, face hidden, riding out the proceedings as legal arguments went back and forth.

Laher's motivation for allegedly selling the guns seems even less complicated than Prinsloo's. He had no gang connections, and the sales lead he had presumably made to the Junior Mafias, and, through them, to the Ghettos, must have been more about whom he knew, rather than wanting to benefit any side in a gangland war. No one has ever raised a political motive for his alleged actions. He was not an ex-apartheid cop, for a start. It seems to just boil down to money. Laher, I believe, was a businessman who had spotted a business opportunity – it was hamburgers one day, guns the next. His response to the effect that, in February 2015, he had 'received information that [he] was involved in a criminal syndicate' smacks of desperation, as though he were suggesting he had been an unknowing or unwilling participant. This was not unlike Prinsloo's far-fetched claim that he was selling weapons to what he thought were security companies engaged in anti-piracy operations.[13]

Again, it seems hard to believe that Laher did not consider the consequences of selling guns to criminals. Perhaps Prinsloo had assured him that they would never get caught, so the price in blood was bearable – as long as it was not their own blood being spilt in the line of fire.

The collector

Laher appeared in court alongside another unlikely partner in crime, Alan Raves, also a Vereeniging-based businessman. While Laher crouched concealed beneath his hood in the dock, Raves sat there openly, for all to see. A short, rotund, balding man he again seemed an unlikely suspect. Raves had been arrested in August 2015 some seven months after Prinsloo. The court proceedings would exact a huge cost on his health.

The connection to Raves had seemed to Project Impi investigators to point to right-wing elements in the guns case. That there were fears of a connection to far-right extremists had been shared with me, and this was one of the lines of investigation pursued by the Project Impi team. The right-wing link, the stuff of conspiracy theory, has never been borne out, at least in public, but it did open a much wider set of issues around the management of weapons in South Africa more generally.

Raves lives in Unitas Park, in Vereeniging, just a kilometre and a half from Prinsloo's own home. He is listed as director of six companies. Like Laher, he was also part of the local network of gun enthusiasts who mixed with Prinsloo. Raves was a gun aficionado and collector. Gun enthusiasts like nothing more than to speak about guns, so the two must have got on well.

Investigators said that Raves would come to the armoury to select guns from the stocks that were to be destroyed. This in itself was not illegal. He had legitimately been appointed as a heritage firearms expert and inspector in terms of the National Heritage Resources Act. That gave him the right to access the storage facilities where firearms destined for destruction were kept and select those of particular historical value. Once he had identified firearms of historical interest, he was obligated under the Act to inform the South African Heritage Resources Agency of their existence.[14] But, instead of declaring them, he allegedly stole them. In simple terms, Raves had seemingly spotted an illegal business opportunity through his relationship with Prinsloo.

He also owned a gun shop that sold military equipment and memorabilia, Gama Arms, situated in a nondescript shopping centre. When you visit the store, you can easily appreciate the notion that he was a right-winger. At the time I was there, there was an old South African flag for sale and items from the Rhodesian war. But there were also military memorabilia from the two world wars. The place is full of all sorts of old army stuff.

For acutely politically conscious officers like Vearey and his investigators, however, Raves seems to fit a perfect stereotype of a white right-winger. In reality, he is probably more barmy-army than state subversive. There is little doubt that he has an active interest in military issues, and that he harbours conservative political views – 'God bless Donald Trump', he says in one Facebook post[15] – but he does not seem to be the type to run a right-wing revolt.

Raves's life was plunged into turmoil after his arrest. His social-media posts rant emotionally about how he became a single parent as the result of what appears to be a messy and painful divorce. But there is an undoubtedly nasty streak to Raves too. When someone called Marc Swanepoel challenges him on social media – 'Helping criminals. You are sick, bro!' – Raves responds: 'You look like you were conceived in an incestuous relationship.' Swanepoel replies: 'And, your mother was raped.' To which Raves counters: 'Your whole poes Bro, I will rape you.'[16]

Later, when the case was presented in the media, Raves, by dint of being in the same courtroom as Laher, was caught in the crossfire. But what he was accused of was something different, and

A small, chunky man with an attitude. Unlike Laher, Alan Raves, accused of illegally buying heritage firearms from the police armoury through Prinsloo, did little to mask his identity outside court. CARYN DOLLEY / NEWS24

it is for this reason that his argument in court has been that his case should be separated from that of Laher's sales of guns to the gangs.[17] Unlike Laher, Raves does little to hide his identity. He has less reason to do so.

The history of colonial southern Africa can be told through different types of guns and their stories. The job of heritage inspectors is to identify these historically significant firearms and remove them, so that they can be retained in museums or bought by collectors. There is an active market of arms collectors eager to buy stock from southern Africa – Americans and Europeans, for example, looking to buy guns from the Boer War, South Africa's various border war conflicts in the 1980s or the Rhodesian Bush War. Guns from all of these conflicts could fetch a high price, depending on their condition and how, where and by whom they had been used. The more history, or the more unusual the firearm, the higher the price it would fetch in the collectors' market.

The point about heritage arms, however, is that once identified, they need to be moved to what is referred to as a heritage unit, essentially an institution such as a museum or state body, where they can be kept for posterity. Raves had several connections in the military and arranged for the establishment of a designated unit at the Durban Light Infantry, one of the oldest military regiments in the country with a pedigree that stretches back before the Boer War. Once the pilfered weapons had been transferred to the Durban Light Infantry, no one took any notice of them. 'It was a place weapons go to die,' one weapons expert explained. Raves registered the weapons as having gone to the Durban military base, but then allegedly altered the paperwork to hide their source and sold them to the collector and enthusiast market at a considerable mark-up. It was the connection to the Durban Light Infantry that also made police investigators nervous about a wider right-wing conspiracy with links to the military and even cross-border arms trafficking.

Prinsloo, who was under surveillance at the time, led the police to Gama Arms early on. He had delivered a set of gun magazines removed from the police stores there. At first, detectives did not appreciate the link. When Raves, however, hired Martin Hood, one of the foremost attorneys in the firearms field, their suspicions were apparently aroused. Unsure of what they were actually dealing with, the police arranged for a more detailed inspection of the stock held by Gama Arms. It was then that the overall extent of what Prinsloo and Raves had allegedly been engaged in became clearer.

Most people I spoke to emphasised that Raves was a collector without overt political affiliations or objectives. His collecting and sale of the detritus of old wars, such as uniforms, flags, military equipment and the like, were to meet both a personal interest and a market demand. In doing so, however, he raised the suspicion of policemen to whom the symbols of old apartheid wars, and the connection to items from the former Rhodesia – Raves apparently had a statue of the former head of the Rhodesian Army, General Peter Walls, at his home – were a red flag.

What of Raves's motivations? Again, money, without a doubt, was a factor. But he was probably also driven by a collector's desire to accumulate unusual items of interest. That the state would have destroyed these anyway probably added to his motivation – perhaps, in his mind, it was not a crime: the guns would become scrap metal, so he was doing a favour by rescuing them from the system. As for any political motivation, although he may have felt disdain for the democratic government, he seems hardly the type to instigate a violent campaign against the state. Raves strikes me as a wannabe. A reference on his Facebook is revealing: '*Gelukkig het my recce opleiding my hard gemaak*' (Luckily, my Recce training [a reference to the South African special forces] hardened me.) But the comment is clearly made tongue-in-cheek: there is no record that Raves served in the special forces.

Four key figures – Naidoo, Prinsloo, Laher and Raves – were revealed by the Project Impi team to have been involved in profiting from selling state guns earmarked for destruction. Naidoo has effectively escaped sanction in return for providing information. Prinsloo, although released early, received an 18-year sentence and, at the time of writing, still has to appear in court to give evidence against Laher and Raves. These two men now await their fate.

If Project Impi had established two clear lines of inquiry both with Prinsloo at the source and through two people with whom he was acquainted – one through Laher to the war-torn Cape Flats, the other through Raves and his criminal business around heritage arms – there still seemed some loose ends. One of these led to KwaZulu-Natal, the place to which Naidoo told investigators he had been involved in moving arms. For the Project Impi investigators, it was just the beginning of their troubles. Vearey and Jacobs made a pilgrimage to Durban to pick up the scent. It was a move that raised strong opposition – and in the end probably cost them their jobs on Project Impi.

CHAPTER 10

THE TAXI ROUTE TO KZN

A t 5 pm on 27 April 2018, a group of heavily armed men stormed the Brook Street taxi rank in Durban. The place is usually a bustling hub of activity as taxis pull in and out, and commuters queue up to get a ride. The men are reported to have let loose with semi-automatic firearms; as shots went off, people scattered in all directions. Security guards at the taxi rank, also heavily armed with semi-automatics, returned fire. The busy rank quickly turned into a war zone before the attackers sped off, later abandoning their car as police gave chase. In their wake, one man lay dead and another two were rushed to hospital.

The taxi rank had been the scene of a similar shooting on 16 September 2015 – this time early in the morning as people on their way to work were beginning to stream through the rank. In that incident, three people had been shot dead and three others injured. It was a miracle that so few had died: police recovered more than 120 spent cartridges, a testament to the scale of the firefight. The police had piled up weapons confiscated after the shoot-out. These were not stolen guns but licensed ones. They included the usual array of 9 mm pistols, but also the Bulgarian-made SAR Dashprod M14, a short-barrelled assault rifle, a favourite for a new generation of security companies protecting the province's taxi associations.[1]

The taxi industry in South Africa has developed distinctively mafia-style attributes.[2] Mafia groups develop in places where state regulation is poor or corrupted, and self-regulation provides an opportunity for those with a capacity for violence to secure market share of illegal economies. Historically, mafia groups emerged, argues Federico Varese, a pre-eminent analyst of mafia organisations, 'during turbulent times, when states were not trusted and were unable to properly govern the economy (legal and illegal)'.[3] This is a situation that applies perfectly to the South African taxi industry. With its rapid growth and poor regulation by the state, internal forms of violent regulation developed in the industry. It is little wonder, then, that the country's taxi bosses have always been hungry for guns. Guns mean profit. It's a vicious cycle, in that profit provides the means to acquire more guns. These two incidents, often referred to as the first (2015) and second (2018) Brook Street shootings, are prime examples of mafia-style attacks, where violence is applied for economic gain.

Looking more closely at these public and shocking events, it is also possible to detect a sign of a new generation of gun use in KwaZulu-Natal (KZN). These weapons, at least for the most part, were licensed and newly acquired, not illegally procured from an old arms cache.

While easy to dismiss as no more than episodes in the endlessly competitive and violent taxi conflicts that plague South Africa, the two Brook Street shootings demonstrate a deeper and longer-lasting problem with firearms control in South Africa. It is one predictably complicated by corruption and political influence, but it is also an example of how badly wrong the process of firearm control and management has gone. It also says much about the development of organised crime and the degree to which a new class of 'untouchable' criminals with serious political connections has emerged in democratic South Africa.

But what does this have to do with the lost guns from the police armoury in Vereeniging? Quite a bit, as it turns out. First, it is more than likely that the organisations that perpetrated the shootings, and which wield enormous influence in Durban and the province, were early recipients of illegal arms from Prinsloo. Second, and in some ways this is potentially more serious, it demonstrates the erosion of the state firearm regulation and licensing system.

KZN was soaked in blood during South Africa's transition to democracy. The Truth and Reconciliation Commission has documented the groundswell of abuse and torture by the police in the province in the mid-1980s as conflict escalated, followed by a surge in violent incidents from 1989 as a vicious political war ensued between the Inkatha Freedom Party (IFP) and ANC sympathisers.[4]

State strategy had shifted from one of direct confrontation between the police and the liberation movement in the province, to the arming of the IFP. Firearms were supplied in bulk by the South African Defence Force to IFP hit squads and other armed groups. At one point, six ten-ton truckloads of weapons were delivered to IFP self-protection units.[5] As the TRC concluded: 'Sufficient evidence is available for the Commission to make a finding that former SAP operatives provided substantial amounts of unlicensed heavy weaponry, explosives and ammunition to senior members of the IFP in the post-1990 period.'[6]

These state-supplied weapons were the forerunner of a later set that were to find their way to KZN some 15 years after the transition to democracy, courtesy, it seems, of Christian Prinsloo. Weapons were also smuggled into the province by ANC cadres to arm self-defence units sympathetic to the movement. A low-level civil war ensued. The province was awash with guns. Many of them were buried in caches to be retrieved only years later.

It is easy to forget now how vicious the violence in KZN was in the transition years. One estimate suggests that over 20 000 were killed in political violence in the province from 1984 to 2002.[7] This 'unofficial war', sustained by a floating stock of weapons, would have long-term consequences for a traumatised population.[8]

The last thing that KZN needed was more guns. But this was a province, as a senior policeman who had served through the blood-soaked 1990s said, that had a well-established gun culture. Lots of groups – whether they were political, criminal or involved in the taxi or private security industry – were eager to get their hands on weapons. KZN had historically topped the provincial list for the number of stolen police firearms.[9] It is perhaps no surprise that anyone looking to sell guns would think of the green and bloodied hills of KZN.

How the Prinsloo guns link to KZN is shrouded in mystery. A good place to start is simply with the number of guns that were sold. That is important because in the admission of guilt that Prinsloo provided to the police, he took responsibility for 2 400 weapons that he had taken from the armoury and arranged to be sent to the Western

Cape. Given that a trail of evidence already implicated Prinsloo in that branch of the gun supply chain, he would understandably want to keep secret the other places he had distributed guns to.

During the research for this book, one thing became clear: the number of guns that Prinsloo had admitted to selling to the gangs was not the real total. There had been many more. Three highly credible sources, one with close ties to Prinsloo himself, said that the number of guns was likely to be nearer to 9 000 – well over three times the number that he had claimed responsibility for. But where had they all gone? From the beginning, there seemed to have been a link to gun-hungry KZN. That link was most likely Prinsloo's former colleague, the mysterious police officer Colonel David Naidoo, who has subsequently disappeared from sight.

Might Naidoo, who was from Durban and presumably had contacts there, have acted as Prinsloo's partner, a Laher-like link to the Indian Ocean province? Naidoo's possible involvement in the gun-running to KZN is surmise. There has been no further record of him or his movements since he gave evidence to the Project Impi investigators, although he has been listed as a witness in the forthcoming trials of Laher and Raves. But given that some of the first consignments of guns made their way to KZN, it seems hard to believe that Prinsloo and Naidoo – two colleagues working together both legally and illegally at the police armoury in Vereeniging, with Naidoo having connections in the province and Prinsloo not – did not cooperate in some way to move the weapons.

But who in KZN would have the appetite (and money) for guns, and the same violent capacity as the drug gangs over 1 500 kilometres down the coast in Cape Town? There seemed only one possible answer: the province's powerful taxi associations.

For the Project Impi detectives, nosing around home turf in Cape Town was one thing, but stirring up the hornet's nest of Zuma's home province, with its complicated and overlapping allegiances and systems of clientelism, including elements involved in the violent taxi business, was something else altogether. The investigators were to find that out in short order.

A Durban trip

As the Project Impi team's work deepened, sometime in early 2015, Vearey and Jacobs journeyed to Durban. They had been asked by the SAPS head office to visit Gauteng and KwaZulu-Natal and present the lessons that they had learnt from the use of South Africa's tough anti-gang legislation, the Prevention of Organised Crime Act, in those crime-ridden provinces. Vearey and Jacobs took advantage of the occasion to see whether they could find any links to Prinsloo's crimes outside of their home province.

A senior KZN detective told me that, to understand better the case in the province, Vearey and Jacobs had asked to see dockets linked to a series of crimes. From these, they detected patterns around the use of firearms. Reportedly, they already had some idea of what they were looking for in KZN, and the docket review was an attempt to drill down into the detail.

Policing in the province had been on the decline for a number of years. At the time of Vearey and Jacob's investigations in Durban, the provincial police were a seething pit of intrigue and corruption. As a former Crime Intelligence officer said, you never knew whom to trust. 'There were good people and some not too good people. It was not a very nice place to work – and very stressful.'[10] The then provincial commissioner, Lieutenant General Mmamonnye Ngobeni, would be suspended, and she later resigned following bribery allegations.[11]

The idea was that the two Cape police officers should brief their KZN counterparts about what they had found and how things could be improved. On the face of it, this was an exercise that reflected an organisation aspiring to self-improvement. In the swirling politics of the SAPS, it was anything but. Their presence was taken as a snub to local authority, perhaps exacerbated by Vearey's abrasive style.

Going through the dockets that had been provided by KZN colleagues in preparation for the seminar soon showed that the state of investigations was, in the words of the Crime Intelligence officer, 'a total fuck up'. Vearey and Jacobs suggested that the fragmented collection of dockets, some related to cases of violent crimes in which guns had been used, should be pulled together to build racketeering cases against the perpetrators.

In their presentation at the meeting, Vearey and Jacobs emphasised the need to identify clearly which weapons had been used and that it was crucial to link multiple crimes to one another. This presumably because they were seeking answers for the Project Impi investigation at the same time as rendering assistance to colleagues. Whatever the case, the issue that they homed in on was the fact that the KZN police were not looking closely enough at the weapons used during violent incidents. They told the incredulous local cops that they should start tracking weapons and linking these weapons to different incidents: basically, a mirror of what had been done on the mean streets of the Cape Flats.

Ballistics data from weapons used in violent incidents in KZN, however, had not been collated in this way. A former senior detective said that one of the challenges in the province was that there were no two crime scenes where the same firearm was used, because after each shooting the components of the firearms and the barrels were changed. Even more sinister was the fact that a senior provincial police officer said that he believed that ballistic results were tampered with: 'There is outside influence even in the lab and so the results are not always reliable.' What this means is that it was impossible to tell for sure whether Prinsloo's guns had been distributed in province and whether they had been used. More investigations were clearly needed.

'That is when the shit hit the fan. It was made clear that cooperation would be limited,' explained someone close to the case in KZN. By the end of the discussions, the two intrepid investigators did not feel welcome in KZN any more. Pushing away the sharp-elbowed Cape cops may just have been irritation at their lecturing style, but it also seemed to be because the local cops felt that Vearey and Jacobs were angling for the province's well-connected taxi bosses. Politically linked police in Durban sent a message to headquarters that the two were stepping on ground, far from their home turf, that was best left untouched. Vearey would later tell others that the KZN trip was the beginning of the end for the Project Impi investigation.

It is worth mentioning here that the Project Impi investigators had steered clear of using official channels for testing weapons that had been retrieved and suspected of being linked to the Prinsloo case. The reason was they had suspected from early on that senior people in the police may have been running cover for Prinsloo (and others who might be involved), so spreading the word about the case would have damaged the investigation. At the time, General Khomotso Phahlane was head of the forensic science laboratory (he would later be appointed acting National Commissioner, and then lose his job on the basis of corruption allegations), and he arranged for Vearey and Jacobs to work directly with certain people at the laboratory who were regarded as trustworthy.

The fear that higher-level police officials may have had a hand in protecting or benefiting Prinsloo somehow was one that had gnawed at the investigators from the start – hence the level of secrecy they adopted. Over time, however, theories of a conspiracy were eroded by evidence that pointed to a greater likelihood that the guns scandal may have been a bureaucratic cock-up, as opposed to a criminal conspiracy. The SAPS, with its high ratio of generals, may have had multiple levels of approval in its processes and operations, but the generals lacked the will and the capacity to conduct any physical checks that the weapons were in fact being destroyed as ordered. 'In the end,' said one exasperated senior police officer, 'provincial commissioners, various commanders within the Central Firearms Registry and generals at head office signed off on weapons to be destroyed and this is nothing more than a paper process.' Remarkably, even in this overly bureaucratic system no one bothered to verify that the guns were actually turned into scrap metal, and not released again into the criminal underworld.

That did not mean that no conspiracy existed – it was just not clear where in the SAPS ecosystem it was located and what its function might have been. That returns us to the intriguing question of KZN. The police generals in Durban clearly would have been none too impressed when the Cape upstarts suggested that they pursue a number of local criminal suspects with racketeering charges, particularly if it were clear to the senior local officials that these were 'untouchables'. Racketeering, by its nature, implies criminal organisation, suggesting bodies with a serious criminal capacity for violence. It is most likely that the Project Impi investigators proposed that a wider investigation should be undertaken into taxi organisations. But, just like the gang bosses in the Cape, taxi bosses have their own police generals on their payrolls and political protection too.

I scratched and scratched and went back to some sources to try to determine what had happened. What I was eventually told was that Prinsloo, it seems, had earlier made a startling admission to Project Impi investigators. He either clammed up on this later, given that he did not want to reveal the number of guns that he had sold, or the investigators believed it was better to focus on the Cape Flats, where they had better evidence of the weapons actually being used to kill people. But what Prinsloo apparently admitted during an interview at some point was that he had supplied weapons to different organisations involved in the taxi conflict in KZN – like those who had orchestrated the Brook Street attacks. He had also started selling the guns in KZN, and not in the Cape Flats, he allegedly said, and other weapons from the armoury had been sent to the Eastern Cape and Gauteng.[12] I had been told by Cape gang contacts that they had first heard of police guns being sold in Durban.

Prinsloo is reputed to have sold guns to some of the most powerful and violent actors in KZN: the politically connected Gcaba and Mpungose taxi factions, key players within the struggle for control over the province's taxi empire. In a KZN version of a *Pax Mafiosa*, the two taxi clans operate in different areas and have reciprocal agreements. Unlike in the case of the gangs of the Western Cape, however, there is no definitive proof, beyond off-the-record interviews, that Prinsloo's guns made their way into the hands of these taxi bosses. The ballistic evidence is not helpful, so the case may never be proven. Clifford Marrion, a former head of SAPS detectives in KZN, did confirm, however, that there had been a flood of state-issue guns, including R4s and R5s, linked to crime scenes around the province from around 2008 onwards. As indicated, the first sales from the firearm registry by Prinsloo are said to have been in 2007, so the timing would seem to tie in.

Intriguingly, a group of Durban metro policemen, several of whom worked undercover, also told me in July 2018 that they estimated that about 20 per cent of the guns they were seizing on the streets of the city were police-issue Z88s, which had also been professionally altered. They had also seized several R4s and R5s. Such illegal fire-arms were often taken from people associated with the taxi industry. The officers were nervous to meet, but when we finally sat down for a coffee, they emphasised how much corruption had permeated policing in the province. Local policing seemed to have become riven with mistrust.

Project Impi investigators firmly believe that the guns investigation was derailed after the focus of their work shifted to KZN. The fact is that the link between Prinsloo and the guns-to-taxi-bosses angle has never been followed up. An investigation that sought to do so was effectively ended under suspicious circumstances. 'We may never now know the truth,' a senior police officer said of the curtailment of the KZN leg of the investigation.

In short, the Prinsloo guns from the armoury may well have found their way into the hands of dangerous people in KZN, but key criminal groups in the province have also been armed with legally licensed weapons, including semi-automatics, such as those used in the Brook Street killings. How this has occurred is an indictment of the state for its inability to regulate the taxi industry, the private security industry and the licensing of firearms – a volatile combination if ever there was one.

The taxi baron brothers

How the KZN taxi industry, and the two organisations that are reputed to have obtained guns from the police armoury operate, is a revealing story in itself. It is a narrative of a mafia-style operation and political protection.

Taxi associations have held a lot of clout for a long time in KZN. Their assets have accumulated, and rival dynasties of taxi bosses have come to the fore, forging crucial links to politics and branching out into new areas of business. The story of taxi kings in KZN may be to some extent a fairy-tale one of rags to riches, but it is also one that is often mired in the daily violent drudgery of killing opponents and muscling in on sought-after routes. In this industry, one taxi family stands head and shoulders above the rest: the Gcabas. Widely feared, hugely influential and close to the political powers that be, including Zuma and Minister of Police Bheki Cele, the Gcaba brothers started out operating taxis and have since built a diverse business empire.

Within that empire, however, taxis remain the core family business of the four Gcaba brothers, Mandla (the head), Royal Roma, Thembinkosi and Mfundo. (Two other brothers, Moses and Frank, lost their lives in the late 1990s.) The Gcabas are not to be messed with. 'They are the most feared family in the entire provincial taxi industry and have a reputation countrywide as untouchable dons,' a senior state official said. Jacob Zuma is an uncle of the brothers, a powerful family connection at the time the brothers were consolidating their power. The Gcabas are like the robber barons of early 19th-century American history – only more violent.

In trying to trace the link to the Prinsloo guns in KZN, I spoke with lots of people about the Gcabas. The overriding sentiment is that they are untouchables. Police officers and people from the National Prosecuting Authority told me that they had the capacity to make cases and witnesses disappear. Their tentacles seem to reach into every corner of the provincial administration and the police headquarters, making it all the more astonishing how seldom their names appear in the press and how seldom they have appeared in discussions on the Zuma era, as they were important players in the affairs of his administration.[13]

From their early days, the Gcabas learnt that violence pays in the taxi industry. The father of the four brothers, Simon Gcaba, together with one Bernard 'Big Ben' Ntuli, his protégé, was one of the forerunners in the sector back in the 1980s. The two had a knack for marketing, parking their 'Zola Budd' – township slang for minibus taxi, after the South African barefoot runner – outside their home in Umlazi, Durban. This was not just any Zola Budd, though: it was the 'granddaddy of blinged-out taxis, fitted with an ear-aching sound system'. The Gcaba boys also threw their weight around, developing a reputation for 'jackrolling' – a euphemistic term for terrorising or abusing girls at clubs.[14]

Simon Gcaba and Big Ben became powerful members of the Durban and District Taxi Association. Ben was president; Simon assumed the role of head of public relations, a catch-all role entailing in reality a combination of alleged extortion-style practices and keeping the cops sweet. A taxi boss who gave evidence to a commission of inquiry into violence in the industry in 2001 reported: 'We were requested to contribute a sum of monies.' Simon Gcaba would use these funds to buy presents, usually meat and drinks. 'He used to visit each and every police station' testified the taxi boss.[15] This way, Simon nurtured a cosy relationship with the police, one senior metro police officer said. Since then, his sons have worked, through a combination of the carrot and the stick, to maintain these relations. This alleged system of complicity stretches from the police station to the highest level of the SAPS.

Big Ben and Simon made good, until, as seems almost inevitable in the industry, greed drove a wedge between them. A fierce rivalry developed. Simon was shot dead outside a Durban ice cream parlour in February 1996. The police, unusually, offered a reward of R250 000 for information in the murder. Big Ben was the primary suspect but was to meet his end after contracting cerebral malaria, remaining beyond the grasp of the law.[16]

After Big Ben's death, the Durban and District Taxi Association split into two and a vicious war for control over the industry ensued – with the brothers on one side and a cluster of other aspirant taxi barons on the other. The mourning sons quickly took over their father's business interests. Around then, the market was rapidly growing for long-distance taxis, particularly between KZN and

Johannesburg, and the brothers worked hard to expand their enterprise into the Durban Long Distance Taxi Association.

Taxi wars

When taxi bosses diversify into other forms of economic activity, they are known to resort to violence – a learnt behaviour in one industry passed to others. The Gcabas appear to be the ultimate exponents of that pattern of ubiquitous, mafia-style violence.

The taxi industry is a complex beast. Although KZN has the highest number of taxi associations – 246 were registered at the time of writing – the industry has been in the process of consolidating for some time, often to the advantage of the Gcabas' market share.

Much of the cause of the vicious taxi conflict in KZN has revolved around entities vying for control of the money-spinning long-distance routes. There are two main competing groups involved, both rubbing up against each other and attempting to muscle in on smaller association turf as the levers of power in the industry are held by fewer and fewer people. That consolidation has been driven by those with access to guns. Every gap in this violent market is taken, with no quarter being given.

The story goes that as Simon was being buried, the family's taxis were being kicked out of the Durban rank by a series of local challengers. The brothers worked hard to regain their place at the table, calling all their rivals to a meeting to try to ensure the survival of the business. Negotiations alone did not work, and tensions simmered. In October 1996, a few months after Simon's murder, Mandla Gcaba was shot at and hit four times but survived. The family were attacked at home again in the same year. In March 1997 the eldest brother, Moses, was shot dead. To compound their loss, their sibling Frank was killed in a car accident the following year.

Nevertheless, by then the Gcabas had managed, using a combination of sharp elbows and cash incentives, to return to the Durban rank and they manoeuvred for control of the Durban and District Long Distance Taxi Association. The story of setback and re-establishment is a legend in the taxi industry. 'They fought tooth and nail to protect the family business in the 1990s. And the blood flowed.' This is how a member of an opposing taxi association, who fled the industry in fear, remembers it. Their taxis, easily distinguished by the Gcaba Brothers logo, today circulate on the routes in their hundreds. Their branding sends a clear message to rivals: 'We own this rank.'

In August 1997, when one of the accused in the Moses Gcaba murder, Michael Phungula, was being brought to the Durban High Court, he was killed. According to evidence heard at the Moerane Commission, Phungile scuffled with the detectives who were escorting him and was shot dead in the process.[17] Rumours swirled that the Gcabas had paid the police to exact revenge.

Despite increased security, the family had a go at the remaining accused a few months later. A group of men, armed with AK-47s, attacked the court. This time a shoot-out with passing police ensued, and the men fled, after killing one of the officers. A grandmother outside the court building was also killed, as were two of the attackers. Others escaped in a getaway car.

The story here turns into pantomime. Eager to arrest the group for killing one of their own officers, the police traced the car, and then, using camera footage, established the identity of the driver. It was a local policeman, one Constable Sibusiso Mpisane. Demonstrating just how brazen the whole attack was, Mpisane had actually driven the shooters to the luxury Gcaba home, a gated estate for the wealthy on the Durban north coast. In police custody, Mpisane made a statement which, while guaranteeing his immunity from prosecution, firmly implicated the brothers. It was crucial to the case. As RW Johnson has dryly observed: 'Those who knew Mandla Gcaba could hardly believe that he would be made answerable to a court, and so it turned out.'[18]

Brothers Mandla and Royal Roma were arrested. Mpisane predictably disappeared, feared dead. Dead he was not – but with no witness available, the judge acquitted the brothers. Constable Mpisane then surfaced again, saying he had been kidnapped. More bizarrely, he claimed to have spent time on an island off the African coast. For a metro police constable, it soon turned out, he had become immensely wealthy, complete with a mansion and array of fancy cars. He also proved to be a regular host to the provincial political elite, including Bheki Cele, who would later serve as both Commissioner of Police and police minister. No gangster novel could have done better. The Gcabas prospered and Mpisane and his wife Shauwn became regular fixtures on the high-roller bling-filled Durban social scene.[19]

The brothers were innovators in a business environment defined by plenty of shades of grey. Taxis had been a foundation for their violent family business empire as they diversified their interests and sweetened their political protection. Mfundo Gcaba, the man widely thought to be behind the first Brook Street taxi rank attack, is regarded as, in the words of one police officer, 'the family's chief enforcer' – a 'violent and unpredictable' operator, and hungry for guns. It is probable, if not provable, that the guns filched by Prinsloo were arming the violent KZN taxi associations, who were also developing a line in accessing legal weapons. The best way to access such powerful semi-automatic weapons legally was to register a private security company and apply for a licence. These weapons fuelled taxi warfare in the province, such as the violent confrontations in Brook Street. KZN's taxi industry soon began to sprout multiple private armies.

CHAPTER 11

PRIVATE ARMIES

The brothers sought to polish the story of their gritty rise to power by appointing a public-relations consultant.[1] A website profile for Mandla, for example, reads: 'Mandla Gcaba is a warrior for peace who bears the physical and emotional scars of the taxi industry's painful transition from its violent past to the prosperous stability we see today.' [2] Stable the industry is not. But the Gcabas became a national taxi powerhouse – in the words of a senior Department of Transport official, 'They elevated themselves to a status above what would normally be the case within the politics of the industry.'[3] Keeping their politics sweet was essential.[4]

Several years into the new millennium, the Gcabas began spreading their business wings. Most notoriously, Mandla Gcaba became involved in a company called Tansnat Durban CC in 2009. Tansnat took over the running of Durban's transport system buses, and operates several other bus and transport interests. Two other shareholders resigned from the company, leaving complete ownership to Mandla.[5] In 2009, at the same time as Mandla acquired his share in the company, it was awarded a contract, without a tender, to run Durban's metro bus fleet. But in fact Mandla already had a contract to do so, through a company called Remant Alton Land Transport, of which he was a director. When Remant effectively collapsed, the city paid out R390 million to purchase over 500 of the company's buses and equipment. This was then handed on to Tansnat. It was a clear insider job.

Following protests from workers, who refused to sign new contracts, and a court challenge from other bus operators, the city seemed to accept defeat, or almost. Instead, it was announced that

Tansnat would run operations on a month-to-month basis. Between 2010 and 2012, the city paid R300 million to Gcaba's company to run the services, money that was then declared irregular expenditure in an audit. Despite this, the contract was not cancelled.

It gets worse. In 2013, Tansnat admitted owing millions to SARS and its drivers went on strike because they were not getting paid. To keep operations going, the city agreed to pay the company R8.1 million for the drivers' wages. Later in the year, the company said that it did not have enough money for diesel, so the city provided a line of credit.

By 2015, even the eThekwini authorities seemed to have had enough and attempted to have the company liquidated, insisting that it owed the city some R53 million. Mandla was accused of using Tansnat as his own bank, reportedly giving himself an unsecured loan of R30.7 million.[6] By 2016, the city announced an 'intervention team' to take control of Tansnat's finances, although how this operated remains unclear. By March 2018, the city was again advising of disruption to the bus service and Tansnat was reported once again to be short of diesel.[7] A series of other financial claims were made against Mandla.

What is interesting about buses in Durban is that, whereas in other South African cities, notably Cape Town, there are regular attacks on bus companies contracted by the city, this is not the case in Durban. When I asked a Durban metro police officer why that was, his chilling response was, 'If you did that in Durban, you would die.' It is little wonder then that Uber has brought the local taxi industry into its city operations, with the Gcabas reputed to have taken a stake. A case of transport and security provision mixed mafia-style.

Violent men

It is Mfundo Gcaba who has led the charge in recent years to expand the Gcabas' taxi empire. People regularly used the word 'thug' when describing him. As noted earlier, he is regarded as having been behind the first Brook Street taxi rank attack and was arrested at the scene.

The Gcabas are also active in the province's private security industry, with links to several companies. (By my count, they are currently directors or members of some 88 companies, several of which are in the private security business.) Interviews with people in the taxi industry, the police and the private security sector point in particular to Mfundo's use of strong-arm tactics to make sure Gcaba-linked companies are used. One company repeatedly reported by many sources to be linked to the Gcabas is an outfit called LK Security Solutions, in which the Gcabas reportedly own shares. (I was told as much by a representative of the company when I phoned to ask. In a follow-up call, a colleague of mine also asked an LK manager for the number of Mfundo Gcaba. He said that he would check if he could provide it, and subsequently did not.) None of the brothers are listed as directors of LK, and the precise relationship between the Gcabas and LK remains unclear. However, 'Whatever is said on paper, Mfundo is definitely involved,' said a well-informed private-security expert. A senior provincial security expert characterised LK's role in the taxi industry as 'deeply problematic'.

Taxi operators say that LK Security is essentially forced onto them to protect ranks and routes. Private security, after buses and construction, is a major area of business development for organised crime, and it's solid territory for the brothers because it has links to strong-arm tactics and, of course, guns.

LK Security has been mired in controversy. In one case, the company was appointed as the service provider for AbaQulusi Municipality in May 2015, without, true to form, any tender process being followed or even a service-delivery agreement being signed. An LK representative reportedly said they followed all the correct procedures on their side, and blamed the municipality for failing to engage.[8] In another, taxpayers effectively paid for two companies to do the same job at King Edward VIII Hospital in Durban. Inexplicably, LK Security reportedly acquired the contract to protect the hospital while an existing company, Kekana Protection Services, did not have theirs cancelled.[9] In March 2019, it was announced that LK was one of the security companies that had had all of its firearms confiscated for ballistic testing by the police task team investigating political killings in KZN.[10]

Another company in which the brothers are reputed to have a financial interest (again, they are not listed as directors) is iHlokohloko Security Services. Representatives of iHlokohloko notoriously accompanied Mfundo Gcaba to the Brook Street taxi rank in September 2015. He was arrested and the firearms of the security guards were confiscated.[11]

Such private security actors have been in the front line of enforcing the interests of the brothers in the taxi industry. The Gcabas control, or have strong influence over, three long-distance associations: the Durban Long Distance Association, which controls taxis running north-west from the city to Johannesburg and is a source of much of the tension in the industry, the Berea Long Distance Association and the Sonke Long Distance Association. (Sonke operates on routes southwards to the Eastern Cape.) The really profitable route is the one that runs from KZN to Joburg. The southern route to the Eastern Cape, however, is also a good money spinner and the Gcabas have long had an interest in taking it over. That has brought them into direct conflict with the Port Shepstone-based Zamokuhle Long Distance Taxi Association, whose minibus taxis operate on that route too. Few people go up against the Gcabas without consequences, and the Zamokuhle Association has had particular courage in taking them on, insiders in the taxi industry explained.

The Zamokuhle Association took Sonke to court in in 2015 in an effort to prevent the association from muscling in on its rank in Durban, threatening its members and generally interfering with its routes down the coast, through Port Shepstone, and on to the Eastern Cape. Concerned about tensions in the provincial taxi industry, the KZN Department of Transport also sought an interdict preventing Sonke from invading other taxi routes. Their efforts have been to little avail.

For his part, Mfundo Gcaba has always said that he is not a member of Sonke Long Distance. He has, however, attended several meetings representing Sonke and on several occasions has demanded that

Sonke be allowed to operate on the routes running south of Durban. Mfundo has also insisted that taxis that are not from eThekwini will not be allowed to operate routes on their own without Sonke.[12]

The first Brook Street incident was widely perceived to be central to targeting the Zamokuhle Association and enabling the Gcabas to take over the southern route. After the September 2015 attack, 12 people were arrested, including Mfundo Gcaba. During the court case that followed, an affidavit from the investigating officer, Major Mandla Dlamini, claimed that the Gcaba group had arrived at the taxi rank in the early hours of the morning and begun taking over the loading bays belonging to the Zamokuhle Long Distance Taxi Association. The Gcabas' legal team countered that the private security company that was patrolling the rank had recognised Mfundo and opened fire. He had acted in self-defence, they argued.[13]

Many people I spoke to were surprised that a case involving a Gcaba had made it to court at all. By contrast, few seemed surprised when, in February 2017, the state withdrew the charges against Mfundo and his co-accused. The state cited inconsistencies in the ballistic report on the firearms used in the shooting as well as their failure to trace – and presumably convince – witnesses who would testify.[14]

The 2015 Brook Street shooting was only one incident in an ongoing war for the southern route. Prior to that, six people had been killed in a series of shoot-outs that could be traced to the dispute, including the deputy chairperson of the Zamokuhle Taxi Association, Mlungisi 'Boro' Ngcobo, who also happened to be an ANC regional executive – highlighting that within the ANC there is division over the Gcabas' role.

Two days after the 2015 Brook Street incident, a fully laden taxi from Port Shepstone was sprayed with bullets on the freeway south of Durban. It was taken as a warning that the Gcabas would not give up. A provincial Hawks policeman said that the conflict would continue as long as the Gcabas, led by Mfundo, were looking to expand their route coverage. They felt, he said, a sense of impunity, that they were 'untouchable'. The Gcabas are also linked to the 2018 Brooke Street incident, through one of the protagonists,

Mkhali Madondo, a known Gcaba ally and a taxi warlord from Ixopo, with whom they have been long aligned. A provincial official with excellent knowledge of the local taxi industry said that Madondo's taxis were prevented from forcing their way to the front of the rank. Madondo was killed in the subsequent shoot-out.

It's who you know

The Gcabas' high-level political connections, which have no doubt served to wrap them in this protective layer, are legion. Several police officers affirmed that they would simply not risk conducting an investigation into the brothers' activities. In the words of one, it would 'go nowhere and lead only to trouble for you'. While Zuma was president, the Gcabas appeared to have a powerful protector. Mandla Gcaba is listed as a director, together with Zuma's son Mxolisi, of Inkanyamba Beverages, and he shares directorships in six companies with a Zuma nephew, Khulubuse.[15]

Michael Hulley, Zuma's long-time (and now one-time) lawyer, was introduced to him by the Gcabas. Hulley had begun his career in the hard-knocks world of the taxi associations, which required a finely calculated sense of risk.[16] When Zuma was fired by Thabo Mbeki as deputy president, he needed a lawyer and the Gcabas are said to have recommended Hulley. He also represented Mandla and Royal Roma when they were arrested for the shooting allegedly aimed at avenging Moses Gcaba's killing. Hulley became their go-to lawyer.

When Zuma was ejected from the presidency and looked around for support and finances, it was inevitable that he would fall back on the brothers. RW Johnson notes in his analysis of post-Zuma South Africa, '[As] ever, Zuma was happy to gather support from any direction, including frankly criminal ones, such as his nephew, the much-feared taxi boss Mandla Gcaba.'[17]

As befits those who see themselves as untouchable, the support was shockingly overt. During Zuma's corruption trial, 80 per cent of the eThekwini municipality's bus fleet, still controlled by the Gcabas despite the disastrous service, was requisitioned to collect supporters from Umlazi, KwaMashu, Ntuzuma and other areas so they could attend. In the process, thousands of commuters were left stranded.[18] The criminal-political nexus could not have been more blatant.

The Gcaba brothers hedged their bets, however, in their patronage network, ensuring a good spread of advantageous connections among influential members of the relatively small circle of new moneyed Durban political elites. One of those is Cele, a former Zuma supporter who subsequently had a falling out with the president after he was dismissed for alleged corruption before later being appointed, after Zuma's exit, as Minister of Police, a job he had long coveted.[19] Cele has a close relationship with Mpisane, the police constable-cum-getaway driver and errant witness in the Gcaba High Court shooting incident. Mpisane played the trusted role of lobola negotiator for Cele's 2010 marriage. Cele, remarkably, also came out in support of Tansnat when the company muscled in to take over the bus transport contract, announcing that Tansnat had 'a very good track record in the province for running bus services'.[20]

When Cele was police commissioner, it transpired that the Gcabas had won a contract that was concluded through the office of the national commissioner to transport attendees to the annual celebration of Police Day. When some of the buses did not arrive, the SAPS used police cars, which should have been patrolling the streets, to ferry thousands of people to the party.[21] This on top of allegations that the Gcaba family benefited from other tenders while Cele was provincial MEC for transport. Cele has long been thought to have an interest in the province's turbulent taxi industry.[22] A senior police officer in the provincial Hawks said that Cele was linked to the Gcabas through a number of commercial dealings. The same officer also stated that the Gcabas had threatened the provincial MEC for Transport and Community Safety, Thomas Kaunda, telling him, Gupta-style, that they could have him removed from office.[23] When the media reported on the outsourcing of the Police Day transport in January 2011, Cele's office denied any suggestion of friendship with the Gcabas.[24]

These overlapping mutual interests raise interesting questions as to why the Project Impi investigation into how Prinsloo's guns had been reaching the province was summarily blocked. The overwhelming weight of suspicion would imply a political veto from above. Had the Project Impi team been able to continue their investigation into whether the Gcabas had been recipients of Prinsloo's guns, their attention would almost certainly have turned to another player: the so-called Sputla Mpungose faction of the Sizwe Long Distance Association. The suggestion is that powerful political and police interests aligned to prevent the investigation from going forward.

The Sizwe Long Distance Association has its centre of gravity in Ladysmith and Newcastle, in northern KZN. It's a complex network operation, made more so by the fact that Sizwe has rank-sharing agreements with the Gcaba brothers. Control over the Sizwe-run KZN – Johannesburg route is hotly contested by different taxi groups. Sputla Mpungose is a key player in the taxi conflict in northern KZN.

Sputla is said to be in business with other men of violent repute. Here the story gets interesting, a reminder that the violent conflicts of KZN stretch back into the past and often involve the same sets of people. Some of Sputla's allies are said to be ex-IFP hitmen, although they have fallen out with the party and indeed have been criticised by the leader, Mangosuthu Buthelezi.[25] Intriguingly, they have subsequently been recruited by the ANC.[26]

Sputla was successful in causing a split in the Sizwe Long Distance Taxi Association, to his advantage. Most of his operations are based in the Ulundi and KwaNongoma areas but he has also sought to advance his interests in the Newcastle and Madadeni taxi associations. He has done this, reportedly, by extorting taxi operators in the area. Sputla's two partners in this arrangement are allegedly both ex-IFP hit squad operators, Mangisi Buthelezi and Nkalankala Zungu.

Sputla's role in the tortuous politics of the Sizwe taxi organisation is complex but it boils down to ensuring access to routes to keep the money rolling in, and violence is meted out to enforce that. There have been allegations that a payment was made by the provincial transport department to keep Sputla away from the conflict within Sizwe, but this, say insiders in the department, is not the case.[27]

Like Gcaba, Sputla has been arrested on numerous occasions for violent crimes. He, too, has never been charged.

All of this goes to show just how the South African taxi industry is so impenetrable by law enforcement and hard to clean up. The industry has, over time, forged links with criminal elements and politics in a way that ensures the protection of key players. All would have had a strong interest in blocking further investigations into the Prinsloo guns in KZN. It was perhaps only a matter of time before two of the fastest-growing industries in South Africa joined forces – the taxi business and private security. The link is important because private security companies can apply to obtain firearms, and under certain conditions semi-automatic weapons.

Hitmen in uniforms

As the taxi industry expanded in the province and later consolidated into a smaller number of powerful controlling interests, the part played by private security companies would become critical. Private security companies that became the gun power in taxi wars and the protection of taxi bosses and ranks have played a key part in the re-arming of KZN, not only with stolen guns but with licensed ones too. The role played by private security companies in the taxi industry began to grow in the late 1990s, explained one of the pioneers of the system, Warren Julie, who began an outfit called, appropriately enough, the Taxi Violence Unit: 'We began looking after ranks, and providing protection to individual taxi bosses, and then that expanded into route protection,' said Julie. His company provided security to the Gcaba brothers at the time. Flourishing business from the taxi industry clients provided other opportunities for private security companies. There are now an estimated 50 to 60 private security companies doing 'taxi work' in KZN and several of these were started by taxi bosses.[28]

Private security firms provide a convenient facade of legality over what is essentially a set of strong-arm, mafia-style operations. As good a measure of that is the number of assassinations, often carried out by

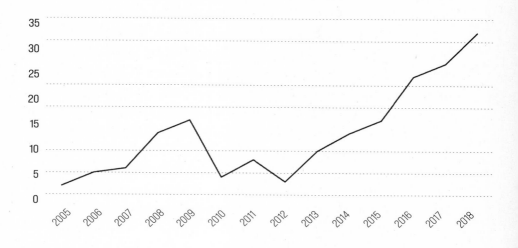

KwaZulu-Natal taxi-related hits, 2005–2018
SOURCE: GLOBAL INITIATIVE AGAINST TRANSNATIONAL ORGANIZED CRIME
Note: Data is from the Global Initiative's project on hits and assassinations, which
seeks to count and record individual cases. These are cases recorded as hits in
media reporting, so they are by no means likely to provide the full picture.

skilled hitmen, in the taxi industry. KZN has the highest numbers of
taxi-related targeted killings of all South Africa's provinces, and these
have soared since 2012, closely paralleling the increase in gang-related
violence in the Western Cape.

A senior provincial government official explained how private
security companies linked to the taxi industry in the province have
been responsible for shielding hitmen. Essentially, taxi operators
will hire private security companies (or create their own) and then
instruct the company to hire known hitmen. The result is that taxi
hits are carried out by private security firms, making them the private armies of the taxi bosses.

Evidence was provided to this effect to the Moerane Commission

on political violence in KZN, although the commission was criticised for not having provided recommendations in this area. Vanessa
Burger, a local activist, acknowledged that if this had been done, it
'would have trodden on the toes of far too many top ANC officials
who have very lucrative private security contracts'.[29] Politics and the
private security industry are increasingly intertwined.

In terms of the legislation, private security companies in South
Africa have to be registered with the Private Security Industry
Regulatory Authority (PSIRA).[30] But not all companies are registered with the authority and some receive light-touch oversight,
depending on the extent of their political connections. Some of the
taxi-linked private security companies in particular appear to escape
government scrutiny altogether.

A study by PSIRA of the links between taxi violence and private
security firms grimly begins by noting that 'there was a high risk' of
the authority's researchers being shot at. It concludes that taxi security
companies have become militarised, including by adopting uniforms

An armed security officer from the Taxi Violence Unit, a Pinetown-based private
security company, patrols a taxi rank in KwaZulu-Natal. PHOTO: SHAUN SWINGLER

similar to those of the army or the police, in contravention of the 2001 PSIRA Act. PSIRA notes that brandishing firearms is 'commonplace in [the taxi ranks]'. It concludes that private security guards behave like members of a 'military wing' of the taxi associations.[31]

Security companies associated with the taxi industry are used as a vehicle for obtaining licences for semi-automatic weapons. The result has been an arms race between the taxi companies and a proliferation of licensed firearms in the province. Since 1994, the stated policy of government has been to reduce gun ownership; in KZN, the opposite has happened. The illegal use of legal firearms is where the problem now lies, said a senior provincial government official. It is a 'problem' that has been enabled by the erosion and corruption of the regulatory system around both firearms and private security.

Taxi associations in KZN are represented by the South African National Taxi Council (SANTACO), an umbrella body established in 2001 under the guidance of Dullah Omar, then the transport minister. Although SANTACO representatives are leery of talking about guns in the industry, a lawyer for the organisation told members of the Portfolio Committee on Police in 2018 that he knew that state weapons had landed up in the hands of *izinkabi*, the local term for hitmen acting for the taxi industry.[32]

Obtaining firearms, including semi-automatic firearms, is permissible for private security companies after a thorough review of their requirements and, in the case of semi-automatic firearms, the presentation of proof (such as commercial contracts) that they will be operating in areas or on tasks, such as cash-in-transit protection, where such heavy weaponry is required.

For large companies operating in the market, obtaining gun licences for these weapons is an onerous process that takes a considerable amount of time. That is not the case, it seems, for several connected companies with links to the taxi industry in KZN. Police officers and PSIRA inspectors told me that these companies escaped scrutiny altogether. The provincial PSIRA is perceived to be compromised and at least one key official there is reputed to have a link to the Gcabas.

Take the allegations made by Thomas Getsemane, the Director of Mvimbeni Holdings, the private security company that was guarding the rank from which Zamokuhle Long Distance Taxi Association operated at Brook Street. Getsemane said that two weeks after Mvimbeni's appointment as security provider, he received a telephone call from Mfundo Gcaba, instructing him 'to withdraw from a contract as a security company alleging that [his] company's presence in Brook Street [was] preventing [the Gcabas] taking over the route'. Getsemane concludes that 'there is clear partiality and protection of one family' by state institutions, and that his company was targeted by PSIRA.[33]

An inspector for PSIRA told me that Getsemane's allegations were valid, and that some taxi companies were given preference: 'There is an understanding that some companies are just left alone. The Gcabas are basically on top of that list.' He continued: 'Many private security companies involved in the taxi industry are nothing more than hitmen in uniforms. There are loads of companies not registered with PSIRA and often guys say they are doing security for taxi bosses and are carrying weapons owned by other companies.' In just one documented case, PSIRA inspectors accompanied by police confiscated weapons when the serial numbers on the guns belonging to guards did not match their firearms permits.[34]

Bizarrely, when a company is deregistered by PSIRA for contravening its regulations, the authority plays no role in confiscating the weapons, which can be retained or hired out to other security companies. Taxi-associated private security companies in particular escape regulation because they either have political protection or are simply unregistered – but have access to licensed firearms nonetheless. When firearms were confiscated after the 2015 Brook Street shooting, the police, an officer involved explained, returned them to iHlokohloko, the company linked to the Gcabas.

Remarkably, firearm licences are granted to some private security companies in the taxi industry within two days, confirmed several in the industry. That is unheard of – some applications take months, even years. Even more remarkably, unregistered private security companies also use firearms, including semi-automatic guns, and obtain licences rapidly, while some unregistered companies hire firearms from companies that are registered.

The net result of this mayhem around weapon use and licensing is that guns, and semi-automatics in particular, have flooded into an industry known for high levels of killings. Such guns have been openly used in firefights, as in the case of the Brook Street attacks. The whole system, insiders say, is in need of a thorough audit.

A new system of police-administered gun control in South Africa was designed at the dawn of the democratic era to restrict the flow of guns. Today, licensed semi-automatics are being used publicly by groups, like the Gcabas' outfits and others, that you would regard as fitting the very definition of organised crime – mafia-style operations that enforce control over their markets by deploying hitmen to eliminate competition.

It is ironic that, of all South Africa's provinces, it was in KZN, with its notoriously violent taxi industry, that the Project Impi investigation into firearms supply and distribution was abruptly forced off the road. The investigation ran dead in the province – seemingly under high-level political pressure to silence it. From research for this book, provided in off-the-record accounts, it is probable that the province's taxi bosses received state guns through Prinsloo's channels, although, frustratingly, there is no ballistics paper trail to show it, as there is in the case of the guns supplied to the Western Cape gangs.

The days of operating with impunity may well be over for the Gcaba brothers. Recently they have become vulnerable, partly because they may have overstretched their capacity to control their business operations. 'The Gcabas,' said one provincial official, who is regarded as being neutral, may 'no longer have the monopoly on fear, and people are standing up to them.'

Ready access to firearms has been central to enabling groups like the Gcaba brothers to maintain their violent grip over their business interests. There is an urgent need to look at the challenges of firearm regulation in South Africa.

CHAPTER 12

SOUTH AFRICA'S GUN CULTURE

South Africa, concluded two historians in a widely referenced 1971 paper, was a 'gun society'. That was because, they argued, guns, and those who had access to them, were a formative part of South African history. Firearms have been crucial to shaping South African society, the environment and politics from colonial-era wars until modern times.[1] Unsurprisingly, therefore, controlling the distribution of firearms has been a prerogative of government policy in the new South Africa.

Under colonial rule, several armed actions were fought specifically over the rights of black people to own guns.[2] Policies that restricted firearm ownership and attempts at disarmament were the source of much conflict. 'Legal restrictions on gun ownership', concludes a history of guns, race and power in South Africa, 'came to mark who was a citizen and who was not'.[3] The authorities believed that firearms in the hands of the wrong people (and during the colonial era and apartheid, that meant black people) represented a danger to the state. During South Africa's transition, guns had been the means and a symbol of liberation, as later popularised by Zuma's performances of *Umshini wami* ('Bring me my machine [gun]'), a struggle song associated with members of uMkhonto we Sizwe.[4] Guns continue to retain a degree of political cachet as a symbol of power and defiance: Julius Malema's apparent unlawful firing of an assault rifle at a political rally in the Eastern Cape in 2018 being a good example.

The history of South Africa is also replete with cases of gun dealers seeking to make a profit by acquiring guns and selling them on. Guns have long had currency, providing status and protection to those who could acquire them.[5] Stockpiles of weapons have historically provided a guaranteed and lucrative market for arms dealers in southern Africa – a remarkably diverse bunch of people, from hunters and traders to gun-dealing missionaries.[6] In that sense, Prinsloo fits into a long lineage of people who have sought to profit from firearms. The guns, neatly packed onto the shelves of the police armoury waiting to be destroyed, may have seemed to the police colonel like a time-honoured means of earning cash. After all, under-the-table gun sales have long been a feature in South Africa, with unscrupulous dealers being known to supplement their income in this way.

The discussion of the historical roots of South Africa as a gun society reveals remarkably close parallels with the situation today. The debate hinges fundamentally on two pools of firearms – those that are legally regulated, or licensed, and those that aren't. The flow of guns between one pool and the other remains a source of much debate – and violence. Historically, periods of conflict and uncertainty in South Africa have seen growth in both legal and illegal possession of firearms. In contrast, phases of stability have seen declines because of state interventions around control and reduced demand.

Firearm ownership in South Africa, both the legal and illegal forms, declined considerably in the 1960s and 1970s from earlier eras. Older stocks of firearms held since colonial days were no longer functional and gun trafficking had been brought under control by the state, limiting the number of firearms in circulation.

This was to change from the 1980s, both in respect of legal and illegal categories of ownership. The civil turmoil in South Africa from the mid-1980s saw a significant volume of unregistered and illicit weapons in circulation. These were the result of the government providing weapons to fuel the liberation conflict, most notably in KZN, and the distribution of weapons to ANC cadres fighting for the liberation movement. Meanwhile, legal firearm ownership, mainly among whites who increasingly feared political uncertainty and growing levels of crime, surged through the 1980s, peaking in the 1990s.

Weapons from neighbouring countries that had experienced conflict, notably Mozambique, were also trafficked to South Africa. The availability of automatic weapons at the time saw a spate of robberies and armed attacks in which AK-47s – which had been distributed both by the state and the liberation forces – were used. The sources of these weapons began to dry up by the late 1990s as age, attrition and state weapon-collection programmes eroded the available stock of illegal weapons.

The importance of achieving a system of effective firearms control was therefore of utmost importance in post-1994 South Africa, when the illegal firearm pool was at its height and presented a huge risk. Regulating a new generation of firearms was seen as essential to long-term crime and violence control. If an effective system could be introduced to control the legal firearm market, and by implication seepage from the legal to the illegal, it would serve as a crucial policy tool to restrict the pool of illegal firearms. Measures included seizures of guns by the police and the voluntary surrender of firearms in amnesties. What few people at the time could have imagined was that the state itself would become a source of illegal firearms.

Black and white

Broadly, three phases have marked state efforts at gun control in the recent past. The figure of Prinsloo stands as a bridge spanning all three. He was involved during all of them, being consulted as a firearms expert, sharing advice and administering the law around guns. In the end, his theft and sale of weapons delivered a blow to gun control, demonstrating the failure of the state itself to secure weapons under its jurisdiction.

In the first phase, in the decade before 1994, gun ownership was tightly restricted to white ownership, although with some loosening of restrictions established earlier during apartheid. The focus of policy was on who, in racial terms, could buy guns, and gun control was designed for a narrowly defined political purpose in the sense that it explicitly favoured one race group over others.

The 1969 Arms and Ammunition Act, the main gun control legislation of the apartheid era, restricted gun ownership to white people. A limit of 12 guns was imposed but there was no system to review whether firearms licensed to an individual remained within their possession. Once granted, a firearms licence required no renewal: it was effectively held in perpetuity.

By the 1980s, government policy, combined with a sense of impending crisis and rapidly growing crime rates, encouraged whites to acquire guns. White men, subject to conscription, were familiar with gun use and owning firearms became commonplace. Revolver ownership grew considerably, including among white women.

The conflict of the late 1980s drove some changes in the race-based system of gun ownership. An amendment to the 1969 Act made provision for certain categories of black people to apply for gun licences. Black police officers, municipal councillors and tribal chiefs, likely to be attacked in their homes and thus having good reason to be allowed the means to defend themselves, were now eligible to own guns. More rigorous vetting was applied in the case of black applicants, however, and the number of guns issued with official licences was relatively small. Meanwhile, ironically, as noted above, illegal guns were being fed into black communities, most notably in KZN, where government stocks were supplied to groups like the IFP, who were in conflict with the liberation movements.[7]

By 1994, there were some 3.5 million licensed firearms in the hands of civilians, the vast majority being white. (With whites numbering 5.2 million in 1994, a significant portion were therefore armed.) Many white people harboured uncertainties around the imminent new political order, which triggered a siege-mentality rush to obtain firearms, with just over 230 000 licences being issued in 1994 alone, mainly to whites.[8]

In the second phase, in the period after 1994, gun control was a key aspect of the new post-apartheid government policy, and a surprising level of consensus was achieved by the various stake-holders involved. Although politics was never entirely absent from gun policy (at least in the eyes of those who had previously had easy access to firearms), the government's main objective now was crime control, and not racial discrimination. As noted earlier, studies concluded that reductions in violence in the country to 2012 were closely correlated with effective gun control.

That did not mean that there was a decline in demand for guns in post-1994 South Africa. Crime continued to be a concern, and owning guns was also seen as a rite of passage to citizenship through a privilege that had been enjoyed by only a few in the old regime – the few who had used firearm ownership as an instrument of control over the many. (I vividly remember working as a monitor for the National Peace Secretariat in 1993 on the volatile East Rand and being stunned when a black colleague lifted his white peace monitoring vest to reveal a revolver tucked into his jeans. His words are as significant now as they were then: 'You see, having a gun is not only for whites. Anyway, making peace does not mean you can't be armed to protect yourself.')

Ensuring effective gun control was nevertheless an important objective of the new democratic state. One of the first actions the new government took was to introduce a high-profile gun amnesty in December 1994, during which illegal weapons could be handed in.[9]

For the Mandela government, reducing the number of firearms in South African society was a key policy priority. In 2000, six years into the new order, Parliament passed a new law for the control of firearms. Significantly, the purpose of the resulting legislation, the Firearms Control Act of 2000, is twofold: first, to protect life and prevent injury; and, secondly, to prevent the spread of illegally owned firearms by ensuring that they are removed from society and by improving the control of firearms that are held legally.[10] An effective system to process firearms licences, ensuring that those who acquire guns legally have the need for them and competence to store and use them properly, and a database to record legal firearms in private and public possession, were some of the tools introduced to achieve this.

At the core of these efforts was creating an efficient registry for firearms, building on that part of the SAPS where data on firearm ownership and related matters was collected and stored, and where a strict system of firearm licensing would be conducted. So complex and onerous was this task that the SAPS asked for a big budget and four years to complete the task. The launch of the new system was scheduled for 2004.

Several people familiar with the gun control framework in South Africa emphasised how, after 1994, the state had a clear and articulated set of objectives that drove its actions. Central to these was the requirement to reduce the number of guns in society altogether, and to significantly tighten the regulatory framework around firearm ownership. 'People may not have liked what the government was doing at the time, but at least the aims of the policy were clear,' a prominent pro-gun lobbyist told me off the record, as he did not want to be seen as praising the government's approach.

One illustration of the success of these efforts at gun control was that government-organised amnesties were well subscribed. The first, in December 1994, saw comparatively few guns handed in – some 900 firearms and 7000 rounds of ammunition, as people presumably hedged their bets in the early days of democracy. The second amnesty, in 2005, however, in which, ironically, Prinsloo had used the press to encourage people to give in their guns, was much more successful, with some 78000 firearms being submitted. The majority of these were licensed guns. A 2010 amnesty collected 30000 firearms.[11]

Converging gun cultures?

A third phase of gun control, or rather declining control, from about 2010 to 2015, saw a loss of that earlier consensus. It was also marked by growth in corruption around the issuing of licences, and an increasingly furious set of legal challenges between gun lobby groups and the government. And more recently, of course, there have been accusations of state failure around the Prinsloo case. Part of the reason for this weakening around gun control has been contradictory messaging and actions by government, reflecting a loss of the clearer vision of gun control that characterised the earlier efforts. It is also a period that has seen the pro-gun lobby gaining momentum.

The loss of confidence and trust in the government on the firearms issue is symbolised by the small number of guns handed in during an amnesty held in late 2019 and early 2020. Despite incentives for those who had not renewed licences to hand in their firearms, very few guns (a paltry 1 500 in the first month) were submitted before the amnesty was suspended during the coronavirus lockdown.

There have also been some recent significant shifts in the trafficking of illicit guns. If you follow newspaper coverage of cases of armed robbery or cash-in-transit heists, you will notice that old weapons of choice, like the AK-47 sourced from Mozambique or internal arms caches, have been overtaken by R4s and R5s stolen from state stocks.

Firearms control in South Africa, as elsewhere in the world, is now a pretty political subject. There are multiple interest groups – with the usual divide between gun-owning enthusiasts and a gun control lobby.[12] There is some common cause, however, between the pro- and anti-gun lobbies as to the requirement for the elimination of corruption, and the promotion of transparency and predictability in the firearms management regime. The Prinsloo case has also been universally condemned by both spheres, although different conclusions have been drawn. For some in the pro-gun lobby, the case has strengthened the argument that the state lacks the competence to manage firearms handed in as the gun-licensing regime continues to be tightened.

The South African gun debate is, in many ways, distinct from the one that has long been raging in the United States, although they are sometimes conflated. For a start, the South African Constitutional Court has recently ruled that an absolute right to own firearms does not exist in South Africa: 'Gun ownership is not a fundamental right under our Bill of Rights. It is a privilege regulated by the Firearms Control Act.'[13] The US gun discussion is fundamentally about the right to bear arms, which is constitutionally guaranteed under the second amendment. But whereas US pro-gun lobbyists argue that the regulation of firearms is the consequence of an overweening government, gun regulation in South Africa prior to 1994 was at heart about protecting the white state itself.

In South Africa, the debate is made more complex (or less complex, depending on your viewpoint) by a number of factors. One is of course the country's high crime rate, widening the divide between those who argue that guns provide necessary protection and those who argue that the possession of guns – and their theft and circulation in the criminal economy – is part of the problem. And there is the inevitable racial lens with which all government policies are viewed in South Africa, including whisperings that gun control is merely a mechanism designed to disarm white people, thereby reducing a potential threat to the state. Race also impinges on the American discussion, of course, with one academic study concluding, for example, that gun ownership is a way of countering the growing economic and social insecurity faced by white men in a rapidly changing America.[14]

In the past, gun control in South Africa, as noted, was designed to keep guns out of the hands of black people. Today, owning a firearm is seen as a democratic right by a wide segment of the population, and not merely a group of white gun owners, enthusiasts and collectors. Gun dealers report that many black people are equally eager to acquire guns for status and protection. Black gun owners at first bought cheaper and more widely available guns, but have reportedly become more discerning buyers.[15] What does appear to differ between black and white gun enthusiasts, however, is what might be termed the culture of gun ownership. White people, accustomed to guns and the fact that they were easily obtainable in the past, and introduced to them by their fathers and grandfathers, almost inevitably make the argument that guns are part of a cultural identity. Prinsloo and Raves, I believe, would have no trouble with this argument.

An interesting piece of research concludes that white respondents would point to their childhood association with guns as an important factor in making them comfortable with firearms. 'Most of us [whites] grew up with firearms and we've been imprinted with the idea of how to deal with firearms in a manner that is safe.'[16] Interestingly, in this piece of research at least, the sense that guns were a cultural part of white identity was highlighted. This was far more prevalent than a sense that the militarisation of white society and conscription had bred familiarity with guns, a point regularly mentioned in the academic literature of the 1990s.[17] I suspect, however, that such opinions have been filtered and the narrative has evolved over time, particularly, as in this case, when the interviewer is not a white person. 'Culture' built through childhood experience with guns (although one can't help raising one's eyebrows here) is much more neutral than saying that a gun culture has been fostered among South African white men by a skewed racial political and institutional order.

My hunch here is that if an emerging gun culture is shaped by past association, the most knowledgeable are those who have had access to guns, both legal *and* illegal. One person with close links to old ANC networks who then served in government told me that she would receive queries from ex-ANC operatives who were familiar with firearms about the process for licensing: 'They would call me up and have a fairly good idea of what they wanted to buy because they already knew what was available ... They had some idea of guns.'[18]

While this seems to suggest at least some convergence around a gun culture among different South African ethnic groups and classes, a point the gun lobby likes to emphasise, the picture is more mixed. It is perhaps more accurate to say that there has been a strong culture of guns among some South Africans, although it is possible that this may actually be in decline across the wider population as gun control restricts the availability of firearms.[19]

It does seem, however, that some powerful and emerging black business groups with government connections, notably within the taxi industry and the associated security industry, which in some cases have quasi-criminal overlays, have become an important source of lobbying and corruption within the firearms licensing system. The debate on the necessity of gun ownership would also shift if significant declines in crime rates could be achieved, including within these industries. This seems an uncertain prospect, however.

When the state is the trafficker

One group of people in South Africa who have of course a strong gun culture are gang bosses and mid-level gangsters. Some of the same people who have told me about their enthusiasm for the various types of guns that Prinsloo introduced to the Cape for their illegal use are also eager to acquire legal firearms. I have, for example, been sent a picture of a gang boss's girlfriend, posing with a collection of new, legal guns – in what is clearly a show of power and influence. Indeed, displays of legally owned guns on Facebook have drawn the attention of police investigators to cases where gang members, including those with criminal records, acquired legal guns. 'They hide the illegal guns, but put the legal ones on display, almost like they are collectors or as a display of wealth and power,' is how one senior police officer described it.

A mid-level gang boss on the Cape Flats once proudly showed me his newly licensed semi-automatic AK-47. He explained that acquiring a licence had been no problem for him. 'It's all legal, sir.' I am unsure whether he has a criminal record, but just a routine check would have revealed that he has strong gang connections.

A recent study of the evolution of gangs in the western areas of Johannesburg found something similar. An older gang member told researchers: 'During the old days, if you had a gun, you were the main man. Now everyone can get a gun. Even myself, who served nine years in prison, I have been able to get a licence for a firearm.'[20]

A gang boss's wife displays the family's wares, all supposedly legally acquired.

According to the law, it's not a walk in the park to acquire a licence for a semi-automatic assault rifle, like an AK-47. It is easier if you are a sports shooter and belong to a club, or if you own a private security company engaged in high-risk work, like cash-in-transit. However, gangsters – in theory at least – need not apply. But they do, and licences seem to be granted to them. Take the case of Ralph Stanfield, the widely feared alleged leader of the 28s, now regarded as one of the most cohesive and organised criminal outfits in the country. (If anything, his glamorous wife, Nicole, is regarded as even more fearsome.) Underworld rumour has it that Stanfield has plenty of state officials on his payroll. In an ongoing court case, which has dragged on intermittently since their arrest in June 2014 on illegal firearms charges, Ralph and Nicole Stanfield, and his sister, Francesca, are alleged to have acquired firearm licences illegally. The details of how this transpired shows both the best and the worst sides of the CFR.

Applying for a firearms licence requires the prospective gun owner to fill out application details at his or her local police station with a Designated Firearms Officer (DFO). The police station should be in the applicant's area of business or residence. The paperwork is then sent via the provincial office, where it is supposed to be reviewed, to the CFR in Pretoria for processing. To commit fraud in the issuing of firearms licences generally requires a criminal conspiracy between a station level DFO and a partner within the CFR, with presumably some support at provincial level too.

Stanfield applied for firearm licences on several occasions: in March 2000, in May 2002 and in April 2006. They were all declined, both at the CFR and at the Mitchells Plain Police Station. His sister, Francesca, also applied at Mitchells Plain in October 2009 but was turned down. The system seemed to work.

Nicole was more fortunate: she applied at the Table View Police Station in July 2010 and obtained approval a year later for the licensing of a .40 Smith & Wesson pistol. She looks like someone who is hard to turn down, and I suppose when she sashayed into Table View Police Station anything was possible. The application went up the bureaucratic chain and down again, and the licence was granted.

Ralph, being an enterprising sort, did not give up. He, Nicole and Francesca, as well as 17 associates (yes, 17, really), all applied at the Olifantsfontein Police Station in Midrand. In the court case, their charge sheet states, however, that the accused had not in fact been to Olifantsfontein Police Station at all. One Priscilla Mangyani, an administrative clerk at the CFR, captured their applications with the assistance of the DFO at that station. If you were sniffing, it would be a rat you could smell.

Even more intriguing, though, is that the charges include the allegation that the Stanfield family obtained firearms proficiency training (in order to meet the competency requirements under the Act), at the Lyttelton Firearms Training Centre near Pretoria (close to where the Z88 was manufactured, incidentally). The truth, it seems, is that they never received any training.[21]

The charges in the Stanfield case were subsequently withdrawn in October 2016, and then reinstated in April 2018. A prominent defence lawyer with knowledge and experience of South Africa's gun control laws told me that the very best defence in such a case would simply be to claim that the accused had in fact applied properly for the licence, placing the burden of proof on the state to prove beyond reasonable doubt that this was not the case. 'The paperwork in the CFR is so chaotic that they would be hard-pressed to do this,' he suggested.

Since 2004, over three million firearms licences have been issued, and insiders say that given the chaos with the firearms registry it is probably now impossible to know how many of these may have involved fraud and corruption. Gun Free South Africa, the vocal anti-gun lobby, has called for a forensic audit of all licences, permits and authorisations issued to ensure that due process was followed.[22]

Has South Africa's failing, corruptible system of firearm licensing in recent years permitted the guns that the early democratic state was so motivated to control and regulate to arm the violent criminal gangs and industries that are contributing to the horrifying homicide rates the country is experiencing today?

CHAPTER 13

LICENCES TO KILL

The police who run the CFR have a siege mentality. By all accounts, it is very hard to engage with them. So I set out myself to try to obtain an interview, but the most I could manage was to talk to people who had worked there in the past. Approaches to the police, including a letter outlining the purpose of my research, were met with stony silence. The SAPS, it seems, does not want to discuss the firearms registry. Police gun experts, like Prinsloo in his heyday, can be patronising: one former chief of the division said with an air of disdain, tilting his head forward to emphasise the point, that the system was just too complex for non-experts like myself to understand.[1] I did, however, manage to talk to several DFOs off the record.

The greatest problem facing the CFR, as the Stanfield gun licence case suggests, is corruption: people pay bribes to make the registry work in their favour. You can easily see how this happened. As the efficiency of the registry diminished, and gun licences weren't reaching those who wanted them, money appears to have exchanged hands to oil the wheels, and then the backhanders gradually became entrenched and part of the way the system came to operate. One of the most serious consequences of this systemic corruption is that criminals now know they can use bribery to obtain gun licences, or obtain them more quickly.

Stanfield is not the only big-name underworld figure who seems to have obtained a gun licence. Self-confessed hitman Mikey Schultz, who admitted murdering mining magnate Brett Kebble (although, bizarrely, at Kebble's request), an ANC funder and fraudster, also managed to get a licence. In Schultz's case, a prominent gun dealer was also implicated.

In an affidavit provided by one witness, it is claimed that Schultz was a regular visitor to Dave Sheer Guns in Johannesburg and 'spent a lot of money there'. Schultz was helped with the firearms licence application by the director of Dave Sheer Guns, Gareth De Nysschen, who then allegedly expedited the process for him with the help of an unnamed lieutenant-general employed at the CFR.[2] Author and investigative journalist Angelique Serrao reported that the same witness, an ex-employee of Dave Sheer Guns, claimed that she had regularly paid bribes on behalf of the gun dealer to the then head of the CFR, Brigadier Mathapelo Miriam Mangwani. Shultz was issued with five gun licences. When this story broke, Schultz handed the firearms in to the police but was later seen in public with guns. The investigation seems to have stalled; while Mangwani was later suspended, charges against Dave Sheer Guns or Schultz have never been brought.[3]

Although information to this effect has never been made public, it is believed that Prinsloo himself was involved in the manipulation of the firearms registry system to issue licences for known criminals. According to one of the Project Impi investigators, 'Applications would flow through identified police stations and then run through the CFR. The local station would be the lowest rung and often people at the CFR would tell the person wanting the licence which station to send their application through.' Olifantsfontein Police Station, where Stanfield applied (nowhere near his Cape Town place of residence), and several others, including Linden, were seen as suspect.

The system at the registry appeared to be wide open to manipulation by insiders who had access. Details of a firearm could be changed, as required, and licences could be issued for firearms that had been destined for destruction or for semi-automatic weapons that were meant to be licensed according to a more rigorous process. In some instances, licences would exist on the system, but there would be no back-up file, making it all but impossible to trace the details of the case. The task of investigators was made even more difficult by the fact that officials at the CFR were able to log on using the passwords of others.

The ease with which insiders could exploit the system, according to a senior police officer, was evident when a raid was conducted on a dealer in Brackenhurst, Johannesburg, as part of the investigation into Prinsloo and Raves. As the raid was happening, someone was busy at the CFR changing the details of guns linked to the dealership.

Disguising fraudulently registered and licensed firearms also involved manipulating the stock held by legitimate gun dealers. Andrew Soutar of the South African Arms and Ammunition Dealers Association explained that dealers' stock lists can be manipulated without their knowledge. The main challenge, he said, is that dealers struggle to get access to the stock lists held by the CFR. The system is archaic and manual: when a dealer acquires new stock, he or she submits it to the CFR on a paper SAPS 350 form. If officials in the registry then add additional weapons to that form, the dealer would never know.[4] The implications of this are serious: many guns can fall between the cracks and float in an unregulated space, making them vulnerable to being distributed into criminal markets. These guns are referred to as 'ghost stock'.

The risk is that ghost stock can be used to license guns that are illicitly acquired by providing the purchaser with what appears to be a legitimate set of paperwork on their origins. Illegal guns are effectively laundered into the legal stock in this way. (Another concern is that, when ghost stock is listed on the system, honest dealers fear being raided by the police, who, when checking on their stock, may accuse them of not having correct records, making the dealer vulnerable to bribery.)

Cases of ghost stock have cropped up too regularly to be written off off as exceptions or clerical errors.[5] One Johannesburg gun dealer provided an example. He explained how he had been approached by a police investigator from Cape Town. 'He asked me about a weapon seized by the police in Grassy Park [an area with a high gang presence] that was listed as having come from my stock. That weapon had never been part of my stock, and, clearly, some official had completed the transfer form to place the weapon as having come from my stock.'

Another dealer said that, in an attempt to avoid this form of fraud, he scratches out in ink the blank space on the form, so no other guns can be entered there by a third party, but he is aware that there have been cases where the second page of the form has been replaced in its entirety at the CFR.

Shockingly, a gun dealer in Johannesburg told me that he had been approached by a police officer and asked to register ghost weapons in his stock list. The dealer said that he politely refused but worried about the implications of declining. Gun dealers are understandably reluctant to discuss these issues on the record for fear of being targeted for inspections or other forms of retribution.

How do gangsters get gun licences?

While street prices for guns sold by gang bosses on the black market have continued to climb, the trend has been the opposite in the legitimate gun market. With a weakening rand, gun imports should have been costing the South African gun buyer more. This is not the case. Guns have been getting cheaper on the legal market since around 2015.[6] The increase in gun prices in the illegal market coinciding with their decline in the legal one means there are now strong incentives for criminals to try to buy legal guns, exploiting a licensing process that is corruptible. 'The reason some criminals are looking at the legal market more is that it is cheaper and they know they can corrupt the process,' said one gang boss matter-of-factly. A gun licence also provides legitimate cover to buy ammunition. Although the number of rounds that can be bought is capped for each licence holder, the lack of an electronic system means that there is nothing stopping a buyer with a gun licence moving from dealer to dealer to circumvent the system.

The system that allows licences to be obtained fraudulently is well illustrated by a case involving Nafiz Modack. Sometime in 2017, Modack's security outfit began muscling in on the Lifman–Sexy Boys alliance in a number of encounters on the street and in various nightclubs.[7]

A February 2019 affidavit currently before the North Gauteng High Court lays bare how firearm licences were acquired by Modack.[8] The police officer who wrote the affidavit, Charl Kinnear, was a mild-mannered, leathery-faced and moustached lieutenant colonel who had cut his teeth at Sea Point Police Station. As his career progressed, Kinnear, who hailed from Bishop Lavis, on the Cape Flats, became well acquainted with the ways of organised crime. (Sea Point was established turf for drug sales and extortion rackets.) Kinnear later joined Vearey's team, although his relationship with the vocal general was prickly at times, before he became a section commander in the newly formed Anti-Gang Unit.

Kinnear's case took on the loudmouth of the underworld, Modack, whose Facebook page was replete with mafia imagery and references to Al Capone. In November 2017, nine firearms were registered to Modack's name, including pistols, shotguns and a rifle. The licences were all suspected to have been obtained illegally. These are cases involving fraud and deception, and the only conclusion that can be drawn from the details is that there is complicity within the CFR in the issuing of these firearms. For a start, and besides Modack's public profile as a self-declared enforcer, he has two criminal convictions, both in 2010. Neither conviction was seemingly declared in the application process, and neither served to block the issuing of the licences, even though one of Modack's convictions was for a firearms-related offence.[9] Modack also repeatedly applied for the licences at police stations within whose service area he did not have a registered address. Two police stations in particular, Edenvale and Kempton Park, seemed to have been amenable to processing Modack's applications. One colonel at the CFR, Selo Solomon Motau, then swiftly approved four of the licences. The CFR turned down one of the licence applications. However, with no record of a fresh application and no appeal having been lodged or processed, Colonel Motau stepped in to approve it.

As if that weren't enough to raise suspicions, there are several other inconsistencies in the application process for the licences.

For one, Modack allegedly did not obtain the competency certification that is mandatory for hunting and sports shooting firearms. In one case, he did not even bother to sign the form – yet the licence was still granted. In two cases, remarkably, there was no record of an application having even been made for the licences.

In another case, the affidavit of the investigating officer notes that 'the application was approved by Lieutenant Colonel BLJ Mokoto of CFR in Pretoria ... only six days after the application was apparently submitted at the police station in Edenvale. That is unheard of as it takes at least months to complete the whole process until a firearm license is approved.'[10]

This is clearly not the case – apparently as long as you know the right people and pay enough.

In October 2019, Modack's wife, Riana Modack, and three others, including Colin Booysen's niece, Nicole Norman, and an owner of a private security company, were arrested in Cape Town. The four were charged in November 2019 in the Germiston Magistrate's Court with fraud and corruption linked to obtaining firearms.[11] The state alleges that the four went to Gauteng to acquire firearm licences, applying through a police station where they knew corrupt officers would oblige. An officer involved in the investigation said that there were officers who 'sell licences for a fee' in Norwood, Boksburg, Boksburg North, Edenvale and Kempton Park police stations. Modack and several of those implicated, including Motau, were arrested in June 2020 on charges of fraud. Modack was released on bail.

There have been numerous cases where people travel from other provinces to specific stations in Gauteng to make their applications, a former senior government security official told me. They know that for the right amount of money their licence will be fast-tracked. In one police station in Gauteng, the going price is R2 000 to obtain a licence in two weeks, R5 000 to get it in one week and R15 000 if you want a semi-automatic rifle licensed in a week.

Gun dealers and lawyers working on firearms-related issues believe the main problem is systemic corruption. If you want something to happen at the CFR, you basically pay to make it happen. There is consensus among the gun-owning and gun-dealing community in South Africa that the CFR is corrupt, and that money either speeds up the application process or ensures that an application is granted, in cases such as those of the Stanfield and Modack families, where questions as to the criminal standing of the applicants would usually, and indeed should, be asked. In October 2020, two SAPS brigadiers, Samuel Maredi and Zoleka

Nafiz Modack on the move with his bodyguards in Cape Town. Modack was the main suspect in a case where bribes were paid to acquire gun licences.

PHOTO: GALLO IMAGES / NETWERK24 /JACO MARAIS

Khuboni, were arrested. They were alleged to have been involved in fraud, defeating the administration of justice and contravention of the Firearms Control Act in relation to multiple cases in Edenvale, Kempton Park and Norwood.[12]

It appears that what enables corruption at the firearms registry is the shoddy electronic system and the fact that it continues to exist alongside a paper-based processing system. Given advances in information technologies over the past decade, it shouldn't be beyond the realm of possibility for a data system like the CFR's to be designed to capture and present gun records in an easy and transparent way, and for track-and-trace technology to link the records indelibly. Apparently it is: the CFR seems to run on a shambolic combination of paper and electronic records; the system is said to be chaotic. The result: criminals easily slip through the cracks and get their guns; legitimate applicants do not receive a proper service, or are even charged.

It seems that the information technology system at the registry has long been a catalogue of error and corruption. The contract for the services was tainted from the beginning. It was awarded to a company called Waymark Infotech in September 2004. Incidentally, Waymark Infotech's website describes itself as having experience in systems development for elections and voter roll management. The company's activity in at least two elections has been questioned, and in 2005 the Zanzibar Electoral Commission went so far as to cancel its contract with the company over allegations of corruption.[13]

This does not appear to have deterred the CFR, however, from contracting the company as a supplier, and the budget for the IT system was set at R93 million, the deadline for its handover stipulated for July 2006. Things got off to a bad start. Over time, the contract ballooned to R412 million, over four times the original amount, and by 2014 the police had paid some R340 million for a system that had still not been fully implemented.[14]

In September 2014, the police cancelled the contract with Waymark without the company having completed the full installation of the firearms management system. An internal investigation was launched into the contract, which, like so much other government information on the failing system of gun control, has never been made public. The Auditor-General concluded in 2015 that the missed deadlines and escalating costs provided a solid basis to hold both civil servants and the company to account.[15]

Some 16 years after the implementation of the legislation designed to transform the system of gun regulation in South Africa, what the CFR has to show is a half-completed and clearly problematic system of gun records, a system that lays itself open to corruption and manipulation. Given that firearms control policy was a central pillar of the new democratic government's plan to reduce crime, it is hard not to hang one's head in despair.

The missing report on the firearm registry

There was no excuse for not picking up the failure of the system. By 2010, it was already becoming clear that the CFR was failing. The Police Minister at the time, Nathi Mthethwa, instructed the Civilian Secretariat for Police Service, a technical advisory body to the minister, to conduct an assessment of the CFR and of how the Firearms Control Act was being implemented more generally. Mthethwa demanded a report, and in comments to the media in November 2010, he gave some insight into its conclusions: 'We want to frankly state to the nation that the current state of affairs at the CFR is far from what and how it is supposed to be. ... Instead of serving as an additional arsenal to our mission [to reduce crime], suffice to say that the CFR currently acts as a bottleneck in our crime fighting initiatives.'[16]

Although the secretariat's report was considered too sensitive for public consumption and never released, extracts of it were later attached to a presentation given to a parliamentary committee, which was provided to me. In an affidavit, the then Police Minister Nkosinathi Nhleko said that the report was 'not intended for pub-lic consumption' but to 'assist [him] to develop policy'.[17] I applied for a full copy of the report under the Promotion of Access to Information Act but was refused.

The sections of the report that I have seen, labelled 'confidential', can only be described as a damning indictment of the work of the South African police in establishing and managing the CFR.[18] The registry, the report says, was troubled by a litany of errors and there was widespread evidence of poor implementation. These included, most critically, a backlog in the processing of licences, with applications, including for renewals, sometimes taking years. Hence, under pressure, the report states, and to hide the backlogs when inquiries were made, the CFR 'randomly issued licenses without proper process'. The impact of these backlogs was to make the system vulnerable to corruption as staff at the CFR requested, or were offered, bribes, to 'fast track' applications.[19]

Police management made a commitment to the minister and to Parliament to implement a turnaround strategy at the CFR to address the issues raised in the 2010 report. Ten years later, no comprehensive strategy has been designed or implemented. One person familiar with the report went so far as to say that things have got worse now, and not better.

According to the report, based on multiple accounts – external allegations made by the legal fraternity and then corroborated with officials and ex-officials who were prepared to talk – by 2010 there was a thriving corruption market smoothing the processing of firearms licences. Corruption seemed to concentrate around three processes. The first was the 'issuing of licences to people who should legally have had their licences refused' – as seems to be the case with the Stanfields and Modack. The second was 'people having to pay bribes to ensure that their licences are issued and to avoid delays'. The third involved applicants who were 'able to license firearms which are then not accurately listed on the system'.[20]

I have some 20 pages of the report, and reading through these findings is like being punched repeatedly in the gut. Effective gun control and regulation were among the most important objectives of government policy, and yet the report describes the processes at the CFR as 'completely dysfunctional',[21] riven by poor management and cost overruns. There is a section on how poorly the registry is structured, and how staff barely understand their place in it. The whole edifice seems to have been constructed to be incomprehensible. Systems have been 'overcomplicated', says one of the conclusions. I was reminded of my previous encounter with the former head of the CFR, who told me in all seriousness that the registry was too complex for ordinary mortals to understand.[22]

The dismal findings of this report do seem to have shaken the registry – but only temporarily. In a response that smacks of defensiveness, the police colonel in charge of the section in the CFR responsible for issuing licences, Sibongile Dorah Kibido, drew up an affidavit in April 2015 in reply to one of the multitude of court challenges that the CFR has been drawn into. In it, she says that 'while there were such difficulties some years back in 2010 ... these problems were since rectified and the administration is running smoothly at present'.[23] You would be justified in finding it derisible, therefore, that, just a month before Colonel Kibido made that statement in her affidavit, the then Deputy Minister of Police, Maggie Sotyu, had visited the CFR. After her inspection, Sotyu addressed a firearms summit convened by the National Assembly Portfolio Committee on Police in May 2015: 'I am very sad to say today,' she said, 'that, with the billions that the SAPS gets every year from government since 1994, we are still plagued with the same problem of a [CFR] that is dysfunctional and in constant decay.' If this were not damning enough, Sotyu continued: 'What I saw [during her visit to the CFR] was horrendous to say the least. It is blatantly obvious that this CFR has not been a priority for a long time.'[24]

The deputy minister's comments to the summit probably marked the zenith of the state's openness about the CFR and the gun-control discussion generally. After that, government strategy seems to have increasingly slid into a denialist one, as reflected by Colonel Kibido's 'the shop is in order' affidavit. At several meetings, turnaround strategies were presented by the police, but there seemed to be a deliberate attempt to slow engagement with the lobby groups, both pro- and anti-gun, on the issue.

There was a brief glimmer of hope when evidence of corruption presented by various stakeholders to the Secretary for Police, the most senior civilian official in the department, responsible for policy development and reporting directly to the minister, seemed to have borne some results. Eighteen CFR officials, including the head, Brigadier Mangwani, were served with letters of immediate suspension related to the fraudulent issuing of firearm licences. The brigadier was found guilty and is no longer in the SAPS. Four of the 18 resigned, and ten were able to return to work after being found not guilty by internal disciplinary processes. The remainder were given warnings. The DFO at Pretoria Central Police Station, Captain Lawrence Mamogobo, was found guilty of 30 counts of corruption and sentenced to 13 years' imprisonment. He was found to have falsified training and competency certificates, and facilitated the issuing of false licences.

But the result of these purges, according to several involved in the process, was that new staff were appointed, and suspicions between the CFR and external stakeholders increased.[25] The overall level of efficiency of the CFR reportedly deteriorated to a level that was 'as bad and even worse than the situation in 2009'.[26] The firearms summit in 2015 had served to clear the air and allowed parties to vent their frustrations. But it was to prove a false dawn for cooperation.

The general approach of the government since that summit has been to limit external engagements and reduce information surrounding the registry,[27] a strategy apparently designed to shut down open discussion. I submitted several access-to-information requests to the SAPS to determine the numbers of firearms that have gone missing from SAPS evidence stores. No responses have been forthcoming. Government and police sources have also taken pains not to draw attention to the Prinsloo case – no doubt because they fear wider civil action on the issue of state control over firearms.[28]

The police have set great store by the promised turnaround strategy for the firearms registry that was discussed in March 2010 at the National Assembly Portfolio Committee on Police. It is hard to judge the success of the strategy, partly because no overall objectives were set against which it can be measured. Some successes against corruption have been recorded. Those engaging regularly with the CFR, however, continue to suggest that corruption remains pervasive in the registry. Keeping quiet about the challenges and blocking external engagement may have shifted the discussion away from the public's gaze, but it has certainly not solved the problems at the registry.

The complicated story of firearms control in post-apartheid South Africa, then, is far from over. The historical origins of our violent 'gun society' continue to cast a long shadow over the country and threaten to destabilise the societal peace that was the aspiration of the architects of the new democratic South Africa. At the time of writing, the enlightened vision legislated for in the Firearms Control Act of 2000 has been severely eroded. This may be partly the result of certain legal challenges (outlined in an annex at the end of the book), which have limited the Act's purview, but it is fundamentally a function of the government's own appalling mismanagement of gun licensing and its defensive communications track record on the issue.

The Prinsloo case is emblematic of and was enabled by this sorry state of affairs in South Africa's gun-control regime. The Prinsloo story is but one case that has undermined trust in the state, and it raises worrying questions about the ability of South Africa's police service to safely and securely manage and control firearms – and to keep them out of the hands of violent criminals. Part of the challenge, as I have indicated, is that the discussion around the licensing system and the gun control regime in general has been increasingly restricted, in part due to the technical nature of the subject matter, but also because the government approach seems to be to deliberately shut down the debate. It is time for the public to ask what we can do to get back our guns.

CHAPTER 14

GIVE US BACK OUR GUNS

On 22 May 2014, members of SAPS Crime Intelligence, the Hawks and some officers from Hillbrow Police Station raided a house in Woodlands Road in Johannesburg's plush northern suburb of Norwood. The police had received information that there were drugs being stored at the house, which was just a stone's throw from the local police station. The officers did find some dagga but, in the process, they inadvertently stumbled on a massive arms cache. They found in the house 112 assault rifles, including state-manufactured R1s, R4s and R5s, 300 handguns and a machine used to manufacture ammunition. Commercial explosives and detonators were also found at the site.

A Ukrainian couple who had long been resident in Johannesburg, Mark and Emma Shumler-Tishko, along with their Malawian domestic helper, were arrested. They were charged with possession of unlicensed firearms, and possession of ammunition in contravention of the Explosives Act.[1] An additional charge of dealing in dagga seemed small bore in comparison.

Speaking during the bail application, State Prosecutor Talita Louw told the court that among the weapons were guns that had been handed in at police stations during a firearms amnesty, which therefore should have been subsequently destroyed. One was an R1 that had been submitted during the amnesty at the Roodepoort Police Station four years earlier. The rifle had been taken out of the police storeroom for destruction, Louw said. 'It is not known how the same firearm was found in the possession of the applicants.'[2] Louw said investigators were checking the serial numbers of firearms handed in at police stations across the country.[3] She told the court how other firearms found at the house were, according to

police records, registered as belonging to the state. 'The only infer-
ence one can draw,' she concluded, 'is that there is more to this case
than meets the eye. Investigations are under way to determine how
these firearms left the custody of the police.'[4]

Although there were high hopes that the arrest and subsequent
trial of the Norwood accused would shed light on corrupt cops and
other state employees who may have been leaking weapons on the
black market, at the time of writing this book, six years later, the
case remains unsolved. A suspended police officer, Thabiso Kubyane,
who has links to the organised-crime figure Radovan Krejcir, is
reported to have links to the Norwood arms cache.[5] The trial has
not gone ahead, and despite a concerted attempt to find out what has
happened, there is little information publicly available.[6]

Although unresolved, the Norwood case does at least provide a
startling example of how huge numbers of firearms from the state
have ended up in the wrong hands. Over half the firearms in that
cache were reported as being state-registered, while others were
from police stores, having been presented as evidence in previous
trials or handed in during the gun amnesties. It should be a national
scandal, yet the case has barely made the news.

In September 2020, Charl Kinnear, the lieutenant colonel who
had been investigating Modack's acquisition of fraudulent gun
licences, died in a hail of bullets outside his Bishop Lavis home. It
was a highly professional assassination, likely to have been commissioned by a consortium of crime figures and their allies in the
police. It was a stark reminder, if one was needed, that the flow
of weapons and corruption within the licensing process implicated
people with powerful interests – who would stop at little, including
the killing of a senior police officer, to protect their tracks. Kinnear
died because he was intent on exposing the alliance that lies between
officers deeply embedded in the criminal economy and their allies in
the dark reaches of a subterranean world, where the ordering of an
assassination is just another transaction in a day's work.

Kinnear's murder provided a symbolic recognition of how the
sale of police weapons to South Africa's underworld has had a

decisive role in the country's spiralling levels of violent crime. This is most notable in Cape Town, where the trend line of rapidly escalating murder rates almost exactly coincides with the period during which the black market guns entered circulation in the city. The gun supplies transformed the nature of the Cape gangs, triggering both internal gang conflicts and a series of inter-gang wars. The ubiquitous Z88s and other firearms, once held in state stores, have wreaked havoc on the streets and many lives have been lost. The loss of automatic rifles, including from the South African military, is particularly damaging, as these are used in the most serious of crimes, such as cash-in-transit heists, taxi industry shoot-outs, armed robbery and the ongoing clashes between groups of heavily armed illegal miners.

As important as controlling how state weapons are registered and secured is the need to manage ammunition under the control of the state. Criminals often say they select guns based on the availability of supplies of ammunition – one reason that has made the Z88 so attractive to gangsters.

In the area of gun-control enforcement and regulation, the CFR is a weak link in the state's response. Corruption and poor management at the CFR have persisted since its establishment, and its processes and information systems are inadequate for the challenge. That known, convicted criminals are able to acquire gun licences is simply unacceptable. Nowhere is this more alarming than in the granting of licences to certain private security companies, often associated with the taxi industry, that operate on the fringes of the law, to put it mildly. The system of regulating the private security industry has also been weak, and is associated with corruption and undue influence, most notably in KZN, where the problems caused by violent operators in the taxi industry and private security companies have been particularly acute.

One of the consequences of the state-guns-to-gangs phenomenon has been the development of an active market for illicit arms and ammunition in the underworld. Guns have become a tradable, lucrative commodity, with the evidence suggesting that gang bosses and other criminal entrepreneurs collude to increase prices to secure profit. There are also rumours that significant quantities of firearms have been stockpiled for this purpose, holding the prospect of a steady future supply of illegal guns for some time to come. The rising price of guns in this illicit market has not stopped their spread: it simply means that the market is now more effectively managed by the crime bosses to their benefit than in the days when large numbers of guns flooded Cape Town and prices were low. The illicit economy in South Africa generates enough cash to be able to pay for these weapons and ammunition, and the firearms sales market, like that of drugs, sustains the underworld through the money it generates.

Pools of firearms and ammunition held by government entities are under threat because they are seen as an easy source of profit: they can be bought cheaply and sold at a good margin. By failing to secure these stocks, the South African state has been arming organised criminals. State actors have also sought to cover up or downplay the extent of the problem, hoping perhaps that it will go away. It will not. While Prinsloo as an individual must take responsibility for his heinous crime, the institutional systems in which he acted, as an ostensible public servant, also carry great responsibility. A failure to secure seized firearms is an institutional failure as much as it is an individual's crime. Remarkably, however, there have been no consequences for SAPS management, no accountability, no responsibility taken, and certainly no public apology. These are overdue.

What is clear from speaking to many individuals and interest groups from different sides of the gun debate is that although there are obviously fundamental differences between pro- and anti-gun groups, there also significant areas of commonality. Both agree, for example, that the current regulatory system is dysfunctional and both often express the need to find a way to seek common ground.

It is worth reiterating: state guns are our guns, paid for with our taxes to be used by responsible agents of the state in the interests of our protection, or, if they are handed in, to be properly secured, managed and destroyed, for the future safety of citizens. They are our guns, and we have lost large numbers of them. That has compromised our safety. We owe it to ourselves to retrieve these weapons and to make sure no more make it onto the streets and into violent underworld markets. A transparently communicated policy and a much stronger response to the leaking of state weapons are required.

Towards a safer South Africa

Unless these problems are addressed, South Africa's excessively high violent-crime rate will not be reduced. I believe that a number of actions are now long overdue. I focus here on the ones that I think are the most important.

If the state wants to promote firearms control, it must sort out its own house first. Without achieving that, there will be no public confidence in policies of gun control. The government is losing the discussion by blundering ahead on firearms control without effective messaging and without a clear policy. The result is considerable uncertainty and lack of clarity in the system, reducing an important policy discussion to a set of court actions. Government needs to recognise this and review its approach to firearms policy in its public statements.

But any attempts by the state to get its house in order on firearms policy and systems has to be accompanied by a more transparent approach that draws in key stakeholders and role players. While there is always likely to be a degree of tension and difference between the state and pro-gun lobby groups when it comes to the regulation of firearms, gun regulation has been most successful in countries where the state has attempted to get buy-in from role players and stakeholders, including both pro- and anti-gun lobbies. The South African government's approach should be to seek to prevent an American-style societal divide on firearms policy. Its failure to engage effectively is leading precisely to this outcome.

There should be an independent inquiry into the number of weapons lost by the SAPS, including the actual numbers of firearms sold on by Prinsloo and his collaborators. Elsewhere, governments would have fallen and senior civil servants would be forced to resign over a national scandal like this, and yet there have been almost no consequences in South Africa. President Cyril Ramaphosa has emphasised that corrupt and unprofessional civil servants will face the music when it comes to corruption around the COVID-19 pandemic. The same should apply to stolen state guns, an equally harmful crime – guilty parties in senior police management should be held to account and lose their jobs if they have failed to fulfil their duty. The public have a right to know how many of their weapons are now circulating on the black market, and how they can be returned to safe storage and ultimately destroyed.

The Firearms Control Act places certain responsibilities on official institutions that possess firearms, and these responsibilities need to be taken seriously. Data on the loss of firearms from state departments should also be scrupulously reported. Current data is often contradictory and is altered over time, raising suspicion that the numbers are being fiddled.

The numbers handed in during gun amnesties, and how the weapons are subsequently stored, should be subject to external independent oversight and review. It is clear, as this book has illustrated, that stockpiles of guns and ammunition provide enormous incentives for criminal actors to corrupt police officials. The SAPS should not see such oversight as an imposition on their authority, but as central to rebuilding trust in their ability to handle the state stocks of firearms. The gun amnesty that began in December 2019 and is ongoing at the time of writing is a case in point – embarrassingly, the SAPS had to exclude stations that they regarded as too steeped in corrupt practices to be suitable for receiving firearms handed in by the public. Given the catalogue of mismanagement of guns in the possession of the state, can the public be secure in the knowledge that the state is acting appropriately to keep them safe? Government should seek to build confidence in this regard and, if there is no fear of leakage, as the SAPS would like us to believe, then there is no reason to fear external oversight.

There should also be an independent audit of the firearm destruction process. The public have a right to be assured that the firearms are in fact destroyed. Prinsloo managed to subvert the destruction process by destroying some weapons but retaining the bulk for illegal sale. Police firearm management systems failed to register that this was occurring for at least seven years. There is a strong argument for establishing a weapons destruction commission, or equivalent body, to certify and report on destruction.

Serious questions need to be asked about how and why police members lose their guns, when, in reality, in some cases they sell or hire them out to criminals. In 2010, the Minister of Police made a commitment to the public that police officers found to have been negligent in the loss of their firearms would be punished. The Firearms Control Act makes provision for people who negligently lose firearms to be declared unfit to possess a gun, and this needs to be adhered to. State officials who lose firearms must therefore face consequences, and there should be management systems in place to enforce this. Again, this system should be subject to independent oversight and reported to Parliament annually.

Although the notion will of course be rejected vehemently by the police, it is worth exploring whether having in place specialised firearms units or officers may not be a better policy option than the current system, which enables officers' guns and ammunition to leak into criminal hands in return for cash. A smaller number of police guns in circulation, more effectively regulated and in the possession of better-trained officers would reduce opportunities for theft and misuse. The first principle of policing surely is to do no harm to ordinary law-abiding citizens; if that is so, should SAPS members, or at least a significant portion of them, carry guns at all? At the very least, officers should not be able to take their weapons with them after hours, or at least this should be allowed only in exceptional circumstances.

The role of SAP13 police station exhibit rooms as a source of illegal guns entering the black market requires urgent attention. The police say that they have stopped this pilfering of guns held at police stations. Interviews conducted for this book and press reports, however, suggest that criminals can still buy guns from these stocks. There are orders in place around the control of guns held in SAP13 storage but often they are not adhered to. Currently, station commanders are able to initiate a disposal process for firearms held in their stores, and systems need to put in place to ensure that such disposal processes cannot be used to hide the trail of firearms removed from stores. It is essential that the SAPS sets up more effective systems to monitor firearms flowing through SAP13 stores and report accurately on the outcome of this monitoring.

The activities and effectiveness of the CFR should be audited. Since the Minister of Police first initiated an investigation into the functioning of the CFR in 2010 (the results of which have never been made public), the police have been talking about implementing a turnaround strategy. However, ten years later there is no evidence that this strategy has had any effect. It may well be time for the police to admit their failure in this regard and to engage with experts in the running of the CFR. Police responses around developments at the CFR often obfuscate as much as they explain. There are now just too many questions about the ineffective information technology systems in place, allegations of corruption and mismanagement, and an approach that does not engage with stakeholders. There is also a strong argument, given the failure of police management to improve the registry's operations, that it should be taken over as an independent body, staffed by civilians and under the auspices of an independent board.

The role of private security companies requires urgent attention, particularly as actors in taxi-related violence and assassinations. As I have stated elsewhere, although the taxi industry has tapped entrepreneurial talent and brought wealth and livelihoods to many, the state must respond much more emphatically to the violence that this industry generates. This means cracking down on the licensing of semi-automatic weapons to companies that are engaged in what are clearly illegal activities. Private security companies should not be allowed to become militia-style groups for the industry. We are heading to more violent and more virulent forms of organised crime in the taxi industry unless the state acts firmly. Restricting the supplies of weapons to this sector is a good place to begin.

Securing state weapons and getting back those that have ended up on the streets must be an overriding priority. If the weapons are off the streets, they cannot be used in crime. By all accounts, the Hawks responded too slowly to the December 2019 case in which 12 were arrested in connection with the disappearance of 19 assault rifles from the Lyttelton SANDF military base, and it is unclear at the time of writing whether these weapons will ever be retrieved.[7] Interviews also suggest that criminal entrepreneurs have stockpiled state guns to be able to regulate supply and keep prices high. A specialised unit or commission that gathers intelligence and evidence, and identifies and retrieves state guns that have been lost, is essential. State failure led to the loss of the guns; there should now be a concerted attempt to get them back.

As I have indicated above, the government's current policy of non-engagement with key stakeholders in the firearms discussion is a big mistake. There is now substantial mistrust between the parties concerned. Previous amnesties received considerable support across all constituencies. This is no longer the case, despite the SAPS trumpeting the numbers of guns handed in during the latest amnesty in 2019/20. The numbers are in fact much lower than in previous years.

In 2011, under the auspices of the Civilian Secretariat for Police Service, a forum was established that brought CFR officials together with stakeholders and role players involved in firearms (including pro- and anti-gun groupings). The forum provided an important mechanism for the police to engage these parties over firearm regulation. The initiative was later disbanded after the police no longer wanted to participate. Government policy is effectively feeding into a growing divide between gun owners and the state. The idea of a firearms indaba has been mooted on several occasions to once again draw in cross-constituency support for an effective system of firearm control. A rethink is certainly required. Getting out of the courtroom and into the conference room is the first step that is needed.

Time to get our weapons back

The inability of the state to manage its own assets, particularly those as deadly as guns and ammunition, is a red flag indicating significant institutional breakdown in the law-enforcement environment. Not only are the safety and security of citizens at risk, but our very attempt to create and maintain a democratic state is also threatened. If the police are routinely criminal, or regularly and systematically promote criminal activity, then, by definition, they are not acting in the interests of citizens. If they respond defensively or refuse to engage on a policy of significant importance to achieving safety – proper firearms control and management – state institutions have only their interests, and not those of ordinary people badly affected by high rates of crime, at heart. Confidence building is urgently needed.

At the time of writing, the case against Irshaad Laher and Alan Raves was still moving at an achingly slow pace through the Western Cape High Court. Five years after the arrest of Prinsloo, the trial is yet to begin. Raves has made the argument that his case should be separated from that of Laher; Laher's legal representation is holding up the joint case with the fact that the state has not supplied all the relevant case dockets linking the sale of the guns to the deaths of people on the Cape Flats. As the grinding legal technicalities have been argued out in the court, interest in the case has waned. That is in the interests of those in the SAPS who do not want attention to be drawn to perhaps the biggest failure of the organisation since 1994. Justice has not yet been done.

By failing to stem the flow of firearms from its own strongrooms, the South African state has triggered significant changes in the country's criminal economy. Ordinary citizens have paid the price. Acting now will have important implications for reducing long-term crime levels. It is time to get our weapons back and under proper control.

THE UNDERWORLD'S FAVOURITE GUNS AND THEIR PRICES

There are many challenges when it comes to probing the illegal gun market. No one wants to be openly identified as a gangland gun dealer, particularly when Laher and Raves are standing trial and the issue is making news. Doing research into the illegal gun market relies on speaking to as many people who are willing to talk as possible and cross-checking the price estimates.[1]

Identifying popular gun types is not particularly challenging, but establishing the price for those guns over time is another matter. People's memory of prices is sketchy, and gang bosses and members are also prone to exaggerating the profit they may have scored in a gun sale. The solution is to try to establish a median price that filters out memory loss and the inevitable underworld overstatement.

Once the price of illegal guns had been established, the figures were compared with the prices of legal ones over time. A review of advertisements in an industry publication (*Man Magnum* magazine) provides a useful guide to the legal market. Gun dealerships also gave information on how prices have changed over time.

Popular pieces

A first step in determining gun prices is to identify which guns are popular in the underworld. The same gun types generally emerged as being popular with criminals, each for specific reasons. Take the ubiquitous Z88: this pistol is popular with gangsters for a combination of reasons. As mentioned, it is a police gun, which appears to confer a seal of legitimacy on its underworld owners. The other reasons this model is attractive are that it can be fitted with an extended magazine of 19 rounds and 9 mm ammunition can be acquired with ease.

A number of other pistols are also popular in the underworld. There is the Beretta, from which the Z88's design was copied. Others that make the grade are the Astra and the Taurus semi-automatic pistols. Both of these guns were imported into South Africa in large numbers during the sanctions era – the Astra from Spain and the Taurus from Brazil. The latter was first brought into South Africa via Lesotho during the sanctions-busting days.

A pistol quite common in the criminal fraternity, and one of the cheapest on the market, is the Norinco, a Chinese army service pistol, which has been ubiquitous in South Africa, particularly among a new generation of black gun buyers. Gangsters like the Norinco for its army connotations;[2] that the magazine can hold up to 20 rounds is an added attraction.

Also highly prized in the underworld are the Glock and the Czech-made CZ75. The Glock is liked in the underworld because of its sleek lines and reputation for indestructibility. Senior gangsters spoke too of their liking for the larger-calibre Desert Eagle, although there are very few of those around and they seem to be something of a status symbol for bosses.

When it comes to revolvers, as opposed to pistols, gangsters point out that they are good at close range, have stopping power and don't easily jam – useful in an environment where people don't always take good care of their firearms. The .38 Special is also easy to conceal. Revolvers don't eject the spent cartridges, a useful feature for hitmen who need to make a quick getaway. The .38 Special, .357 Magnum and .44 Magnum are listed by the criminal fraternity as being desirable items for experienced hitmen.

AKs and all that

Long guns, as the term denotes, comprise rifles, including automatic and semi-automatic guns, such as the AK-47 and the old South African army R1, as well as the R4 and R5. These guns all have considerable appeal for the underworld because of their impressive firepower. They are, however, much larger than handguns and more difficult to conceal. Nevertheless, every gang appears eager to have a stock of long guns for emergencies, and they have regularly disappeared from state weapon stores for this reason. Long guns are favoured in certain types of armed robbery or where intense shooting may be required, notably attacks on cash-in-transit vehicles, taxi shoot-outs and conflict between illicit mining groups.

Automatic rifles, like the state-manufactured R1, R4 and R5, are now widely used in the South African private security industry, including the grey fringes of the industry that are contracted by the taxi business. The security industry and cash-in-transit guarding companies deploy converted, semi-automatic versions of these guns because full automatics are not available for civilian sale. The modified guns are referred to as LMs, so the R4 is an LM4 and the R5 an LM5.

About half a million LMs have been sold in South Africa, and because they are no longer manufactured in the same numbers, they are highly sought after by second-hand dealers. Given the demand, there have been several new entrants, one replacement being the Dashprod, a Bulgarian weapon that can take R4 and R5 ammunition. This is used mainly by small security companies. Another is the American AR-15.

The AK-47 is one of the most widely known guns in southern Africa. It appears, for example, on the national flag of Mozambique, a tribute to its use in the regional wars of liberation. It is estimated that around 200 million AK rifles have been produced, meaning it accounts for about one out of every ten guns in circulation globally.[3] The apartheid state distributed large quantities of AK-47s in Angola, Mozambique and South Africa in the 1980s and 1990s in a strategy that sought to undermine liberation movements. Mozambique has long been a key source of AK-47s used by criminals in South Africa.[4]

Use of the AK-47 in the underworld has changed over time. Older AK-47s, smuggled in from Mozambique or from old ANC arms caches, were widely used until the mid-2000s. For example, the dominant firearm used in cash-in-transit robberies between 2003 and 2006 was the AK-47. As in the case of revolvers, their durability is an important attribute.

As Anneliese Burgess outlines in her study of cash-in-transit heists: 'The weapons of choice are AK-47s and R4 and R5 rifles. The AK-47 is used because, according to respondents, it is reliable and instils fear when shots are fired. The R4s and R5s are used because *they are easy to obtain*.'[5] (The emphasis is mine, highlighting the South African state's poor record on managing its firearm stocks.)

From 2006, there was a shift in the pattern of guns used in cash-in-transit robberies. At that point, government-manufactured R4s and R5s started to become the weapon of choice and began to appear on the streets. The shift appears to be the result of various factors. Notably, they became more available, leaking from state sources because key underworld figures had developed connections to the state.[6] These guns also have the advantage of using armour-piercing ammunition, enabling them to be used to attack the increasingly robust vehicles used to transport cash in South Africa.

The last two years have seen another change in the use of firearms in cash-in-transit heists: the reintroduction of the AK-47, this time newer versions. Some security companies now make use of these modern AK-47s and it is likely that there has been some seepage from them to the underworld too.

Comparative pricing

Gaining an idea of the prices of guns used in the underworld may tell us something about their availability and value for criminals. The chart provides an overview of prices for pistols. This includes the price when bought in bulk by a gang boss (labelled the 'boss price'), the price for sales in the underworld (the 'sale price'), and prices when purchased new and second-hand on the legal market.

Take the case of the Z88. Going on the information received from interviews, a gang boss is able to buy a Z88 for around R5 000. The legal price for the same firearm is about R6 750 new and about R3 850 used. The same Z88 can then be sold on illegally on the streets for about R15 000.

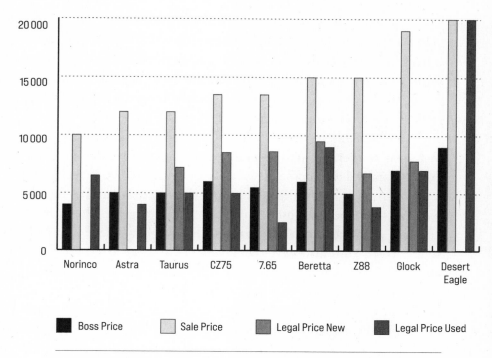

Comparative underworld and upperworld pricing estimates for selected pistols, 2019 (in rands)

This pricing distribution applies to most other firearms that are favoured by criminals. A CZ75 pistol, for example, is priced on the legal market at R5 000 used. Bosses say they can buy this gun for R6 000, well under the legal price for a new CZ75 pistol at R8 500. But willing buyers in the underworld can purchase a CZ75 for R13 500. More or less the same price variations apply to every other pistol favoured in the underworld.

The next chart provides the same sets of figures for revolvers and a selection of long guns. This time, the position is more complicated. The pricing data for revolvers in the legal market is more inconsistent than for pistols. The same seems to apply in relation to the price differentials between underworld and upperworld markets. For example, the data for the three most commonly sought-after

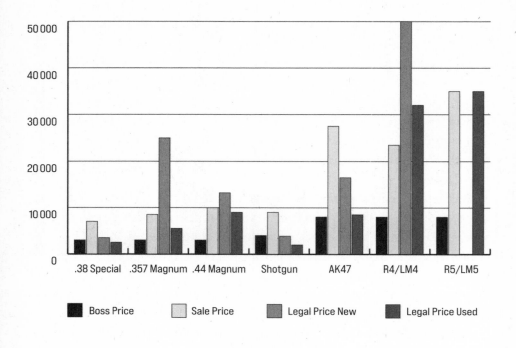

Comparative underworld and upperworld pricing estimates for selected
revolvers and long guns, 2019 (in rands)

criminal revolvers – the .38 Special, the .357 Magnum and the
.44 Magnum – all suggest that the guns are sold relatively cheaply
in the criminal market, at least compared to pistols. It has been
suggested that this may simply be a question of greater availability:
there are more older revolvers around and the market is limited to
a practised set of hitmen. Ordinary gang members would rather
have a pistol.

On the legal market, the prices of revolvers seem to see-saw much
more than those of pistols. The reported price of a .44 Magnum
increased dramatically in 2018 and 2019, having stayed fairly consistent before then. The price of a .38 Special fluctuated between 2014
and 2019 from around R7 800 to under R2 000. Again, it is difficult
to know exactly the reasons for this variability over time. Gun dealers,

however, report that revolvers are becoming less and less popular in the buyers' market.

One of the main sources of revolvers is the SAP13 stores. The .38 Specials were once a very popular choice of gun for self-defence in South Africa. They are less popular now, given the growth in the pistol market, so they are regularly handed in as part of deceased estates and stored in the station SAP13 stores before being transferred to the main armoury. The Prinsloo caches contained .38 Specials for this reason.

In the case of shotguns, the legal and illegal sale price are the same, as is the price for which they are purchased both by underworld dealers and legal users wanting a second-hand model. The reason for this is that shotguns are not really gangster guns. There is little demand, so the legal and illegal prices are relatively similar. One gang boss said that shotguns are thrown into deals as an extra to 'sweeten the pot'.

Intriguingly, automatic and semi-automatic long guns, like the R4, LM4 and AK-47, are bought cheaply by gang bosses, suggesting ready availability of underworld supply. They are then sold at a good profit. In the case of the R4/LM4, however, the guns are worth more in the legal market, partly because of demand from private security companies for the LM4. The R5/LM5 appears to have real value in the underworld; such guns are purchased at around R8 000 by crime bosses and then sold in the criminal market for approximately R35 000. This seems close to the legal price of around R35 000.

In the case of the AK-47, they are sold on the illicit market at a higher price than on the legal market. The 'boss price' for the AK-47 is around R8 000, whereas the street price is considerably higher at R27 500. Given that there is some data on global prices for illegal AK-47s it is interesting to compare these with South African prices. In dollar terms, at 2019 prices and currency conversion rates, an AK in South Africa at a 'boss price' would be around US$550, and for street buyers something in the order of US$1 900. In Afghanistan, an AK is said to sell for US$600 – a figure that is close to the South

African 'boss price'. On the Mexican border and in Pakistan, the rifle is said to be traded at around US$1 200. Similarly, in Belgium, the perpetrators of the attack on the offices of Charlie Hebdo in 2015 bought their AK-47 for $1 135.

The graph shows the divergence between the 'boss' price and the sale price, integrating the average cost of eight pistols. The prices for most pistols on the illegal market have increased over time. Take the case, for example, of the Taurus 16. In 2000, this gun would have cost you around R2 415, with a steady increase in the price to R9 743 in 2015. The price then dropped to around R6 600 in 2019. The Astra 18 has a similar trend: a price of around R1 250 in 2000, peaking at around R9 000 in 2014, and then declining to R4 000 in 2019. The Glock could be purchased for R4 355 in 2000, with the price peaking in 2016 at R11 300, and then declining to R9 032 in 2019. The Beretta shows a steep increase from 2000 (when it sold at R975), to a price of R11 198 in 2016, falling to R9 833 in 2019. The CZ75 follows a similar trajectory, with a price of R1 250 in 2000 and a peak of R9 000 in 2014, before dropping to R4 000 in 2019. The Z88 also follows this trend, although the drop in price is less steep than for other types of pistols. A Z88 is listed as costing R3 666 in 2000, peaking at R7 500 in 2015 and then dropping slightly to R6 750 in 2019.

Oddly, the two pistols that seem to be an exception to this trend are the Norinco and the 7.65. The former shows a consistent increase from a 2003 price of R1 175 to a 2019 price of R6 500, while the latter increased slowly from 2002, when it was priced at just over R1 000, to 2016, when it went for R800, before increasing to R3 450 in 2018. It is not exactly clear why this is the case.

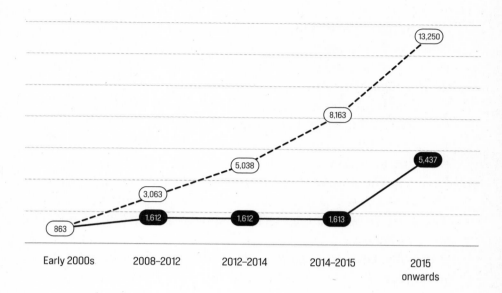

Early 2000s	2008–2012	2012–2014	2014–2015	2015 onwards

Divergence between average gun dealer and gun buyer prices averaging eight pistols in the criminal underworld, early 2000s to today (in rands).

Note: the black line shows the average reported prices for which illegal pistols were bought (often in bulk) by underworld gun dealers and the dashed line is the price for which they were sold on (generally individually) into the wider illegal market.

ANNEX II

PAPERS DRAWN – RECENT LEGAL BATTLES AROUND GUN CONTROL

The inefficient functioning of the CFR, combined with the government's increasing unwillingness to engage on gun control, led to a well of frustration and a rallying cry from pro-gun groups who used the state's weak and inconsistent approach to gun control to mobilise support. Government was soon embroiled in a series of court challenges driven largely by the ineffective, unpredictable and uneven activities of the SAPS, and the CFR in particular.

Two issues in particular have significantly restricted the number of licence holders falling within the provisions of the Firearms Control Act. Although the reasons are technical, they are central to understanding how the system is being eroded.

The status of these licences is the first issue causing uncertainty. There are some 1.75 million private citizens who possess firearm licences, and more than 3 million licences have been issued under the Firearms Control Act. Approximately 700 000 (Gun Free SA suggest the figure may be over a million[1]) people hold licences issued under the previous Act which have not been converted to the post-2000 licensing regime.[2]

Green and white licences
The licences issued under the 1969 Arms and Ammunition Act are commonly referred to as 'green licences', given that they were attached to the green South African identity book. It was envisaged that on the passing of the new Act in 2000 green-licence holders would have to take steps to convert their licences to so-called 'white licences' (issued under the 2000 Act) during a transitional phase. As

per the stipulations of the new gun-control regime, this would mean that licence holders would have to apply for a renewal, the timing of which would be dependent on the type and purpose of the firearm.

A court challenge in 2009 by the South African Hunters and Game Conservation Association to determine the constitutionality of certain provisions of the 2000 Act resulted in an interim interdict under which green licences remained valid. There were thus no steps required of their holders, including no requirement to renew them, until such time as the case could be heard. The judge in that case was Bill Prinsloo (no relation to Christiaan Prinsloo, I assume) of the Gauteng High Court, widely seen as sympathetic to gun owners. Bizarrely, since the government has never lodged an answering affidavit, no date for the hearing has ever been set down, and the interim interdict has remained in force, effectively creating two classes of gun licences – green and white.

The government's thinking on this issue remains unclear, although it has been suggested that the failure to lodge an answering affidavit is based on a recognition that the current system would not be able to manage the volume of green licences that would then be submitted for renewal. In theory, at least, renewal may require firearms to be handed to the SAPS for safekeeping. No public statement from the CFR or the ministry has been forthcoming on the issue. In effect, holders of green gun licences fall outside of the renewal provisions of the Act.

The second, and related, issue weakening the current system is the question of renewals of firearm licences granted under the 2000 Act. An important provision of the Firearms Control Act was that licences could be valid only for a limited period of time and then require renewal, based on the owner demonstrating again that he or she was competent to handle and store the weapon, and was in need of it. The old licensing system was for life: once granted, it required no renewal.

The new approach to firearm ownership, then, is similar to the one that all South African drivers are familiar with, whereby a new driving licence has to be applied for every five years. The same period applies to a licence to possess a firearm for self-defence.[3]

If a renewal is not granted, is delayed or is not applied for, then effectively the firearm is held illegally.

Constitutional Court ruling

The provisions around the renewal of firearm licences were challenged in court by the South African Hunters and Game Conservation Association on several grounds, including that they are vague and violate the protection of property. In June 2018, the Constitutional Court unanimously ruled that gun owners must renew their licences or forfeit their guns. Significantly, as noted in Chapter 13, the Constitutional Court ruled unanimously that gun ownership is not a fundamental right, but a privilege regulated through legislation.[4]

While the Constitutional Court did note that 'the apparent problems in the administration of the Act are of legitimate concern', it held that this was not something that required consideration in a case that effectively was only examining the legal provisions of the Act.[5] The reality is that the system of firearm control, in other words the CFR, is not able to process such a large number of applicants. As a result of the judgment, one important question that has arisen is where and who should store the firearms when the application for renewal is being processed. DFOs acted in different ways to different licence holders applying for renewal, causing much confusion. There were also contradictory statements issued by the SAPS.

The ruling of the Constitutional Court threw a cat among the pigeons. A considerable number of gun owners had not applied for a renewal of their licences – the number could be has high as 450 000. Things have recently become even more complicated. A new application was made to the Gauteng High Court by Gun Owners of South Africa, which again challenged the system of renewals. Remarkably, Bill Prinsloo was again the judge in the case. He issued an interim order to the effect that the police could not seize the guns of those whose licences had not been renewed. Gun owners could be excused for getting confused. In any event, the pressure on them to renew their licences was lifted. The Minister of Police appealed.

In May 2020, the Supreme Court of Appeal in Bloemfontein issued a scathing judgment, which labelled the actions of Bill Prinsloo 'unusual, troubling and regrettable'. The judge, it seems, had worked with Gun Owners of South Africa to make amendments to the order they had proposed. The Appeal Court said that Prinsloo had not acted as an independent and impartial judge. The Appeal Court ruled that a court of law could not in effect change what was the purpose of the legislation, in this case that firearm licences required renewal.[6]

While there is now more clarity, the impact of this legal back-and-forth over time, and of the frustration among several interested parties as to the level of communication from the government, is a general impasse in the firearms control regime. On one hand, at the time of writing, old (green) licence holders are effectively excluded from the provisions of the 2000 Act; on the other hand, the renewal requirements, a key provision of the new firearms control regime, apply to post-2004 (white) licence holders. What has also occurred in this period is that new licences continue to be issued, causing the overall number of licences to grow. This is ironic given that the objective of gun-control policy since 1994 has been to reduce the number of privately held firearms.

GETTING RID OF THE GUNS?
FIREARM AMNESTIES

A firearm amnesty is declared in terms of section 139(3) of the Firearms Control Act, which makes provision for people to hand in their guns without fear of prosecution for illegal ownership. This does not apply if the gun has been used in a crime, and no one handing in a gun is exempt from prosecution if it was found to have been used in an unlawful act. Ballistic testing will be conducted to determine this, although it is largely a waste of time, and it would in any event be impossible to make the link to criminal cases even if murderers were to hand in their weapons.

The experience of previous amnesties is worth some consideration. The first was held for a single day, on 16 December 1994, in the context of South Africa's transition to democracy. Some 900 weapons and 7 000 rounds of ammunition were handed in – a relatively small number given the volumes of guns circulating at the time. This amnesty was a bold but essentially symbolic event, and people who owned legal or illegal firearms may have been inclined to hold onto them, not yet confident that the new democracy was secure.[1]

The second amnesty was for six months, January to June 2005. Police figures show that 78 893 firearms and firearm parts were handed in during this period. Interestingly, in this case, most of the firearms submitted were licensed, at just under 60 per cent.[2] The vast majority of the rest were cases where owners had not properly registered their firearms or they were from deceased estates. The amnesty was accompanied by a publicity campaign. It is fair to say that very few firearms from the criminal underworld made their way to police stations as a result of the amnesty.

The third amnesty took place for four months from January to April

2010. In this case, just under three-quarters of all firearms collected (30 442) were held legally, while the remainder[3] were not properly registered or were from deceased estates rather than from criminals.[4]

The results of the three amnesties, particularly the 2005 one, made some dents in the numbers of guns in circulation. Large quantities of legal and illegal ammunition were also handed in – 1 880 710 rounds in the 2005 and 2010 amnesties. There is consensus, however, that none addressed the issue of illegal guns in criminal hands.

It is worth noting here too that the law provides for the handing in of legally owned guns at any police station at any time. Although the available data does suggest that around 5 000 such cases occur every year outside of amnesties, and 15 000 firearms were handed in in the 2016/17 reporting period without an amnesty being called,[5] it is clear that the amnesties have the positive effect of publicising the possibility of handing in weapons.

During the 2019/20 amnesty, the response has been poor. Although the police have talked up the amount, with some 1 500 guns handed in during December 2019, the figure is well below that of previous amnesties. (The previous amnesty saw some 13 000 fire-arms being submitted every month.)[6] The spread of the coronavirus and the subsequent lockdown intervened and, at the time of the writing, the amnesty has been extended.

This success of the first three amnesties is somewhat clouded by evidence that the guns that citizens handed in were not prop-erly disposed of. To reiterate, if an amnesty results in a pooling of firearms without their being destroyed it is counter-effective, as it creates greater risk than if these guns had been held in people's homes. Large stores of firearms are vulnerable to bulk purchase by criminals eager to make a significant mark-up.

In the case of the 2019/20 amnesty, the suggestion from the gov-ernment that the police should retain control of citizens' firearms while the licence renewal process runs its course poses particular dangers. It would be far safer to find a way to renew licences while firearms remain in the custody of their owners.

Amnesties and public trust

Regulation 93(4) of the Firearms Control Regulations of 2004 stipulates that firearms handed in during an amnesty must be destroyed within six months of the completion of the amnesty. So far so good. There are, however, numerous reports, including of oversight visits conducted by the National Assembly Portfolio Committee and the Civilian Secretariat for Police Service to police stations and facilities, that found guns that had not been disposed of well after this period. Firearms handed in have been found unattended in police station SAP13 stores. Criminals are well aware of the SAP13 system as a good source of firearms that are easy to acquire.

Shockingly, and besides the Prinsloo case, there are numerous cases where firearms handed in during the 2005 and 2010 amnesties have landed up in the criminal underworld. A tragic example is that of a firearm handed in during the 2010 amnesty at the Tugela Ferry police station in KwaZulu-Natal that was then used during an armed robbery of a Gauteng Spar, in which the owner was shot and killed.[7] The notorious Norwood guns, the story of which was recounted in the concluding chapter, is another case.

Little is known of the leakage of ammunition that was handed in, but it is highly likely – given that ammunition is less easily recorded than a gun – that it is relatively easy to remove and sell. Gangsters report that they have bought ammunition from the police.

Unsurprisingly, given the politics now surrounding the issue of licensing and gun control in general in South Africa, the process around the 2020 amnesty has been fraught. The police said that on this occasion a special effort would be made to secure the guns. But then their actions immediately undermined this.

Certain police stations, for example, were identified as high risk because of their history of losing firearms. Police management told Parliament that there were 46 stations that senior officers did not think were up to collecting and storing firearms that might be handed in. It's worth dwelling on that number: 46 stations that the police themselves would not trust with the task of safely storing firearms. These stations, it was said, would not be allowed to accept amnesty firearms.[8] However, the number of unsafe stations was rapidly reduced to just three: Isipingo in KwaZulu-Natal, Bellville South in Cape Town, and Kanyamazane in Mpumalanga.[9]

In the presentations to Parliament in October 2019, SAPS management also admitted that there were police officers with criminal records dealing with ballistics and firearms processing.[10]

There are other questions that suggest that the process may be less secure than hoped. The police have rejected the idea of independent monitoring of the amnesty process (in the past this was done by the civilian secretariat) and, instead, the SAPS has developed an internal monitoring and audit system. How could this even be contemplated, given the evidence available of police complicity, quite apart from the Prinsloo case? Independent oversight of the process should therefore be a prerequisite.

NOTES

PREFACE

1 Zeederberg was by all accounts one of the most skilled and resourceful individuals in the employ of the South African arms industry. He was reputed to spend hours on the factory floor inspecting production and interacting with technicians. It was his efforts that were to make the Z88 a long-enduring firearm. The Beretta 92F was re-engineered by Lyttelton Engineering to a high standard. Lyttelton would eventually make the pistols available to the commercial market too, with the Z88 also forming the basis for a better and highly successful follow-on series, the SP, and a compact version called appropriately the Baby Z. A small number of cosmetic changes were introduced in the design, but the Z88 was essentially a sophisticated, durable and high-quality copy of the Beretta.

2 The best overview of the history of the Z88 is in C Lotter (ed.), *Firearms Developed and Manufactured in Southern Africa 1949–2000: A Reference Guide by the Pretoria Arms and Ammunition Association*. Pretoria: PAAA, 2017, 89–125.

3 Laher is currently facing charges but has denied guilt.

4 A copy of the video is in the author's possession. It may be found online at https://vimeo.com/86853059.

5 These numbers have changed over time as the court case against Prinsloo has proceeded. The numbers here are taken from an affidavit, JV10 of 3 October 2016, in the case of POPCRU, Vearey and Jacobs vs the Minister of Police and others, case number C671/2016.

6 The police shootings at Marikana, for example, resulted in the deaths of 34 people. The comparison is not intended to detract from the impact of the massacre at Marikana, but only to show how deadly the theft and sale of police firearms have been.

7 R Matzopoulos et al. A retrospective time trend study of firearm and non-firearm homicide in Cape Town from 1994 to 2013, *South African Medical Journal*, 108, 3 (2013), 197–204.

8 BBC News, South Africa crime: Can the country be compared to a 'war zone'?, 18 September 2018, https://www.bbc.com/news/world-africa-45547975. The United Nations Office on Drugs and Crime (UNODC) has an online database of homicide statistics by city. When comparing Cape Town's homicide numbers with those of other cities which are in non-conflict zones but notorious for violence, it is evident that Cape Town is among the most dangerous cities. See UNODC, Global study on homicide, 2019, https://www.unodc.org/unodc/en/data-and-analysis/global-study-on-homicide.html. The book explores this issue later.

9 Interview with Dale Michler, former subcontractor to Netstar vehicle tracking, Johannesburg, 21 November 2019.

10 As an illustration, and for recent cases, see: N Seleka, Two JMPD officers and a police constable among five suspects arrested for armed robbery, *News24*, 28 November 2019, https://www.news24.com/SouthAfrica/News/two-jmpd-officers-and-a-police-constable-among-five-suspects-arrested-for-armed-robbery-20191128; Staff reporter, Cops bust two Cape men for stolen furniture, appliances worth R72 000, *IOL*, 23 December 2019, https://www.iol.co.za/capeargus/news/cops-bust-two-cape-men-for-stolen-furniture-appliances-worth-r72-000-39664972; ANA reporter, Three arrested for illegal firearms as crackdown on Mitchells Plain continues, *IOL*, 17 December 2019, https://www.iol.co.za/news/south-africa/western-cape/three-arrested-for-illegal-firearms-as-crackdown-on-mitchells-plain-continues-39345969.

11 This was mentioned by serving and retired police officers in the course of researching the book.

12 See, for example, Police bust four suspects in Krugersdorp for illegal mining and possession of unlicensed firearms, *iReport South Africa*, 3 October, 2019, https://ireportsouthafrica.co.za/2019/10/03/police-bust-four-suspects-in-krugersdorp-for-illegal-mining-and-possession-of-unlicensed-firearms/.

CHAPTER 1

1 This is the groundbreaking study of organised crime in Chicago by John Landesco published in 1929, cited in V Ruggiero, *Understanding Political Violence: A Criminological Analysis*. Maidenhead: Open University Press, 2006, 74.

2 M Wiener, *Ministry of Crime: An Underworld Explored*. Johannesburg: Pan Macmillan, 2018, 393.

3 N Prince, Alleged gang boss shot in arm, leg, *IOL*, 10 May, 2013, https://www.iol.co.za/news/alleged-gang-boss-shot-in-arm-leg-1513702.

4 The best record of this important period in gang evolution is from the well-informed Irvin Kinnes. See I Kinnes, From urban street gangs to criminal empires: The changing face of the gangs in the Western Cape, Institute for Security Studies, June 2000, https://issafrica.s3.amazonaws.com/site/uploads/Mono48.pdf.

5 These attempts to build a united gang boss front are fascinating, and Stanfield was key. See W Schärf and C Vale, The firm – organized crime comes of age during the transition to democracy, *Social Dynamics,* 22, 2 (1996), 30–36.

6 See R-L Francke, LOOK: Alleged gang kingpin dishes out money to community, *IOL*, 18 April 2017, https://www.iol.co.za/news/south-africa/western-cape/look-alleged-gang-kingpin-dishes-out-money-to-community-8703134.

7 Murder of Cape Town gang leader Rashied Staggie brings an uneasy peace as assassination theories abound, Global Initiative Against Transnational Organized Crime, Risk Bulletin of the Civil Society Observatory of Illicit Economies in Eastern and Southern Africa, March–April 2020, https://globalinitiative.net/wp-content/uploads/2020/04/RB6.03.04.web_.pdf.

8 Hassan's sister was quoted in F Villette and D Adriaanse, Lawyer Hassan laid to rest, *IOL*, 8 November 2016, https://www.iol.co.za/capetimes/news/lawyer-hassan-laid-to-rest-2088194.

9   Interview with Noorudien Hassan's mother and brother in Cape Town in August 2018.

10 L Brolen, D Wilson and E Yardley, Hitmen and the spaces of contract killing: The doorstep hitmen, *Journal of Investigative Psychology and Offender Profiling*, 13 (2016), 220–221.

11 I was a young recruit to the national Secretariat for Safety and Security at the time. I was tasked with following up and reporting on police successes in the investigations.

12 This statement is consistent with interview material provided by several gang members and leaders about PAGAD. In this case, the interview was conducted in Mitchells Plain in July 2018.

13 There do not appear to be any media reports of this incident. Given the volume of police activity and crime on the Cape Flats, this is perhaps no surprise.

14 Personal communication, Cape Town, September 2018.

CHAPTER 2

1   D Middleton and M Levi, Let sleeping lawyers lie: Organized crime, lawyers and the regulation of legal services, *British Journal of Criminology*, 55 (2015), 647–668.

2   L-A Daniels, Who was Pete Mihalik?, *IOL*, 30 October 2018, https://www.iol. co.za/news/south-africa/western-cape/who-was-pete-mihalik-17698131.

3   'Drip by drip, the rock of their integrity is eroded away' by the lure of drug money, concluded an authority on the issue. See S Taylor, Criminal lawyers and lawyers who turn criminal, *The New York Times*, 19 March 1985, https://www. nytimes.com/1985/03/19/us/criminal-lawyers-and-lawyers-who-turn-criminal. html. A former Cape Town defence lawyer, now a prosecutor, told a Global Initiative conference in Cape Town in November 2019: 'When I started out, I was a criminal defence attorney and I worked for gangsters and even competing gangsters. Often we would get paid off the books. We were on a sort of retainer for them, that if they got caught we would have to get out of our pjs in the middle of the night to go bail them out. And they paid you well for it. But I couldn't do that forever because they are difficult to work with and demanding.' GI-TOC, USAID, Centre of Criminology - University of Cape Town and Institute for Security Studies, Criminal Market Convergence in Southern Africa: An assessment and innovative responses, UCT Business School, 8 November 2019.

4   See, for example, the case of Dutch lawyer Evert Hingst, covered in H Nelen and F Lankhorst, Facilitating organized crime: The role of lawyers and notaries, in D Siegel and H Nelen, *Organized Crime: Culture, Markets and Policies*. New York: Springer, 2008, 127–143.

5   A Hyman and P Nombembe, Shot Cape Town lawyer 'died because he failed to deliver', *Times Live*, 9 December 2019, https://www.timeslive.co.za/news/south-africa/2019-12-09-shot-cape-town-lawyer-died-because-he-failed-to-deliver/; on the murder of Advocate Vernon Jantjies, see also P Nombembe, Lawyers are under siege: Friend of advocate gunned down in Cape Town, *Times Live*, 2 December 2019, https://www.timeslive.co.za/news/south-africa/2019-12-02-lawyers-are-under-siege-friend-of-advocate-gunned-down-in-cape-town/.

6   See Violence aimed at lawyers threatens to undermine the criminal-justice system in South Africa, Risk Bulletin of the Civil Society Observatory of Illicit Economies in Eastern and Southern Africa, Issue 7, April–May 2020, https://globalinitiative.net/wp-content/uploads/2020/05/GI-Risk-Bulletin-007-04May1845-proof-5.pdf.

7   Section 252A of the Act provides that the police 'may make use of a trap or engage in an undercover operation', the evidence from which would be admissible in court if a number of conditions are met. Among these are whether permission had been sought and obtained, whether the crime was of a serious nature and the 'degree of persistence' of the state in attempting to persuade someone to engage in the crime.

8   C Dolley, *The Enforcers: Inside Cape Town's Deadly Nightclub Battles.* Johannesburg: Jonathan Ball Publishers, 2019, 82.

9   It is still a little unclear exactly what was found. References are made to an 'investigation diary', 'documents' and 'records'. I have used material here from an interview with a senior police officer and someone close to Hassan. For press coverage, there is a good summary in C Dolley, 'EXCLUSIVE: Confidential info leak in stolen cop guns case involving 3 028 dockets', *News24,* 26 May 2017, https://www.news24.com/SouthAfrica/News/exclusive-confidential-info-leak-in-stolen-cop-guns-case-involving-3-028-dockets-20170526.

10 I am joined in this opinion by several senior gang bosses who provided their views on the likely culprits.

11 Interview with Yaseen Hassan, 16 August 2018, Cape Town. Interestingly, Nafiz Modack also claimed in 2018 that Vearey had been behind the murder of Hassan, but for different reasons. See C Dolley, *The Enforcers: Inside Cape Town's Deadly Nightclub Battles.* Johannesburg: Jonathan Ball Publishers, 2019, 83.

12 G Serra, China Town guard killed for his gun, *Daily Voice,* 7 November 2016, https://www.dailyvoice.co.za/news/western-cape/china-town-guard-killed-for-his-gun-6618422.

13 See M Duval, 'Closet killer' gets 30 years for murder and robbery spree, *IOL,* 5 March 2020, https://www.iol.co.za/news/south-africa/western-cape/closet-killer-gets-30-years-for-murder-and-robbery-spree-44167323.

14 See, for example, M Duval, 'Closet killer' robbed me, *Daily Voice,* 24 August 2018, https://www.dailyvoice.co.za/news/western-cape/closet-killer-robbed-me-16714735.

15 As the sentences will run concurrently, Haywood will effectively serve a 30-year sentence. See M Duval, 'Closet killer' gets 30 years for murder and robbery spree, *IOL,* 5 March 2020, https://www.iol.co.za/news/south-africa/western-cape/closet-killer-gets-30-years-for-murder-and-robbery-spree-44167323.

CHAPTER 3

1   This data was compiled by researchers at the Global Initiative Against Transnational Organized Crime, drawing on interviews with gang members, community members and police across the Cape Flats.

2   The figure of 100 000 was given during several interviews with SAPS representatives and matches the Global Initiative Against Transnational Organized Crime's calculations of gang membership numbers.

3   See https://vimeo.com/86853059 A copy of the video is also in the author's possession.

4   AmaBhungane, Zuma's 'deal' with Cape gang bosses, *Mail & Guardian*, 20 November 2015, https://mg.co.za/article/2015-11-20-00-zumas-deal-with-cape-gang-bosses/.

5   Interviews, people close to the gang and the family, August 2019.

CHAPTER 4

1   See the 5 March 2011 post at https://bruindamaged.wordpress.com/.

2   Based on legal advice at the time, we did not name him directly. See M Shaw and K Thomas, Ending the cycles of violence: Gangs, protest and response in Western Johannesburg, 1994–2019, Global Initiative against Transnational Organized Crime, 2019, https://globalinitiative.net/gang-cycles-johannesburg/.

3   While it was reported in the media that Boonzaaier himself was subsequently shot and killed hours after Staggie, he is, at the time of writing, still very much alive.

4   C Dolley, *The Enforcers: Inside Cape Town's Deadly Nightclub Battles*. Johannesburg: Jonathan Ball Publishers, 2019, 30.

5   Personal communication, senior member of an organised criminal group with good knowledge of these activities, November 2020.

6   Cape gangster gets VIP invite to Zuma's party, *News24*, 27 April 2014, https://www.news24.com/SouthAfrica/Politics/Cape-gangster-gets-VIP-invite-to-Zumas-party-20140427 Accessed 16 January 2020.

7   C Dolley, EXCLUSIVE: Duduzane Zuma's mystery meeting with underworld figure Nafiz Modack, *News24*, 10 January 2018, https://www.news24.com/SouthAfrica/News/exclusive-duduzane-zumas-mystery-meeting-with-underworld-figure-nafiz-modack-20180110.

8   N Jele, Businessman Mark Lifman loses SCA appeal bid in tax row with SARS, *News24*, 1 March 2020, https://www.news24.com/news24/southafrica/news/businessman-mark-lifman-loses-sca-appeal-bid-in-tax-row-with-sars-20200301.

CHAPTER 5

1   SAPS Annual Report 2006/2007.

2   Ministerial answer in Parliament, April, 2010.

3   Something seems seriously wrong with SAPS firearms data management. The figures for Gauteng for the year 2010/11 show 1 344 SAPS firearm losses. The national figure provided for the same year is 1 355. The same applies in the following year, 2012/13: the figure for Gauteng is 840, while the total SAPS firearms reported as lost for the year was 834. At first, the SAPS Annual Report for 2012/13 suggested 2 200 police firearms were lost or stolen, but this was adjusted down to 834 in the following year's report. According to data released by the police under a Promotion of Access to Information Act request by AfriForum, the

SAPS could not account for 7 829 police issue firearms between 2009 and 2014. For the same period, the figures of lost or stolen SAPS firearms in the official data show just under 1 000 more firearms, at 8 662.

4   If a police officer was transferred from one station to another, the officer would take the firearm with him or her, although, in theory at least, it seems that they should have left it at the station where they had worked. An audit would have shown that firearm to be missing or unaccounted for, and the firearm would have been recorded as such. The figures from 2011 show only those firearms officially reported as stolen or lost.

5   In Jacomina van Niekerk's detailed study of three stations, approximately 40 per cent of all incidents could be regarded as negligent, with the rest classified as a result of 'unlawful acts perpetrated against' police officers. However, Van Niekerk concludes that 'these figures should be treated with caution, as there are indications that members are often untruthful about the circumstances under which they lose their firearms.' See J F van Niekerk, Control of state firearms by members of the South African Police Service in three cluster areas in Gauteng, thesis submitted in partial fulfilment of the requirements for Magister Technologiae: Policing, Tshwane University of Technology, 2017, 88.

6   Ibid., 109.

7   Ibid., 146.

8   It should be noted that this percentage does not refer to the same set of firearms: those guns being recovered in a specific period were not necessarily lost in the same period. During this period, 3 841 police-issue firearms were reported as lost or stolen, and 688 were recovered. The 66 per cent recovery rate for civilian guns announced by the police can be tested by looking at those year-by-year figures that the police have provided on civilian gun recoveries. Numbers for civilian firearms lost and stolen, combined with a number for recoveries (again, to emphasise, these are not necessarily the same firearms, but year-by-year corresponding totals), are available for four recent years (2013/14, 2014/15, 2015/16 and 2017/18). Over those four years, a total of 28 471 civilian guns were reported as lost or stolen, and 16 947 were recovered. That is a recovery rate of some 60 per cent: below what the police reported, but still high.

9   From figures provided by the SAPS, the number of individual guns reported as stolen by police officers was 27 128 over the period from 2001 to the end of the 2017/2018 financial year. According to numbers reported to the Small Arms Survey, the service owns 258 066 guns (see A Karp, Estimating global law enforcement firearms numbers, briefing paper. Geneva: Small Arms Survey, June 2018). So that is around 10 per cent, assuming the number of guns that the SAPS owned remained relatively constant.

10   This point was raised in several interviews but there is no clear evidence that he did so.

11   Just how hard it is to get an accurate sense of what may have gone missing from SAP 13 stores is illustrated by the complicated way such thefts are recorded. If a theft of a firearm from the stores is detected, then a case of 'theft of firearm' is opened in the Crime Administration System and a docket opened

by an investigating officer. There is no reference in the electronic system to the fact that the firearm was stolen from police custody itself (this would require a specific crime code), so there is no way of determining which police stations, for example, showed the greatest problems.

12 Laher has denied the charges and his case is still pending.

13 The phrase was used in several interviews with gang members who had knowledge of the gun transfers.

CHAPTER 6

1 The community activist in question is very well informed and reliable. Personal communication, 2018 and 2019.

2 Laher's alleged involvement is consistent with evidence presented during his ongoing trial. Laher has denied the allegations, saying he was targeted because of his love of weaponry and hunting.

3 SAPS statistics show that, nationally, in 2007/08, there were 13 335 cases of illegal possession of firearms and ammunition. This had increased to 16 134 ten years later. The rate of increase is lower in the Western Cape, but still present, from 2 299 cases in 2007/08 to 2 929 in 2016/17. There is also a notable jump in the numbers in 2010/11, with 2 886 cases.

4 A D Emmert, G Penly Hall and A J Lizotte, Do weapons facilitate adolescent delinquency? An examination of weapon carrying and delinquency among adolescents, *Crime & Delinquency*, 64, 3 (2018), 355.

5 Interview with a senior executive responsible for mine security and formerly a state security official, Johannesburg, November 2019; interview with a private security manager involved in vehicle tracking and armed response, Johannesburg, November 2019.

6 9,5m rounds of SAPS ammunition lost in six years – Pieter Groenewald, *PoliticsWeb*, 11 August 2019, https://www.politicsweb.co.za/politics/95-million-rounds-of-ammunition-lost-in-six-years-.

7 A Plüddermann, B Myers and C Parry, Surge in treatment admissions related to methamphetamine use in Cape Town, South Africa: Implications for public health, *Drug and Alcohol Review*, 27, March 2008, 185.

8 S Haysom, Hiding in plain sight: Heroin's stealthy takeover of South Africa and what to do about it, ENACT, April 2019, https://enactafrica.org/research/policy-briefs/hiding-in-plain-sight-heroins-stealthy-takeover-of-south-africa.

9 See the numbers and explanation in A Kriegler and M Shaw, *A Citizen's Guide to Crime Trends in South Africa*. Johannesburg: Jonathan Ball, 2016, 178–179.

10 It should be noted that calculating murder rates gets difficult at local station level, because the census boundaries don't match the police station boundaries. For the areas included (Manenberg, Delft and Elsies River) where the policing boundaries were bigger than the census boundaries, the populations of the additional surrounding neighbourhoods (which weren't included in the census boundaries) were added to make the population match that of the jurisdiction of the policing boundaries. Population numbers are based on the most recent census of 2011.

11 The BBC has done a useful fact check on the subject. See South Africa crime: Can the country be compared to a 'war zone'?, *BBC News*, 18 September 2018, https://www.bbc.com/news/world-africa-45547975.
12 These numbers are from the official SAPS crime statistics reports per station area.
13 Based on a detailed review of crime statistics per station area across the Cape Flats.
14 This is a theme that emerges from multiple interviews, including with parents of children who have been killed.
15 A Braga and P Cook, The association of firearm caliber with likelihood of death from gunshot injury in criminal assaults, *JAMA Network Open*, 1, 3 (27 July 2018), 1–10.
16 This data is from a presentation given by Bronwen Davies of the Division of Forensic Medicine and Toxicology at the University of Cape Town at the Safety and Violence Initiative Conference, Preventing Violence and Promoting Safety in Fragile and Insecure Environments, Cape Town, 27–28 November 2017.
17 See, for example, N Campbell, J Colville, Y van der Heyde and A van As, Firearm injuries to children in Cape Town, South Africa: Impact of the 2004 Firearms Control Act, *South African Journal of Surgery*, 51, 3 (August 2013), 92–96. Data for 2007 appears to be consistently low, with an increase thereafter.
18 The study noted in its conclusion, however, that an upswing was occurring. See R Matzopoulos et al, Where have all the gun deaths gone?, *South African Medical Journal*, 106, 6 (June 2016), 589–591.
19 R Matzopoulos et al, A retrospective time trend study of firearm and non-firearm homicide in Cape Town from 1994 to 2013, *South African Medical Journal*, 108, 3 (March 2018), 201.
20 The data is from A Wichers, Firearm fatalities examined at Salt River medico-legal laboratory in 2009 and their investigative outcome by 2014, thesis submitted to the University of Cape Town in partial fulfilment of MPhil in biomedical forensic science, February 2016.

CHAPTER 7

1 A Faull, *Police Work and Identity: A South African Ethnography*. Oxford: Routledge, 2018.
2 In the High Court of South Africa in the matter between Irshad Laher and the Director of Public Prosecutions, Western Cape: The Respondent's Heads of Argument in Opposition to an Interlocutory Application for Access to Police Dockets, case No: CC 21/2016, 14 November 2019, 2.
3 Details of Jeremy Vearey's career can be found in several places, but a good overview is in his own affidavit to the Labour Court, in the matter between the Prison and Police Civil Rights Union and others and the Minister of Police and others, sworn on 3 October 2016.
4 A Hyman, Suspected underworld boss accuses would-be top cop of asking for bribes, *Sunday Times*, 13 October 2019, https://www.timeslive.co.za/sunday-times/news/2019-10-13-listen-suspected-underworld-boss-accuses-would-be-top-cop-of-asking-for-bribes/.

5 T Simpson, *Umkhonto We Sizwe: The ANC's Armed Struggle.* Cape Town: Penguin Random House South Africa, 2016.

6 AC/99/0027, Truth and Reconciliation Commission, Amnesty Committee, Application in Terms of Section 18 of the Promotion of National Unity and Reconciliation Act No. 24 of 1995, Jeffrey Theodore Benzien, Applicant (AM 5314/97), Decision.

7 Some details of Peter Jacobs's career are to be found in the Khayelitsha Commission evidence. See Commission of Inquiry into Allegations of Police Inefficiency in Khayelitsha and a Breakdown in Relations Between the Community and Police in Khayelitsha Phase One, Major General Peter Jacobs, 6007–6355 of Commission transcript, 28 March 2014.

8 Q Myala, Zille arrest claims nonsense, says Vearey, *IOL*, https://www.iol.co.za/news/zille-arrest-claims-nonsense-says-vearey-2079344.

9 J Vearey, *Jeremy Vannie Elsies.* Cape Town: Tafelberg, 2018, 1.

10 Affidavit, Jeremy Alan Vearey, In the Labour Court of South Africa, Cape Town, in the matter between the Prison and Police Civil Rights Union et al and the Minister of Police, sworn on 3 October 2016, 10.

11 For example, senior SAPS investigator Charl Kinnear, testified in court during a bail application for Modack between December 2017 and February 2018, that Modack had identified Tiyo as a senior police officer who could "sort it out" when he had problems. See C Dolley and S Sole, SAPS Wars part 1: The blurry blue line between the cops and the Cape underworld, *amaBhungane*, 4 March 2019, https://amabhungane.org/stories/saps-wars-part-1-the-blurry-blue-line-between-the-cops-and-the-cape-underworld/.

12 C Dolley, Exclusive: Duduzane Zuma's mystery meeting with underworld figure Nafiz Modack, *News24*, 10 January 2018, https://www.news24.com/SouthAfrica/News/exclusive-duduzane-zumas-mystery-meeting-with-underworld-figure-nafiz-modack-20180110.

13 Interview with Noorudien Hassan's brother, Cape Town, July 2017.

14 Sworn statement of Clive Joseph Ontong (labelled JV10) attached to court documents in the Labour Law case between Vearey and Jacobs and the SAPS, 13 September 2016.

CHAPTER 8

1 The SAPS' strategic vision and mission to 'prevent and combat crime' can be found in the organisation's 2020-2025 Strategic Plan, https://www.saps.gov.za/about/stratframework/strategic_plan/2020_2021/saps_strategic_plan_2020to2025.pdf.

2 Police investigators did not say this directly, but in interviews I was left with the impression that Naidoo must have been providing information before Prinsloo's arrest.

3 See the references in A Kirsten, Simpler, better, faster: Review of the 2005 firearms amnesty, Institute for Security Studies Paper 134, April 2007.

4 Amnesty nets mostly legal guns, *News24*, 17 January 2005, https://www.news24.com/News24/Amnesty-nets-mostly-legal-guns-20050117

5   Personal communication, Jenni Irish-Qhobosheane, researcher, May 2020.
6   The way in which police officers join the SAPS as a way to achieve upward mobility, both for themselves and their families, is conveyed in Andrew Faull's *Police Work and Identity: A South African Ethnography*. Oxford: Routledge, 2018.
7   The 2020 pre-tax annual salary for a police colonel was in the region of R840 000 (correspondence with SAPS human-resources officer, 17 August 2020).
8   Interview with Martin Hood, Johannesburg, December 2019.
9   The bail was set at R5 000, which seems very low under the circumstances.
10 Quoted in M Mortlock, WC community pickets against alleged gun peddlers, *EWN*, https://ewn.co.za/2016/05/20/WC-community-pickets-against-alleged-gun-peddlers-outside-court.
11 Quoted in M Baadjies, They are murderers, *Daily Voice*, 25 July 2016, https://www.dailyvoice.co.za/news/watch-they-are-murderers-5391344.
12 M de Wee, Former cop who sold guns to gangs seemingly released before serving third of sentence, 20 October 2020, *Netwerk24*, https://www.news24.com/news24/southafrica/news/former-cop-who-sold-guns-to-gangs-seemingly-released-before-serving-third-of-sentence-20201020.
13 Ibid.
14 Personal communication with Adèle Kirsten, Gun Free South Africa, May 2020.

CHAPTER 9

1   Interview, senior police investigators, Cape Town, October 2017.
2   G Serra, Spur owner accused of selling guns to gangsters, *IOL*, 29 June 2016, https://www.iol.co.za/news/spur-owner-accused-of-selling-guns-to-gangsters-2039689.
3   See the South African Hajj and Umrah Council's accreditation list, https://www.hajjumrahinfo.co.za/sahuc_accreditation/2020/Accreditation_List-1st-release-3430-090120-web-list.pdf.
4   By late 2017, Modack was much in the news, but that was a decade later. As noted earlier, he had seemingly emerged out of nowhere in an attempt to muscle in on an established set of players in the private security-cum-extortion industry, which dominates Cape Town's nightlife. See C Dolley, *The Enforcers*. Cape Town: Jonathan Ball, 2019, 59.
5   Junior Mafia killed, *The Voice*, 11 October 2017, https://www.dailyvoice.co.za/news/junior-mafia-killed-11545380.
6   R J Scholes, Illegal drug use, in particular tik, and criminal groups in the Western Cape, dissertation submitted in partial fulfilment of MA, University of Cape Town, February 2007, 42.
7   Junior Mafia killed, *The Voice*, 11 October 2017, https://www.dailyvoice.co.za/news/junior-mafia-killed-11545380.
8   Quoted in P Saal, Cape mortuary backlog causing further anguish for grieving families, *Times Live*, 17 October 2017, https://www.timeslive.co.za/news/south-africa/2017-10-17-cape-mortuary-backlog-causing-further-anguish-for-grieving-families/.

9   References to stockpiles were made in several interviews and discussions. No self-respecting gang boss is likely to give away the location of such stockpiles but I have little doubt that they exist.

10   The issue of storage is obviously somewhat of a sensitive matter. But it emerged in several interviews that gang bosses have kept in storage a number of guns, both to sustain the market and to keep prices high. There is talk of containers of guns kept in hidden locations.

11   G Serra, Spur owner accused of selling guns to gangsters, *IOL*, 29 June 2016, https://www.iol.co.za/news/spur-owner-accused-of-selling-guns-to-gangsters-2039689.

12   Ibid.

13   Ibid.

14   Regulation 104(5) of the Firearms Control Regulations states that 'No person including the State may destroy a firearm without the prior written permission of the Registrar. The Registrar shall only consent to the destruction of a firearm with due regard and compliance with the provisions of the National Heritage Resources Act, 1999 (Act No. 25 of 1999) as imposed by the South African Heritage Resources Authority or their nominated agent.'

15   Alan Raves public Facebook page, post dated 4 January 2018.

16   Ibid.

17   On 14 November 2019, Raves argued for a stay of prosecution in respect of case number CC21/2016. In the alternative, he sought a separation of his trial from Laher's. On 28 November 2019, Judge Slingers' judgment denied the application. For more, see: Alan Raves v The Director of Public Prosecutions, Western Cape and the National Director of Public Prosecutions, case number 4659/2019.

CHAPTER 10

1   The SAR M14 is a type of AK-47. The 'Dashprod' tag is in fact a South African addition, as the gun is imported by Dave Sheer Guns: a contraction of 'Dave Sheer Product'. It is a clever bit of marketing.

2   See M Shaw, *Hitmen for Hire: Exposing South Africa's Underworld*. Johannesburg: Jonathan Ball, 2017, 60–82.

3   F Varese, *Mafia Life: Love, Death and Money at the Heart of Organised Crime*. London: Profile, 2018, 6.

4   Truth and Reconciliation Commission of South Africa Report, Volume 3, October 1998; see the graphs presented on pp. 160–161. https://www.justice.gov.za/trc/report/finalreport/Volume%203.pdf

5   Truth and Reconciliation Commission of South Africa Report, Volume 2, October 1998, 609.

6   Ibid., 610.

7   O'Malley Archives, Justice denied: Political violence in KwaZulu-Natal after 1994, https://omalley.nelsonmandela.org/omalley/index.php/site/q/03lv02424/04lv03275/05lv03336/06lv03344/07lv03353.htm.

8   M Kentridge, *An Unofficial War: Inside the Conflict in Pietermaritzburg*. Johannesburg: David Philip, 1990.

9 The data was released after a court compelled the SAPS to hand over information requested by AfriForum under the Promotion of Access to Information Act. See M Besent, Police lose over 500 firearms this year, *SABC News Online*, 10 August 2019, http://www.sabcnews.com/sabcnews/police-lose-over-500-firearms-this-year/. Although the numbers had fallen dramatically by 2018/19, KZN still tops the list, with 142 firearms of the 505 reported as lost or stolen, or 28 per cent of the total.

10 A good feel for the level of intrigue can be had from J Pitchford, *Blood on their Hands: General Johan Booysen reveals his truth*. Johannesburg: PanMacmillan, 2016.

11 Ngobeni was accused of having a cosy relationship with a Durban businessman linked to Zuma, see J Evans, KZN police commissioner resigns just as inquiry into her fitness to hold office was due to start, *News24*, 2 November 2018, https://www.news24.com/SouthAfrica/News/kzn-police-commissioner-resigns-just-as-inquiry-into-her-fitness-to-hold-office-was-due-to-start-20181102.

12 I confirmed this point several times with investigators. This is also the view of others close to Prinsloo.

13 Both of RW Johnson's recent books are an exception to this. See RW Johnson, *Fighting for the Dream*, Johannesburg: Jonathan Ball, 2019 and RW Johnson, *How Long will South Africa Survive? The Crisis Continues*, Johannesburg: Jonathan Ball, 2017 (2nd ed).

14 Staff writer, Everything the family touches turns to gold, *Sunday Times*, 18 October 2009.

15 Quoted in C Goodenough, The Taxi Commission of Inquiry: Cleaning up the taxi industry in KwaZulu-Natal, *Perspectives on KwaZulu-Natal*, 1, 1, March 2001.

16 Ntuli went into hiding after the shooting, knowing that the Gcabas would exact revenge. He never stood trial for the crime.

17 E Anderson, Taxi hitmen paid up to R1m, *News24*, 11 January 2011, https://www.news24.com/xArchive/Archive/Taxi-hitmen-paid-up-to-R1m-20010111.

18 RW Johnson, *How Long will South Africa Survive? The Crisis Continues*, Johannesburg: Jonathan Ball, 2017 (2nd edition), 20.

19 See, for example, N Moore, The rise and fall of Shauwn and S'bu Mpisane, Durban's Teflon couple, *Daily Maverick*, 11 February 2013.

CHAPTER 11

1 This was Vuyo Mkhize of Kapital Mindz, who also served as acting communication manager and spokesperson for Tansnat.

2 See Profile of Mandla Gcaba, SA Profiles, 20 October 2008, https://saprofiles.wordpress.com.

3 Interview, Pietermaritzburg, August 2018.

4 In national taxi politics, although they do not hold leadership positions in the South African National Taxi Council (SANTACO), they are said to pull strings in the organisation through proxies. One of these is said to be BB Zondi, KwaZulu-Natal provincial chair of SANTACO, who has had national leadership aspirations.

5 A company search confirms that Mandla Gcaba owns 100 per cent of the membership interests in Tansnat Durban CC, registration number B2009/159544/23.

6   T Broughton, Durban bus service on the skids, *The Mercury,* 13 January 2015.
7   J Wicks and Y Naidoo, Wheels come off again for Durban's bus service, *IOL,* 15 March 2018.
8   Companies milking the municipality will be given the boot, *Vryheid Herald,* 11 November 2017.
9   R Sheik Umar, Battle over security at hospital, *Daily News,* 16 August 2011.
10 See https://www.saps.gov.za/newsroom/msspeechdetail.php?nid=19875.
11 A Khoza, Durban taxi accused will have to wait on bail decision, *News24,* 1 October 2015, https://www.news24.com/news24/southafrica/news/durban-taxi-shooting-accused-will-have-to-wait-on-bail-decision-20151001.
12 Interview, senior official from the provincial Department of Transport, Pietermaritzburg, August 2018.
13 Testimony given by Major Mandla Dlamini in the Durban High Court, 1 October 2015.
14 S Masuku, Zuma's nephew escapes taxi violence rap, *IOL,* 14 February 2017, https://www.iol.co.za/news/zumas-nephew-escapes-taxi-violence-rap-7755124.
15 K Serino, Keeping it in the family, *Mail & Guardian,* 19 March 2010, https://mg.co.za/article/2010-03-19-keeping-it-in-the-family/.
16 A lawyer who does similar work told me that one that one of the biggest problems is to get his clients to pay.
17 R W Johnson, *Fighting for the Dream.* Johannesburg: Jonathan Ball, 2019, 69.
18 V Burger, 100% not behind Zuma, *Daily Maverick,* 8 April 2018.
19 A court set aside Zuma's decision to dismiss Cele; see E Mabuza, Court sets aside Jacob Zuma's 2012 decision to axe Bheki Cele as top cop, *Times Live,* 9 April 2019, https://www.timeslive.co.za/news/south-africa/2019-04-09-court-sets-aside-jacob-zumas-2012-decision-to-axe-bheki-cele-as-top-cop/.
20 S Sole, National security: Beware of a state of disgrace, *Mail & Guardian,* 22 June 2012.
21 G Khanyile, Another Zuma relative nets R1m, *Sunday Independent,* 27 June 2011.
22 See, for example, RW Johnson, *Fighting for the Dream.* Johannesburg: Jonathan Ball, 2019, 42.
23 Interview, Durban, August 2018.
24 G Khanyile, Zuma's nephew in Police Day rumpus, *Sunday Tribune,* 26 June 2011, https://www.pressreader.com/south-africa/sunday-tribune-south-africa/20110626/281543697554158.
25 X Mbanjwa and S Ngalwa, I am no assassin, *IOL,* 20 February 2005, https://www.iol.co.za/news/politics/i-am-no-assassin-234437.
26 See B Mthethwa, Assassin or charming man of the people, *Sunday Times,* 20 May 2007, http://www.pressreader.com/south-africa/sunday-times-1107/20070520/281732675055749.
27 For example, a State Security operative made this allegation in an interview, Empangeni, September 2018.
28 Interview, senior official from the KZN Department of Community Safety and Liaison. The numbers were subsequently confirmed in interviews with an inspector at the Private Security Industry Regulatory Authority and an owner

of a security company doing work on taxi related issues in KZN. All interviews were conducted in August 2018.

29 S Mtshali, Blood on security firms' hands, *Sunday Argus*, 7 October 2018.

30 The Private Security Industry Regulation Act 56 of 2001.

31 PSIRA, 'Caught in between': The involvement of the private security sector in the taxi violence in KwaZulu-Natal – Focus on Ntuzuma, Piesang and other areas (undated).

32 Briefing by SANTACO on taxi-related crimes to the National Assembly Portfolio Committee on Police, 10 August 2018.

33 The letter was submitted to PSIRA, headed 'A complain [sic] of unjust actions against Mvimbeni Holdings', 29 April 2018. In the author's possession.

34 PSIRA, 'Caught in between': The involvement of the private security sector in the taxi violence in KwaZulu-Natal – Focus on Ntuzuma, Piesang and other areas (undated).

CHAPTER 12

1 S Marks and A Atmore, Firearms in southern Africa: A survey, *Journal of African History*, 12, 4 (1971), 517–530.

2 See, for example, T Stapleton, *A Military History of South Africa*. Oxford: Praeger, 2010, 70–74.

3 W K Storey, *Guns, Race and Power in Colonial South Africa*. Cambridge University Press, 2008, 1.

4 Although often referred to in English as 'Bring me my machine gun', the song does not in fact use the word 'gun', although the implication is pretty clear.

5 W K Storey, *Guns, Race and Power in Colonial South Africa*. Cambridge University Press, 2008.

6 J Laband, *Zulu Warriors: The Battle for the South African Frontier*. Yale University Press, 2014, 19.

7 See the regional profile of Natal and KwaZulu in Volume 3 of the Truth and Reconciliation Commission of South Africa's Report, Cape Town, October 1998.

8 A Kirsten, The role of social movements in gun control: An international comparison between South Africa, Brazil and Australia, Centre for Civil Society Research report no. 21, September 2004, http://ccs.ukzn.ac.za/files/kirsten.final.pdf.

9 Gun Free South Africa, *Gun Control and Violence: South Africa's Story*, Johannesburg, 2018, 19.

10 The purpose of the Act is set out in section 2.

11 The numbers for guns handed in during amnesties, and outside them, are provided in the annual reports of the SAPS. Curiously, the police stopped this practice from 2016/17.

12 On the gun owners' side, there are several organisations representing a diverse group of stakeholders. These include the South African Hunters and Game Conservation Association; Gun Owners South Africa (GOSA); the South African Arms and Ammunition Dealers Association; and the Black Gun Owners Association of South Africa. GOSA is the most vocal of the associations in promoting

a looser regulatory framework. On the anti-gun lobby side is Gun Free South Africa, which, although a small entity, is highly active and often supported by a loose coalition of education, health and related experts. It has a preference for the declaration of gun-free zones.

13 See Judge Froneman, Constitutional Court of South Africa, case CCT 177/17 in the matter between the Minister of Safety and Security (Applicant) and South African Hunters and Game Conservation Association (Respondent) and Fidelity Security Services (Pty) Limited (First Amicus) and Gun Free South Africa (NPO) (Second Amicus). Unanimous judgement made on 7 June 2018, www.saflii.org/za/cases/ZACC/2018/14.pdf.

14 E Anker, Mobile sovereigns: Agency panic and the feeling of gun ownership, in J Obert, A Poe and A Sarat (eds), *The Lives of Guns*. New York: Oxford University Press, 2019, 22.

15 Interview with Andrew Soutar, Classic Arms Dealership, Witbank, 28 November 2019.

16 R Stoffels, Differences in discourses of black and white gun owners as a function of socially constructed identity, unpublished monograph, Department of Psychology, University of Cape Town, 2009, 16.

17 J Cock, Fixing our sights: A sociological perspective on gun violence in contemporary South Africa, *Society in Transition*, 1, 1997, 70–81.

18 Interview with Jenni Irish-Qhobosheane, researcher and former head of the Civilian Secretariat for Police, Johannesburg, 18 November 2019.

19 Perceptions of a racial bias being present in the issuing of gun licences are a hot topic among white pro-gun lobbyists. Although it may not be publicly expressed given the sensitivity of the subject, several white gun dealers said that black people applying for gun licences were likely to see their applications processed much more expeditiously than white applicants. The Black Gun Owners Association vigorously deny that this is the case. The actual number of black gun owners seems to be impossible to determine, although the Black Gun Owners Association claims to have 700 000 members. While some black people did acquire licences pre-1994 under the old legislation, these are a small number and that data seems no longer available. Government data on who holds firearm licences no longer includes the race of the holder. The Black Gun Owners Association suggests that the figure of black gun owners could be close to 900 000, although there is general agreement by most in the industry that this number is vastly inflated.

20 Global Initiative Against Transnational Organized Crime, Gangs, protest and response in western Johannesburg, 1994–2019, 2019, 25

21 All of these allegations are to be found in the charge sheet of the case The State vs Ralph Israel Stanfield and 22 other accused, Khayelitsha Regional Court, original trial date set of 26 April 2018.

22 See the recommendations in the Gun Free SA pamphlet, Cape Town proves strong gun laws save lives, poor enforcement kills, 2019. In interviews, several representatives of the pro-gun lobby agreed with this.

CHAPTER 13

1 Interview with former head of the firearms registry, Pretoria, July 2018.
2 A Serrao, Kebble's killer named in guns scandal, *The Star*, 7 October 2013.
3 Ibid.
4 Interview with Andrew Soutar, Witbank, April 2019.
5 This is the conclusion of several dealers and lawyers active in the debate.
6 The prices and changes in prices of these firearms over time were found by accessing old copies of *Man Magnum* magazine. Three copies per year, from 2000 to 2019, were consulted, and the cheapest price per make and model of firearm recorded for each year. Various gun dealerships were contacted and enquiries made as to whether staff could recall the prices of firearms during the period, but none were able to remember prices with accuracy. Internet records were also hard to come by. For these reasons, looking through old gun magazines was deemed to be the best way to find and compare historical prices. Gun dealers whom I spoke to confirmed the drop in prices for pistols in the last couple of years. The explanation generally provided is that several big players in the small-arms market have imported pistols in bulk and have been able to offer lower prices to consumers. But there is not full agreement on that. At least one gun collector and dealer (who did not want to be named) felt that the business models of dealers offering much lower prices in the pistol market did not entirely make sense.
7 See M Wiener, *Ministry of Crime: An Underworld Explored*, Macmillan, 2018.
8 Affidavit of Charl Adam Kinnear, signed on 8 February 2019, in the matter between Nafiz Modack, Rehana Ismail and the National Commissioner of the South African Police Service, and others. Case no: 82048/18.
9 One of the convictions was for dealing in second-hand goods without a valid licence, and the other for not producing a valid firearm licence and for not carrying the firearm in a holster.
10 Paragraph 82 of the affidavit.
11 R Francke, Modack's wife appears in court, *Daily Voice*, 7 November 2019, https://www.dailyvoice.co.za/news/modacks-wife-appears-in-court-36810881.
12 H Rossouw, Kempton Park and Roodepoort station commanders granted bail, *Kempton Express*, 28 October 2020, https://kemptonexpress.co.za/299697/kempton-park-and-roodepoort-station-commanders-granted-bail/.
13 The other case was that of Guinea in 2013, where opposition parties lodged complaints over the company's receiving and handling of the voters' roll. See L Louw-Vaudran, SA firm focus of Guinea poll misgivings, *Mail & Guardian*, 16 August 2013, https://mg.co.za/article/2013-08-16-sa-firm-focus-of-guinea-poll-misgivings/.
14 D Knoetser, SAPS R400 million firearms control system in shambles, *Mail & Guardian*, Johannesburg, 18 October 2018.
15 Ibid.
16 Remarks of Minister of Police, EN Mthethwa, MP, to the National Press Club on the current challenges affecting the SAPS firearms application and licensing processes, Sheraton Hotel, Pretoria, 2 November 2010.

17 Paragraph 48 of the responding affidavit of Minister Nathi Nhleko in the matter between The South African Hunters and Game Conservation Association and the Minister of Safety and Security before the High Court of South Africa, Gauteng Division, Pretoria, Case No 21177/16, signed on 1 June 2016.

18 Civilian Secretariat for Police Service, Enquiry into the Functioning of the Central Firearms Registry and the Implementation of the Firearms Control Act, 2000 (Act 60 of 2000) (incomplete copy and without page numbers).

19 These statements are in an extract of the report, the section of which is unclear. It is possibly 4.2.

20 Ibid.

21 The statement is made at 5.4 in the extract in my possession.

22 The registry systems seem to have created an Orwellian world of paperwork. Take one example outlined in the Civilian Secretariat for Police Service's investigation. The forms to be completed when one applies for a gun licence make provision for a brief motivation statement. When some applicants did not include a further, extended motivation (presumably on a separate sheet of paper and not specifically asked for), they were turned down for not having attached sufficient motivation. But when other applicants did submit detailed motivations, these were removed, as they were told that they were not necessary.

23 Answering affidavit, Sibongile Dorah Kibido, in the High Court of South Africa (North Gauteng Division: Pretoria), Case No: 13528/15, signed and sworn on 8 April 2015.

24 These words, which are to the deputy minister's credit, were part of a prepared speech: Remarks by the Deputy Minister of Police, Hon. Ms Makhotso Maggie Sotyu (MP) at the National Firearms Summit 2015, Cape Town, 25 March 2015.

25 This is the conclusion of several external stakeholders in the process, confirmed by former SAPS and Secretariat officials.

26 Applicant's founding affidavit in the matter between the South African Hunters and Game Conservation Society and the Minister of Safety and Security, Case No 21177/16, paragraph 5.19, signed 15 March 2016.

27 Again, this is the conclusion of several participants with whom I consulted.

28 An angry exchange of papers between the South African Hunters and Game Conservation Association and Nhleko suggests that the deputy police minister's comments at the summit were not welcomed by the government. SAHGCA emphasised how the government's own minister had found the CFR in a shambles – to which Nhleko responded testily that 'it has always been the policy and approach of my Ministry to acknowledge problems and challenges where they exist'. His replying affidavit, however, seeks to do exactly the opposite, arguing that firearms are not disappearing at an 'alarming rate' and denying that they are not properly safeguarded. This exchange is revealing, in that the minister provides figures for firearm losses from SAPS stores – for example, it is claimed that only six firearms went missing from police stores across 1 500 police stations in 2015/16 – information that seems designed to deliberately obscure the reality.

CHAPTER 14

1   The couple claimed in the Johannesburg Magistrate's Court that they had let the room where the weapons were found to an Eastern European man. They said they had no idea the weapons were in their home. See J Lee, B Roane and B Molosankwe, Police seeking eastern European man in weapons case, *The Star*, 28 May 2014, http://dvqlxo2m2q99q.cloudfront.net/000_clients/129863/file/childplay.pdf.

2   G Hoskin, Cops leaking guns, *Times Live*, 4 June 2014, https://www.timeslive.co.za/news/south-africa/2014-06-04-cops-leaking-guns/.

3   Ibid.

4   Ibid.

5   See 'Corrupt' Sandton cop stands to face charges, *The New Age*, 2 December 2014, http://southafricanpoliceservicecrimes.blogspot.com/2016/01/crimes-of-south-african-police-service_72.html.

6   Attempts were made to contact the prosecutor in the case concerned, but none were successful.

7   N Shange, Suspects questioned after weapons theft at Lyttelton SANDF base, *Times Live*, 24 December 2019, https://www.timeslive.co.za/news/south-africa/2019-12-24-suspects-being-questioned-after-weapons-theft-at-lyttelton-sandf-base/.

ANNEX I

1   We interviewed some 90 respondents on the Cape Flats during 2019, including gang bosses and gang members. Our methodology involved asking the prices that they would charge, would expect or had paid, and what they had heard were the prices being offered by other sellers. In cases where a price was a clear outlier, either too expensive or too cheap, we excluded it. In Johannesburg, ten interviews were conducted.

2   As in the case of the Z88, the symbolism of firearms that have wider institutional meaning (in this case, the connection to the Chinese military) is striking.

3   V Brenan, AK-47: The poster boy for killing, *The Sunday Herald*, Glasgow, 18 November 2018, 41. See also CJ Civers, *The Gun: The Story of the AK-47*. New York: Simon & Schuster, 2010.

4   M Keegan, The Proliferation of Firearms in South Africa, 1994–2000, Gun Free South Africa, 30 April 2005, 61–82.

5   A Burgess, *Heist! South Africa's Cash-in-transit Epidemic Uncovered*. Johannesburg: Penguin, 2018, 97.

6   Although it is hard to identify the exact period, the development of gun supply lines from the state coincides with the shift in gun use in cash-in-transit heists.

ANNEX II

1   Gun Free South Africa, Constitutional Court unanimously rules regular gun licence renewal is constitutional, Firearms Control Briefing 3 of 2018, 12 June 2018.

2   It is worth noting here that the figures provided over time and at different briefings are often at variance.

3   The Act provides for different periods, depending on the type of weapon. Hunting and sport-shooting firearms require a renewal every ten years; a restricted firearm (for example, a semi-automatic rifle) that is used for self-defence requires a renewal every two years.

4   Minister of Safety and Security v South African Hunters and Game Conservation Association [2018] ZACC 14.

5   See paragraph 12 of the judgment.

6   National Commissioner of Police and Another v Gun Owners of South Africa (561/2019) [2020] ZASCA 88 (23 July 2020). The reference to Judge Prinsloo's behaviour is in paragraph 29 of the judgment.

ANNEX III

1   A Kirsten, Simpler, better, faster – Review of the 2005 firearms amnesty, Institute for Security Studies, April 2007, 2.

2   South African Police Service: Briefing to the Select Committee on Security and Justice Firearm Amnesty 2019/2020, 30 October 2019.

3   A Kirsten, Simpler, better, faster – Review of the 2005 firearms amnesty, Institute for Security Studies, April 2007, 9.

4   Brand South Africa, Firearms amnesty 'a success', *BuaNews*, 13 April 2010, https://www.brandsouthafrica.com/governance/services/gun-130410.

5   While the data on firearms surrendered to the police used to be regularly reported in the SAPS Annual Report, this was stopped after 2016/17.

6   M Jordaan, Nearly 1,500 guns handed in under firearms amnesty, *TimesLive*, 1 January 2020, https://www.timeslive.co.za/news/south-africa/2020-01-01-nearly-1500-guns-handed-in-under-firearm-amnesty/.

7   Interview with Martin Hood, Johannesburg, 6 October 2019; see also M Baloyi, Surrendered guns 'used by criminals', *IOL*, 27 January 2007, https://www.iol.co.za/news/south-africa/surrendered-guns-used-by-criminals-312672.

8   Presentation made to the NCOP Select Committee on Security and Justice on 30 October 2019.

9   Government Gazette Notice, Vol. 6, Notice 42858, 27 November 2019.

10 South African Police Service: Briefing to the Select Committee on Security and Justice, Firearm Amnesty 2019/2020, 30 October 2019.

ACKNOWLEDGEMENTS

This book has been in the making for over three years. It would not have been possible without the support of the extraordinary staff of the Global Initiative. They have all helped in various ways – small and big. I am particularly indebted to Kim Thomas, who gathered data, found people, arranged interviews with them and kept the work ticking over year after year. She is an absolute star. Jenni Irish-Qhobosheane, colleague and friend, has been a pillar of support too, putting me in contact with sources of information and conducting interviews, and answering my Saturday-morning phone calls.

Tuesday Reitano read the manuscript when it was 30 000 words longer than it is now, and suggested revisions and cuts that saved the author from himself. She has been engaged in doing that judiciously for over a decade now. Peter Gastrow read the final manuscript and provided his usual wise words. They are probably beyond being thanked now, but I do it anyway.

Rukshana Parker and Michael McLaggan provided crucial research assistance, which went beyond the call of duty. Lyndsay Johannisen, in her beautiful and gentle way, laughed softly next to me in the car while phoning the underworld. Matt Skade was my lively KZN companion. Julian Rademeyer took fine pictures of a Z88 at the last minute. Shaun Swingler contributed the cover and other pictures. Claudio Landi drew the graphs – and drew them again as I changed my mind. Theresa Hume has been doing my travel arrangements and other support for as long as I can remember.

Nate Roloff and Colin Arendse provided key research assistance, including introducing me to the mothers of children killed by the guns – a depressing and too easily forgotten reminder for me of why the book needed to be written. Too many children have died in the crossfire in Cape Town and I have dedicated the book to them.

At Jonathan Ball, Jeremy Boraine stuck with the book through its ins and outs, and knew exactly how to pitch it. Ceri Prenter helped pull it together. Mark Ronan is an editor extraordinaire and I am indebted to him for the time, effort, skill and good humour that he put into the manuscript.

Many other people helped without wanting their names made public. I am in particular grateful to one person who opened doors when others could not. I am thankful beyond measure and I hope I have done justice to the stories he and his contacts told me.

My close family is sick of gun stories but hopefully not yet sick of me. They are honestly a joy to live with. My parents asked anxiously about the book's progress on our Sunday-evening phone calls. They have provided a lifetime of support.

Thank you to you all for contributing. Any mistakes and oversights are, naturally, my own.

Finally, Dimitri Vlassis, the UN official who played a decisive part in bringing the UN Convention against Transnational Organized Crime to fruition, and long a source of encouragement to me, died while this book was being written. Wherever he is, I can see him twitch his moustache and say, 'You see,' when I tell him that it is done.

INDEX